Abbas Vali is Professor of Modern Social and Political Theory at the Department of Sociology, in Boğaziçi University, Istanbul. He previously taught Political Theory and Modern Middle Eastern Politics at the Department of Politics and International Relations, University of Wales, Swansea, before moving to Erbil, Iraq to serve as the first Vice Chancellor of the University of Kurdistan Hawler from 2006 to 2008. His writings include *Pre-Capitalist Iran: A Theoretical History* (I.B.Tauris, 1993), *Essays on the Origins of Kurdish Nationalism* (Mazda Publishers, 2003) and *Modernity and the Stateless: The Kurds in the Islamic Republic* (I.B.Tauris, forthcoming).

KURDS AND THE STATE IN IRAN

STATE IN IRAN

THE MAKING OF KURDISH IDENTITY

ABBAS VALI

I.B. TAURIS
LONDON · NEW YORK

Published in 2011 by I.B.Tauris & Co Ltd
6 Salem Road, London W2 4BU
175 Fifth Avenue, New York NY 10010
www.ibtauris.com

Distributed in the United States and Canada Exclusively by Palgrave Macmillan
175 Fifth Avenue, New York NY 10010

International Library of Iranian Studies, vol 36

ISBN: 978 1 84885 788 9

A full CIP record for this book is available from the British Library
A full CIP record is available from the Library of Congress

Library of Congress Catalog Card Number: available

Typeset in Adobe Garamond Pro by Free Range Book Design & Production Limited
Printed and bound by CPI Group (UK) Ltd, Croydon, CR0 4YY

The history of the world is not the theatre of happiness.
The periods of happiness are empty pages.

G.W.F. Hegel, 'Introduction' to *The Lectures on the Philosophy of History*

This book is dedicated to those students and colleagues of mine at the University of Kurdistan in Erbil whose studies and direction of life were interrupted by a destructive and self-serving government. I will always remember them for their integrity and courage.

CONTENTS

Acknowledgements   ix

Introduction   xi

1 The Formation of Kurdish National Identity in Iran   1

2 Komalay JK to the Republic: The Formation of
the KDPI   25

3 The Republic: The Formation and Structure of
Political Power   49

4 Ambiguities and Anomalies in the Discourse of
the Republic   83

Conclusions: The Kurds and the Reasons of the State   113

Notes   139

Selected Bibliography   181

Index   199

ACKNOWLEDGEMENTS

This book was written over a period of a few years during which I moved from Swansea to Erbil and from there to Istanbul where I live and work at present. Writing was almost completely interrupted during January 2006–May 2008 when I was in the employment of the University of Kurdistan in Erbil, only to be resumed in September 2008 when I took up a professorship in the department of Sociology at Boğaziçi University in Istanbul. The resumption of writing also inevitably meant rethinking and revising what had already been written. My special thanks go to Katharine Hodgkin. She was actively involved in the preparation of this text throughout this period. She greeted various versions with enthusiasm and patience, reading them with her usual care and acumen. Her incisive reading and comments proved crucial to the final form and presentation of the chapters in the text. I am indebted to her. I am also grateful to Maria Marsh of I.B.Tauris Publishers for her support, interest and good advice in the preparation of the final text.

Introduction

This study examines the formation and development of Kurdish national identity in modern Iran, from its inception in the Constitutional era to its development under Pahlavi absolutism, and its maturation in the Kurdish Republic, centred in Mahabad in 1946.

Although the events constituting the foci of this investigation take place in the past, this study is not an exercise in historiography. It does not intend to construct a history of the formation and development of Kurdish nationalism in Iran from 1905 to 1947. The method of investigation deployed in this study is removed from the historians' practice, in so far as they use a conception of the past as the uniform origin of historical discourse/narrative. The category of the past informing this study does not signify a uniform process, a continuum constituted by a single origin unfolding in time, animating the process and giving meaning and direction to it. It does not lend itself to causal explanations charting the development of its object from its origin to the present. The category of the past deployed in this study is constituted by the relations of forces with diverse histories which cannot be reduced to a uniform origin, subjective or objective. The past, conceived as such, lacks discursive unity either as a conjuncture or a process.

This conception of the past amounts to more than a defensive theoretical shield or discursive strategy to avoid the all-round charge of essentialism often used by the contemporary post-structuralist theorists to distance their own engagement with history from historicism. The reference to the relations of forces as constitutive of the past in discourse offers us a means to go beyond mere scholastic concerns about the historicity of the subject and the essentialism of historicist discourse prompted by the post-structuralist critique of identity as presence, while the focus on the struggle for and against domination emphasizes the necessity of power, not only to the construction of the Kurdish identity, but also and more importantly to the Kurds' struggle for freedom. Furthermore, this conception of the past is also at the same time a necessary theoretical provision for the genealogy of Kurdish identity in Iran attempted in this study. This genealogy is constructed as stages in a 'lineage of difference' produced by historical encounters between the sovereign power and the Kurdish community. It is represented in terms of the effects of strategies of domination and control deployed by the Iranian state to suppress Kurdish difference in various stages of its historical encounter with the Kurdish community. A brief explanation is necessary to clarify the theoretical framework of the study.

The method of inquiry and the theoretical framework deployed in this study both presuppose the concept of sovereign identity, that is, the identity of political power in Iran in the period under consideration. The genealogy of Kurdish identity is therefore primarily an investigation of the lineage of its constitutive difference with sovereign identity in modern Iran. The narrative of this lineage is constructed in terms of the formation and working of sovereign power in modern Iran. This suggests that the strategies and techniques deployed by the sovereign power to secure domination over the Kurdish community in various phases of their encounter operate as a force threading them together in a process connecting the past to the present. The process in question here lacks a unitary causal logic and dynamics, for it is set in motion by power and is constantly grounded and interrupted by it. It is torn apart and joined together, reshaped and started again by strategies of domination and control. The historical process conceived as such is not given to the analysis; it is an effect of power as 'relations of force' in the political and cultural field. The strategies and policies deployed to ensure the subjugation of the Kurdish community change over time, thus traversing the episodes of this process, underpinning its progression and ascent. In this sense, therefore, this book is to be seen as an 'ontology of the present' in Foucauldian terms, that is, a 'history of the ontology of the present' constituted by this struggle for domination and its significations in the political, cultural and military field.

The term 'Kurdistan' used in this study denotes an ethnic-linguistic community under Iranian sovereignty. It lacks specified contiguous geographical boundaries. Nor does it have a juridical-political unity as a cohesive provincial administrative entity. It lacks the authority to issue uniform administrative and social and cultural processes and practices. Modern nation state and sovereign power have deprived Kurdistan of its territorial and political unity as a single contiguous province within Iran. The territory has been divided and subdivided into smaller and mostly unviable administrative and geographical units attached to adjacent provinces by different governments, first under the Pahlavi rule and then by the Islamic state. The community is now territorially dispersed, with parts located in different provinces and subject to their administrative and legal jurisdiction. The territorial division of the community, however, has not affected its ethnic and linguistic unity and cultural cohesion. The ethnic and linguistic unity of the Kurdish community in Iran is constituted by its otherness, and hence its differences with the sovereign identity. In this sense, therefore, the sovereign identity is constitutive of the Kurdish community and the processes and practices which reproduce Kurdish otherness also at the same time define its unity and cohesion.

The primacy of ethnic-linguistic difference in the construction of the Kurdish community means that Kurdish ethnicity and language were already principles of political legitimacy defining the terms of its encounter with the sovereign power before the advent of the Kurdish Republic in 1946. That sovereign power had already targeted ethnic-linguistic difference, and Kurdish resistance to the strategies of domination and control was expressed in terms of a struggle for the defence of ethnic and linguistic rights. This defence of Kurdish ethnicity and language in terms of a discourse of rights (natural rights) meant that they were already being invoked and deployed as principles of political legitimacy in the Kurdish community. This argument has important implications for the conceptualization of ethnicity and the nation in this study. It means that ethnicity is primarily a political construct, and that the political import of ethnicity in nationalist discourse and practice depended primarily on its role as the principle of political legitimacy in the community. It means by implication that ethnic relations in their pre-political mould were no more than a means of individual identification, essentially devoid of historical significance. The idea that ethnicity is not self-significatory, in turn, means that it always needed a political force outside it to animate it, to set it in motion in the historical process of nation formation. This force is nationalism.

Nationalism not only links ethnicity with rights, but also connects rights with power. But if nationalism is constitutive of ethnicity as a principle of political legitimacy, if it serves to forge a conceptual relationship between rights and power in the process of nationalist struggle, it follows that the outcome of this process, too, must be constituted by nationalism. This amounts to saying that the nation should also be perceived, analysed and theorized at the level of nationalism, a theoretical argument which underpins constructivist conceptions of the nation in contemporary political and social thought. The constructivists argue for the primacy of nationalism as the principal cause of the nation and national identity. For them, the nation is an effect of nationalist politics, a political invention and hence a modern phenomenon. The modernity of the nation and national identity is the defining feature of all constructivist approaches to the origins of nationalism.

I have argued elsewhere in my writings that while I am in agreement with the general theoretical direction and political ethos of the constructivist conceptions of the nation and national identity, I refuse to accept the positivistic thrust of their empiricist epistemology, which appeals to the authority of the historical fact-evidence as the means of validation of historical argument, the only proof of its truth and falsity. This mode of validation of discourse, I have argued, rests on an essentialist conception of historical fact-evidence as self-contained and self-significatory, which seriously undermines the theoretical claims of the constructivist conceptions of the nation and national identity elaborated in the pioneering works of Ernest Gellner, Benedict Anderson and Eric Hobsbawm. In my opinion the constructivist refutation by these writers of the primordialist and ethnicist definitions of the national origin rests on an equally essentialist conception of historical fact-evidence as given and self-explanatory. It is therefore justified to argue that the constructivist conceptions of the national origin entail a notion of the past which is given to the discourse, exists in the present and is capable of animating it. The constructivist histories, therefore, start from the present and return to the present, but through a conception of the past firmly chained to the essentialist conception of historical fact.

The analysis in this book draws on a large collection of primary and secondary sources, both viewed as conceptual representation, though of different kinds, of the real historical conditions they purport to signify. The primary sources include the PRO material covering major events and diplomatic relations regarding the period under consideration, the main Kurdish newspapers of the period 1942–6, and official documents of the Kurdish republic compiled and edited by contemporary historians and archivists. These materials do not define the structure or direction of the narrative of the book; they are not a substitute for political and theoretical analysis and argument, but rather they are used to illustrate or support the main political and theoretical arguments and analyses in various phases of the genealogy of Kurdish identity. English translations from the Kurdish original are all mine, unless otherwise indicated.

In the process of researching, planning and writing this book I have had many long conversations with numerous people; friends, acquaintances and colleagues have shared their time, knowledge and opinions with me. I am very grateful to them for their interest and help, which have greatly enriched the book. They mostly wish to remain anonymous, but some have been mentioned in the endnotes. I know that many of them will be in disagreement with me about the conclusions I have drawn from our conversations, and will dispute many of the arguments in this book, but I nonetheless wish to thank them for their input. I remain solely responsible for the arguments and views expressed in the chapters of this book.

Abbas Vali
Istanbul

1

THE FORMATION OF
KURDISH NATIONAL IDENTITY IN IRAN

An influential body of opinion on Kurdish historical writing traces the origins of the nationalist movement in Iranian Kurdistan to Shaikh Ubaidollah's rebellion against the Ottoman Empire in the late nineteenth century. This rebellion, it is contended, spilling over the Iranian border in the course of its eastward expansion to engulf the territory northwest of Lake Urmiya, planted the seeds of modern nationalism in Kurdish soil in Iran. The nationalist movement then developed in a cumulative process that culminated in the events leading to the establishment of the Republic of Mahabad in 1946.[1] The political activities of the Kurdish forces *vis-à-vis* the Iranian state during the period 1882–1946, active or reactive, are thus characterized as nationalist, irrespective of their social structure, political organization, discursive formation and strategic objective.[2]

The present study challenges this historicist view of the genesis and development of Kurdish nationalism in Iranian Kurdistan and the essentialist conception of the Kurdish nation on which it is based. It argues that Kurdish nationalism in Iran is a modern phenomenon, an outcome of the socio-economic and cultural dislocations caused by the blighted and perverse modernity that followed the advent of Pahlavi absolutism after the First World War. The Kurdish responses to the politics of

1

territorial centralism and the cultural process of the construction of a uniform Iranian 'national' identity pursued by the Pahlavi state defined the discursive and non-discursive conditions of formation of the nationalist movement, culminating in the Republic of Mahabad. The republic, it is further argued, marks the advent of modern nationalism in Kurdistan; its social and institutional structures, and its political and ideological organizations, were determined by a multiplicity of diverse relations and forces that cannot be reduced to a uniform historical origin.

Iran entered the twentieth century in the process of the gradual integration of its pre-capitalist economy into the capitalist world market, a process that effectively had been at work since the early decades of the nineteenth century. The expansion of commodity production and the money economy had drawn the bulk of the landowning class to the market, and swelled the ranks of a powerful mercantile bourgeoisie in major urban centres. Economic development had created social dislocation and ideological strife, generating political dissent among the social forces that had been affected by the new culture of modernity. The large landowners and the prospering mercantile bourgeoisie, although not strong enough to shed their pre-capitalist values, found themselves in a position to oppose the crumbling structure of the Qajar autocracy which, in dire need of extra revenue, was increasingly encroaching upon their sources of income. The debasement of silver currency, rising taxation and high tariffs were curbing agrarian production for the market, the source of both land revenue and mercantile profit. The political alliance subsequently formed between the two classes had a solid economic foundation, political form, discursive cohesion and popular representation. It proved effective when the intelligentsia, traditional and modern, lent their active support to the alliance and backed its call for socio-economic and political reform. The revolution of 1905–6, which replaced autocratic rule by a constitutional monarchy, also marked the birth of Iranian nationalism. The concept of the Iranian nation, which in the course of the Constitutional movement had signified the crystallization of popular democratic opposition to autocracy, entered the official political discourse. Sovereignty, the Constitution declared, was indivisible and permanent, and the unity of the Iranian nation and the territorial integrity of Iran were the conditions of its indivisibility and permanence. It was bestowed on the government by means of popular franchise exercised in periodic elections.

The Constitution of 1906 had already forged a conceptual link between nation and state on the democratic basis of the separation of powers and popular sovereignty. Although the institutional form and the organizational structure of the state had been clearly laid out in the Constitution, the document was quite ambiguous on the nature and conditions of citizenship in the new state. Neither in the text of the Constitution signed by Muzaffaradin Shah in December 1906 nor in its two supplements (the Supplementary Constitutional Law, signed by Muhammad Ali Shah in October 1907) is there any reference to the concepts of citizen and citizenship in the modern democratic sense of the term. The concept of *shahrvand*, commonly used to refer to 'citizen' in contemporary Iran, is a relatively new construct in the Persian language; it emerged in popular democratic and left-wing literature in the 1960s, and only since then has found currency in political and juridical discourse in Iran. The 1906 Constitution considered the Iranians as subjects (*atba'*) of the monarch, but the notion of the subject here implies the rights and obligations commonly associated with the concept of citizenship in democratic theory.[3] Thus, although the concept is not explicitly present in the discourse of the Constitution, the specific rights and obligations associated with it in democratic theory nonetheless feature in it.

This democratic concept of citizenship as the locus of the rights and obligations defining the relationship between the individual and the state was undercut by two sets of qualifications relating to the conditions of popular sovereignty and national

3

identity respectively. The Constitution restricted the franchise to the literate male population, thus excluding women and the illiterate from the formal political process. Given the condition of Iranian society in the early twentieth century, the gender and literacy qualification effectively restricted the exercise of popular sovereignty and the democratic rights of participation in the political process to a very limited body of citizens, primarily the literate, male, middle-class residents of the major urban centres. Iranian women and the overwhelming majority of the male rural population remained in obligation to the state without having any rights to affect the political process.

The definition of the constituent elements of national identity, in as much as they were defined at all, imposed further restrictions on the conditions of citizenship in the constitutional state. The Constitution specified Persian as the official language of the nation, the language of administration and education, elevating it above other local and regional languages, Kurdish included. These languages were neither recognized nor denied; and the same was true of the non-Persian ethnicities. The Constitution remained silent on the subject of ethnicity (see note 4 below). Ethnic relations were subsumed under the general notion of the Iranian nation, whose identity was in part defined by the Persian language (and Twelver Shi'ism), and in part remained obscure. Persian thus became the language of the sovereign, of politics and power, the means of access to knowledge, and an instrument of modernity and progress.

Iranian national identity so defined was the identity of the citizens, the means of their incorporation into the nascent democratic polity, and the basis of their civil and political rights and obligations. It required unity and permanence, which entailed the marginalization of ethnic differences and their expulsion from the political process. Thus, although the Constitution of 1906 did not contain an ethnic definition of the conditions of citizenship, the exclusion of ethnic difference from the political process amounted to the denial of ethnic identity and the severance of its link to the sphere of civil and democratic rights. This denial was hidden behind the silence that marked the formal position of the Constitution on the ethnic and cultural diversity of the nation. Soon, however, the emergent Iranian nationalism broke this silence in the official discourse when the argument for national revival and progress was premised on the urgent need for political and economic modernization. The nationalists perceived modernization as requiring above all political and administrative centralism: a modern bureaucracy, a national army, a uniform tax regime and secular education. The intertwining of political centralism with modernity in the official discourse meant that the decentralizing forces and tendencies could now be designated traditional, signifying backwardness and obscurantism, and anti-historical, in as much as they advocated a real or alleged return to the past. The emphasis on political centralization, although it had a strong justification in the socio-economic and political conditions of Iranian society in the Constitutional era, revealed the latent authoritarianism of the discourse of modernization, which subsequently became the hallmark of official nationalism under the Pahlavi rule.[4]

In the Constitutional era, the Kurds of Iran were not in a position to oppose the denial of their identity in the constitution of the new state. It is no exaggeration to say that a Kurdish collective national consciousness, in so far as this signifies a common awareness of a common existence in history and a common end in politics, did not exist among the Kurds of Iran. Nevertheless there is little doubt that the political and ideological developments in the Kurdish territory of the neighbouring Ottoman Empire did indeed affect Iranian Kurdistan. Shaikh Ubaidollah's movement, which reputedly campaigned for a united Kurdistan, engulfed a substantial part of the Kurdish territory in Iran. The movement may well have led to the germination of the nationalist idea, which was strengthened further by the collapse of the Iranian central authority and by repeated Turkish incursions and interventions during the constitutional period.[5] However, the fact is that during the turbulent years of the

Constitutionalist movement in Iran no Kurdish intelligentsia with a nationalist orientation in politics or literature emerged in Kurdistan. Nor did there emerge a cohesive Kurdish political force, with a modern political organization pursuing nationalist objectives, however parochial or rudimentary. The nationalist idea may well have been present in a rudimentary form among a few informed individuals or even circles, but no political or literary discourse emerged to indicate the existence of nationalist political and literary processes and practices.[6] Despite claims to the contrary, the Kurds had largely remained aloof from the revolutionary process, and in most documented cases any Kurdish participation was counter-revolutionary.[7] Kurdish tribal chieftains joined forces with the counter-revolutionary forces in Azerbaijan in unsuccessful attempts to maintain and restore the *ancien régime*.[8] Their aim was to safeguard the feudal structure of domination of which they had been a part at least since the sixteenth century and which had ensured their financial and administrative autonomy *vis-à-vis* the central political authority.[9] However, the chief reason for the Kurds' absence from the political scene in the Constitutional period was structural, lying in the very foundations of the Kurdish community of the time.

The Community and Its Boundaries

The Kurdish community in the late nineteenth and early twentieth centuries was predominantly pre-capitalist and agrarian. Commodity relations had hardly affected the pre-capitalist structure of agrarian production, which also dominated the urban economy. Trade and commerce were thus underdeveloped, providing little impetus for the development of productive forces, social differentiation and cultural progress. Kurdish urban life, for the most part, was dominated by the primordial relations, loyalties and values characteristic of the tribal landowning class. The urban population was relatively small and largely dependent on agrarian production and the landowning class. It was not developed enough to engender a cohesive urban culture receptive to the ideas of social reform and political modernization espoused and preached by the Azeri and the Persian intelligentsia at the turn of the century. The upper stratum of the traditional mercantile class, who, by way of involvement in long-distance trade with major urban centres in Tsarist Russia and the Ottoman Empire, had come into contact with ideas of reform, progress and the culture of modernity, were too few and too weak to effect a meaningful change in the cultural organization of urban life in the major Kurdish cities in Iran. The tribal chieftains, with their armies and local retinues, which often included elements of the traditional intelligentsia (mainly young Sunni clerics well versed in Persian, Arabic and, to a lesser extent, Turkish literature and history), were by and large the only politically active sector of the Kurdish population. Iranian Kurdistan was comparatively the most underdeveloped part of the Kurdish territory, and, unlike the Ottoman Kurds, the Kurds of Iran had failed to produce a secular intelligentsia by the beginning of the twentieth century.[10]

Tribal politics, prominent as they were, characteristically operated through lineage, and the complex network of loyalties stemming from lineage formed the most cohesive structure for the organization and exercise of authority.[11] The hierarchy of command and obedience within the tribal organization stood vertically, and authority flowed downwards from the top to the bottom. The vertical structure of command had a matching horizontal network made up of sub-clans or sub-tribes with their own political organization, which bolstered the power of the ruling clan or lineage. The political and military organization of the Kurdish tribes was underpinned by an economic structure which was fundamentally similar to that prevailing in non-tribal agriculture in Kurdistan and other parts of Iran at large.[12] With the exception of the nomadic tribes, which were largely engaged in pastoral production, agrarian production in tribal lands was organized around the household, usually nuclear family-based, which obtained the right to use the land in return for a portion of the product that had to be surrendered to the landlord. The right to use the land was mostly a function of the lineage which was vested in the household. Production relations were regulated by rental contract, share-cropping or fixed rent in kind, which was the mechanism of economic exploitation within the tribe. Tribal land was the private property of the tribal leader, and the foundation of his economic power. It was also the primary means by which the Kurdish tribal leadership and the political and military organizations of the Kurds were incorporated into the wider structures of power and authority within Iranian state and society.[13]

Tribal lineage as the principle of political organization in Iranian Kurdistan was a product of the conditions which followed the forced destruction of the Kurdish principalities after the first division of Kurdistan in the sixteenth century. These principalities, existing on the periphery of the Iranian state, retained a tributary relationship with it in a specific system of vassalage that guaranteed them internal organizational and functional autonomy.[14] The relationship between the Kurdish tribes and the Iranian state was also fashioned on a feudal basis, sustained by the exchange of the land for armed contingents between the sovereign and the tribal leadership. The connection between land revenue and military service was the most crucial aspect of the relationship, and other financial relations such as taxes and dues were often very loosely defined, thus giving the tribal leaders a significant degree of autonomy in regulating their relationship with their tribesmen in the economic and political spheres.

The structure of domination was sustained and reproduced by an articulation of landownership and lineage that ensured the extraction of the economic surplus from the tribesmen; this surplus in turn paid for the upkeep of the lord's armed retainers. This tripartite relationship between the Iranian state, the Kurdish tribal leadership, and the tribesmen was not specific to Kurdistan, but a general feature of agrarian relations in tribal lands in Iran.[15] The main factor distinguishing the state-tribe relations in Kurdistan, however, was the strategic position of the region, bordering the Ottoman territory. The Ottoman state had already annexed a large part of the Kurdish region to its territory in 1514 by forming a political-military alliance with major Kurdish principalities, which had grown increasingly wary of the Safavid dynasty's drive to centralization and Shi'ification. The promise of political autonomy and religious freedom by the Sunni Ottomans had been effective in persuading the Kurdish rulers to change their allegiance. Successive states in Iran feared the repetition of this bitter experience, and this fear was the main reason behind the rapid destruction of the remaining Kurdish principalities, as well as the new system of security and control, operating via the political organization of the tribes, that gradually replaced the principalities after 1514.

The Iranian state thus adopted a distinctive attitude towards the Kurdish tribes, subjecting them to stricter political and looser financial control than the tribes in other parts of Iran.[16] The main aim of this policy was to ensure the political and military support of the Kurdish tribes in the cross-border relations with the Ottoman state, while preventing the formation of large and powerful tribal confederacies in Iranian Kurdistan. Such confederacies had been the bedrock of the political organization of the Kurdish principalities and the source of their military power. Although the actual relationship between the Iranian state and the Kurdish tribes depended largely on the political and military balance of power between them, the policies of the Iranian state had a lasting effect on the structural development and the political orientation of the tribes in Kurdish politics in subsequent periods.

The provision of military contingents to the state within a decentralized political structure was not the only function of the Kurdish tribal leadership. Tribal leaders also filled the power vacuum created in the Kurdish urban centres after the destruction of the Kurdish principalities. They were appointed as local governors, and Kurdish towns became seats of tribal power. Lineage and primordial relations were thus extended to underpin their rudimentary political and administrative structures, with retarding effects on the development of Kurdish urban culture. This practice continued until the end of the nineteenth century, when the Qajar government, caught in the throes of an irreversible political and economic decline, adopted the policy of replacing the Kurdish tribal chiefs with members of the ruling family. This policy may have been in part adopted for security reasons, in response to the after-effects of the Shaikh Ubaidollah movement, as well as being in part an extension of the by then common practice of the sale of office to remedy plummeting state revenues. Whatever the reason, the policy was unpopular and exacerbated the existing state of disorder and lawlessness. The Qajar governors were outsiders, lacking any local power-base or influence. They governed towns which remained largely under the political and economic control of the tribal chieftains, without whose consent and co-operation the business of government would come to a standstill. The Qajar governors, therefore, began playing the local chiefs against one another in order to sustain their flagging authority – a practice that was in full swing when the Constitutional Revolution broke out.

The tribal leadership's participation in counter-revolutionary politics in the Constitutional era was undoubtedly largely motivated by conservative and restorative aims. It was an attempt to maintain or to restore the feudal autocracy that had safeguarded their powers and privileges for the past four centuries, to maintain the existing structure of landownership in the countryside, and to restore the lost political leadership in the towns. Considerations such as the defence of the Kurds and their ethnic identity and rights, subsumed under the general concept of Iranian identity in the document of the Constitution and in the official discourse of the Constitutional government, were simply beyond the political vision of the tribal leadership. It is no exaggeration to say that in the Constitutional era the political leadership of Kurdish society lacked national consciousness.

The specific character of the economic and political relations which served to sustain and reproduce the preponderance of tribalism in social and political organizations of the Kurdish community also at the same time defined its boundaries. That is, the increasingly opaque boundaries separating the Kurdish inside of the community from its non-Kurdish outside: from the neighbouring communities with whom the Kurds had historically maintained a flourishing, though uneasy, social, economic and cultural relationship. This relationship at times involved violence, ranging from tribal skirmishes to large-scale communal wars, and often stemming from religious conflicts between the predominantly Sunni Kurds and their overwhelmingly Shi'i neighbours. Religion was the main element of communal identity in Kurdistan in the Constitutional era, especially in the growing urban centres, where it often prevailed over ethnic relations. In the countryside, however, the situation was different. Here, in particular in tribal lands, kinship and primordial relations were the fundamental elements of communal cohesion and identity, almost always defining the course and direction of communal discourse and practice for decades after the Constitutional revolution.

Pahlavi Absolutism and the Prelude to Kurdish Nationalism

The Constitutional government was the main achievement of the popular movement which had sought to restrain the powers of the autocratic sovereign by the rule of law, signifying the collective will of the nation. But now, barely a few years after the revolution, this liberal democratic ideal, already emasculated constitutionally by the juridical conditions of sovereignty and citizenship, seemed increasingly far removed from the rapidly evolving political conditions in the active sectors of society. The Constitutional government was fighting for survival, and the course of events after the revolution had taken the democratic soul out of its constitutional body before it was finally strangled

11

by Pahlavi absolutism. The political alliance between large landowners and merchant capital, and the active co-operation between traditional and modern intelligentsia in the political and ideological field, which had ensured the triumph of the Constitutional movement, did not last long. Both disintegrated soon after the last effort by the deposed Qajar autocrat and his internal and external allies to restore the *ancien régime* was crushed by the Constitutionalist forces in 1912. The power struggle between the landowning class and the mercantile bourgeoisie, and its political and ideological ramifications in the ranks of the still active segments of the traditional and modern intelligentsia, effectively prevented the institutionalization of state power in the country. Repeated attempts to create a modern army, a uniform tax regime and universal secular education failed. The government proved unable to create an effective level of territorial centralism, necessary for the uniform exercise of sovereignty in the country. The modern institutional shell lacked the content to support the political and cultural processes of the construction of a uniform Iranian identity. The Constitutional Revolution had all the general features of a passive revolution, in the Gramscian sense of the term.[17]

This failure to institutionalize state power created growing political instability and social disorder, which was further exacerbated when Iran was quite unwillingly drawn into the First World War. Kurdistan became a battlefield for the contending forces. Turkish, Russian and British forces invaded the territory and occupied various parts of it, in turn or together, leading to the total collapse of authority and administration and the disruption of agrarian production and trade in the region.[18] The mounting social chaos and economic crisis effectively severed the already tenuous link between the Kurdish territory and the centre, thus setting the stage for the first major Kurdish revolt in Iran.

Following the end of the war, Ismail Agha Shikak, known as Semko Shikak, the leader of the Abdui clan of the Shikak tribal confederacy, led a movement against the Iranian government that has been defined variously as nationalist, autonomist, tribal, and as sheer large-scale brigandage. The characterization of the movement as nationalist and separatist is common to both opponents and proponents, as are the more negative perceptions of it as tribal and brigandist.[19] These differences in definitions of the movement and the characterizations of its objectives arise primarily from different interpretations of its political history and of the recorded utterances of its leader in different occasions and contexts. Among Kurdish commentators, characterizations of the movement and its objectives are closely related to their conceptions of Kurdish nationalism, its genesis and development; little attention is thus paid to the social structure, political organization, ideological formation and strategic objectives of the movement itself, in the wider context of Iranian history and politics at the time.

The social structure, political organization and leadership of Semko's movement were predominantly tribal. The political conduct of the movement, leadership and rank and file alike, was also thoroughly tribal: armed sorties and pillage of the urban and rural population of the region, including the non-tribal Kurds, Azeris, Armenians and Assyrians, seems to have been the most common and effective way of raising revenue to pay for the upkeep of tribal solidarity. However, there is a body of evidence, cited by both opponents and proponents of Kurdish nationalism, which suggests that the tribal leadership – and in particular Semko himself – entertained the nationalist idea of a united and independent Kurdistan. According to its editor, Mulla Ahmad Ghizilji (Turjanizadeh), the idea was at times expressed in the *Roj i Kurd*, a journal published in Urmiya from 1919 to 1926. This journal, published in the Sorani dialect, signified the earliest official use of the Kurdish language in Iranian Kurdistan.[20]

Although the idea of a united and independent Kurdish homeland may well have been espoused by the leadership, there is little doubt that it never formed the strategic objective of the movement. The political discourse of *Roj i*

Kurd remained largely alien to the most basic concepts and principles of popular democratic politics characteristic of modern nationalist discourse, even though such concepts were fairly common in the discourse of the Kurdish intelligentsia in the late Ottoman period. The nationalist historical writing which disagrees with such characterizations of the movement more often than not explains its ideological formation and strategic objectives with reference to the vision and actions of its leadership, who defied the central political authority and challenged its representation in Kurdistan. The striking absence of the idea of the Kurdish nation as sovereign, the subject of the historical process of liberation and independence, from the political discourse of the tribal leadership in both its rhetorical and its diplomatic statements – where these have survived the vicissitudes of Kurdish and regional history – does, however, seem to dent the movement's nationalist credentials. This crucial absence points to an apparent paradox in characterizations of Semko's movement as nationalist: the paradox of the struggle against national oppression which does not deploy concepts of popular sovereignty, national rights and legitimacy. It is a paradox appropriate to the tribal and autonomist nature of Semko's movement.

Semko's movement achieved a degree of popularity and support in Iranian Kurdistan before it was finally defeated by the modernizing absolutism founded by Reza Shah in 1925. Reza Shah had succeeded in restoring order to the country by resolving the ongoing power struggle in favour of the conservative social and political forces represented by the growing number of large landlords and traditionalist clergy in the Majlis since 1912.[21] The upper and middle strata of the powerful mercantile bourgeoisie and the bulk of the liberal intelligentsia, who had represented the radical and progressive wing of the Constitutionalist movement, now joined forces with the conservatives. The rise of radical social movements in Azerbaijan and Gilan, along with the Semko movement in Kurdistan, had effectively split the liberal-progressive alliance in the Majlis, and the growing perception of a need for a strong centralized state tilted the already precarious balance of forces in favour of stability, law and order. Reza Shah's state, which was supported by this new regrouping of the forces in the political spectrum, was essentially the large landlords' regime. It reconstituted the traditional pre-capitalist power structure and redeployed it on a modern basis. The structure sustaining this curious amalgam was that of expanding commodity relations, which derived its impetus from the articulation of capitalist landed property and a pre-capitalist labour process in the organization of agrarian production.[22] The modern state apparatus that was created by Reza Shah was structured primarily on large landownership, bolstered by monopoly prices for agricultural produce on the one hand and the protectionist policies of the state on the other. The modernist absolutism that initiated the process of capitalist industrialization and development nevertheless stood firmly upon an economic base which was predominantly agrarian in form and pre-capitalist in character.

Reza Shah created the institutional structure necessary for the territorialization of the centralizing functions of the state in a predominantly agrarian social formation. The main instrument of his drive for political centralization was a modern army, which was institutionally supported by a new uniform tax regime and the restructured agrarian landed property. The destruction of the political structure and military organization of the tribes as the main centres and instruments of dissent and rebellion was the primary strategic objective of his policy of centralization. The scope of the policy was far wider than Kurdistan: it concerned tribalism in Iran in general. In fact, in political and military terms the southern and southwestern tribes, specifically the Bakhtiari and the Qashqai, posed a far greater threat to the political authority of the central government than the Kurdish tribes. The emergence in Turkey of a strong centralized military state hostile to the Kurds and their political aspirations, and the developments ensuring the consolidation of Hashemite rule in Iraq, had substantially reduced the danger of possible ethnic or nationalist movements among the Kurdish tribes. It was thus the destruction of the political and military organization of the Kurdish tribes, rather than of their ethnic identity, that formed the strategic objective of the politics of territorial centralism under Reza Shah. The absence of an effective Kurdish political organization with a coherent nationalist ideology and programme in Iranian Kurdistan as a whole supports this argument. Kurdish ethnicity posed little immediate danger to Pahlavi absolutism during the 1930s. Tribalism was the main source of political instability and the main threat to the authority of the state in Kurdistan.

This is not to say, however, that the state under Reza Shah was oblivious to the Kurdish threat to the 'national' sovereignty and territorial integrity of Iran, or overlooked its potential development as a disruptive factor in the processes of territorial centralism and institutional modernization. On the contrary, recent academic research shows that the Iranian state as early as 1920 was concerned about the developments in the Kurdish territory of the neighbouring Ottoman state, and especially watchful of the Kurdish representation and consideration of the Kurdish question in the League of Nations. Having evaluated the threat posed by an independent Kurdish state in the Ottoman territory, Foroughi, the Iranian representative to the League, advised the government of Tehran to adopt a policy of cultural assimilation rather than political coercion and suppression of Kurdish ethnic identity. In 1927, having been shaken by the scale and the strength of Shaikh Said's movements in Turkey and the destabilizing effects of Semko's activities in the region, the very same Foroughi, now the Iranian ambassador to Turkey, proposed measures for joint Iranian-Turkish co-operation against Kurdish movements.[23] After the consolidation of power by the mid-1930s, the Iranian state had little need to worry about the Kurdish threat. The disarming of the Kurdish tribes, coupled with the absence of an effective Kurdish political organization with a significant following in the major Kurdish urban centres, had largely marginalized (although not eliminated) the Kurdish threat to the political stability of the absolutist state. However Iran's participation in the Sa'dabad Pact in 1937, which regionalized the Kurdish question in the context of an anti-communist alliance, signifies the persistence of an anxiety about the possible threat Kurdish ethnicity could pose to the state, should the regional conditions prove favourable.

The politics of territorial centralism and the consolidation of state power in Kurdistan in the aftermath of Semko's death in 1930 revealed most vividly the dual character of Pahlavi absolutism: the capitalist form and pre-capitalist nature of state power. The centralization and consolidation of state power had a double effect on the socio-economic structures and political organization of Kurdistan. On the one hand, it dealt a massive blow to the political and military organization of the Kurdish tribes and to tribal landlordism, weakening substantially the traditional political base and military prowess of the hostile and potentially hostile tribal leaders; on the other, it restructured the juridico-political framework of tribal landownership, consolidating the economic foundation of their power. It was a typical example of the policy of carrot and stick, which the tribal landlords accepted grudgingly but without resistance. The Kurdish landowning class was thus reintegrated into the economic and political structures of power under Pahlavi absolutism.

The disarming of the Kurdish tribes and the redefinition of the political status of tribal landlordism were followed by attempts to reconstruct Iranian national identity on a uniform cultural foundation. The introduction of national conscription, whereby the defence of the realm was considered as a natural obligation of every male subject regardless of his ethnic origin, creed or social status, was the first step in this direction. This sense of national obligation was the ideological foundation of the modern army. The state was entitled to demand military service, and failure to comply was a crime tantamount to treason. Kurdish men were thus drafted into the new army and served under the new national flag. Traditional primordial loyalties had to be replaced by allegiance to the state, which embodied national sovereignty. The ideological function of national conscription was to create a new uniform loyalty that superseded ethnic and primordial loyalties.

This was reinforced by the introduction of universal primary education, which was the most powerful ideological instrument in the dissemination of the official discourse, now unmistakably nationalist in character. The state schools and the new national curricula were deployed to create a sense of national identity in the new generation, which was to provide the functionaries of the Pahlavi state. However, neither the new national army nor the new national education could function without a uniform official language. The dominance of Persian, which had already been declared the official language of Iran, was now to be reinforced by the suppression of all other languages spoken in Iran. A decree issued in 1935 thus marked the end of Kurdish as a written language, and the most significant element of Kurdish ethnic identity was suppressed.[24] The suppression of Kurdish along with other regional languages was a discursive condition of the constitution of the uniform Iranian identity. The new national identity was also given a new appearance to mark its break with the ethnic and primordial past, and the appearance of the new national identity was European. The state banned local dress for men and women, ordering them to wear European dress.

The conception of nation and national identity as uniform and indivisible constructed by the Pahlavi state thus denied ethnic difference and cultural pluralism, and ethnic difference accordingly became the strategic target of the discourse of national identity. The Kurd was different, and the discursive expression of this difference violated the identity of the sovereign (i.e. the dominant Persian ethnos) and the territoriality of its indivisible authority. The suppression of Kurdish language, history and culture and the denial of Kurdish ethnicity were, therefore, integral to the discursive strategies of national identity in Pahlavi Iran. The official discourse, grounded in the positivist logic of authoritarian modernization, was instrumental in converting the Kurd to the other of the sovereign. Contrasting images of the two proliferated in the discourse of modernity, which counterposed the tribal-rural to the urban-civilized. Kurdish was no longer the language of difference but of otherness, of antagonism and subversion. It questioned the identity of the sovereign and the legitimacy of the new order.

The suppression of Kurdish identity was thus intrinsic to the self-definition of the emergent nation state in Iran, whose brief and troubled history was not preceded by capitalist enterprise and liberal political culture. The suppression of the Kurdish language meant the expulsion of the Kurd from the sphere of writing. It was symptomatic of the imminent death of civil society in Iranian Kurdistan, the sudden disappearance of a nascent discursive formation which mediated between the political and the personal. The demise of civil society as such meant that public expressions of difference, of the ethnic identity of the Kurd, could not be without violence.

The official discourse stripped the Kurds of their ethnic identity. As Iranians they acquired a new identity, the constituent elements of which were derived from Persian ethnicity, culture and history. It was the Kurdish resistance to this forced identity and insistence on the expression of their difference that laid the foundation for the emergence of Kurdish nationalism in Iranian Kurdistan. Their attributed otherness from the sovereign thus became a source of their common identity as Kurds, counterposed to the hegemonist discourse of Pahlavi absolutism. The authors and the practitioners of the new nationalist discourse were the urban intelligentsia, who had their education in Reza Shah's schools and military garrisons. The politics of territorial centralism and the institutional processes and practices of the construction of Iranian national identity had already shifted the centre of Kurdish politics from the countryside to the towns. The formation of the *Komalay*

Jiyanaway Kurdistan (Society for the Revival of Kurdistan) in 1942 marked the advent of modern nationalist thought and practice in Iranian Kurdistan.

The Beginning: The Formation of the Komalay JK

This semi-clandestine organization, it is widely held, was founded on 16 August 1942 in Mahabad. It emerged out of *Komalay Azadixwazi Kurdistan* (Society for the Liberation of Kurdistan), another clandestine organization which had been founded in the summer of 1938 in the Mukrian region of eastern Kurdistan, very likely also in the town of Mahabad. The founders of the Komalay Jiyanaway Kurdistan came from the ranks of the Kurdish urban petty bourgeoisie, both traditional and modern, though predominantly the latter. The majority of the founding members were engaged in occupations which were either created by or associated with the development of the political, economic and administrative functions of the modern state in Kurdistan, and the organization included no landlord or mercantile bourgeois representation of any significance.[25] The formation of the Komalay Jiyanaway Kurdistan signified the revival of civil society in Kurdistan following the abdication of Reza Shah and the collapse of the absolutist regime in September 1941. Writing in Kurdish, which soon dominated the intellectual scene, was the major indicator of this revival. Kurdish became the language of political and cultural discourse among a small band of Kurdish intelligentsia, whose presence in the political field signified the development of commodity relations, secular education and modern administrative processes in Iranian Kurdistan.

The Komalay Jiyanaway Kurdistan insisted on an ethnic qualification for membership: Kurds from all parts of Kurdistan were eligible to join. Although the Christian inhabitants of Kurdistan, especially the Assyrians, could also become members, the constitution of the Komala regarded Islam as the official religion of Kurdistan, and a Quranic verse was inscribed in the emblem of *Nishtiman*, its official organ.[26] But the discourse of *Nishtiman* remained primarily secular, and its appeal to religion was mostly populist and functional. The Islamic credentials of the organization were often invoked to counteract the charges of atheism and communism increasingly levelled at it from within traditional sectors of Kurdish society, in particular the landowning class, the mercantile community and the clergy, who were made insecure by its radical populist-nationalist rhetoric.[27]

The ideological rhetoric of the Komala often invoked social and economic issues associated with the class structure of Kurdish society. *Nishtiman* contains frequent references to social inequality between 'haves and have-nots' in Kurdish society, and the poverty and ignorance of the Kurdish masses, especially the peasantry, contrasted with the accumulation of wealth among the landowners and merchants. Such references, combined with the occasional article or poem praising Lenin and the achievements of the Soviet Union, were clearly sufficient to provoke charges of communism and atheism. However, the discourse of *Nishtiman* did not include class categories.[28] The social and economic issues raised were attributed to the subjective qualities and interests of the economic agents in Kurdish society. For example, economic exploitation in agriculture – extortionate rents and over-exploitation of the peasantry – was attributed not to the prevailing structure of property relations in the countryside, but to the personal greed and immoral conduct of the landlords. Similarly, an economic notion of mercantile profit was absent in references to the accumulation of wealth and growing economic inequality in towns. Nor did the discourse of *Nishtiman* advocate social reform to alter the existing conditions and redress the sufferings of the poor and exploited. Instead, it appealed to the benevolence and humanitarianism of the landlords to reform harsh conditions by easing the burden of exploitation. The perceived radicalism of the Komala remained wrapped in a moral critique of Kurdish

21

society, of a kind traditionally associated with agrarian populism in transitional societies. The concept of 'the people' deployed in the discourse of *Nishtiman* possesses the essential attributes of this category in the conceptual structure of populist discourse. The nationalist character of the discourse of *Nishtiman* does not differentiate it from mainstream agrarian populism. In fact, it is the constant overlapping of the two notions of the Kurdish people and the Kurdish nation in the discourse of *Nishtiman* that accounts for the radical character of its nationalist message, often mistaken for the hidden influence of Marxism-Leninism on the ideological formation of the organization.

In the discourse of *Nishtiman* the two concepts of Kurdish people and Kurdish nation are synonymous and frequently used interchangeably. The concept of the Kurdish people/nation is central to its highly heterogeneous narrative, unifying it around the common theme of an independent Kurdish homeland. This theme forms the main strategic objective of the Komala, and is clearly expressed in its constitution.[29] It informs the conceptual structure of the narrative of *Nishtiman*, prose and verse, assigning to it a specifically nationalist character. The creation of an independent Kurdish homeland is further perceived as an aim to be realized through the united efforts of the Kurdish nation, the subject of Kurdish history. Although the subject of Kurdish history as such signifies a uniform and undifferentiated whole in a strictly nationalist mould, the political strategy by which the nationalist objective set out in the Komala's programme and constitution was to be achieved indicates otherwise.

The most striking aspect of this political strategy is its rejection of armed struggle: Komalay Jiyanaway Kurdistan advocates a nationalist strategy that is strictly civil-political, involving no military/armed practices. This radical break with the classical Kurdish military-political method hitherto prevalent in all parts of Kurdistan is highly significant.[30] It demonstrates not only the Komala's view of the futility of military action against numerically, logistically and technologically superior forces in a landlocked terrain, but also its radical assessment of the social structure, political organization and ideological orientation of military power in Kurdistan. Such power was traditionally possessed, controlled and exercised by the Kurdish tribal leadership, and armed tribal contingents were its backbone. Thus to advocate a nationalist strategy involving military power would have meant sharing power with the tribal leadership, and ultimately succumbing to the conservative political whims and the short-term personal interests of that leadership – a factor that would prove decisive in the rapid demise of the Kurdish Republic centred on Mahabad. The predominance of lineage and primordial loyalties in the social structure and political organization of Kurdish movements had proved detrimental to the development of national consciousness and modern nationalist political practice in Kurdistan. The painful realization of this structural feature of Kurdish society and politics was clearly reflected in the constitution and the political structure of the Komala. The refusal to view the armed struggle as a means of achieving the nationalist objective amounted to the exclusion of the landowning class and the tribal leaders from the political organization and the leadership of the movement.[31] The Komala's assessment of the role of the Kurdish landowning class in general and the tribal leadership in particular remained consistent with its political practice during its brief existence, before it was transformed into the Democratic Party of Kurdistan in 1944.

Ideologically, the exclusion of the landowning class and the tribal leadership from the process of the realization of the nationalist objective signifies an attempt to redefine the concept of the Kurdish nation on political grounds. In Komala's discourse there is a difference between the concept of the Kurdish nation as the uniform subject of national history, and the concept of the Kurdish nation as the differentiated subject of nationalist political practice. The former, which informs Komala's ideological rhetoric, is defined by ethnic relations, and functions to marginalize existing socio-economic and political differences within the nation, presenting it as a uniform and homogeneous subject of nationalist history endowed with the

23

mission to create a united independent homeland in Kurdistan. The latter, which underpins Komala's political strategy, invokes these socio-economic and political differences, which cut across ethnic relations. This difference between the uniform outside and the differentiated inside is the mark of modern political identity. It is never stable or fixed, but constantly redefined in the course of the struggle among the forces and relations that participate in nationalist politics. The vacillation between ethnic nationalism and agrarian populism and the constant overlapping of the concepts of the Kurdish nation and the Kurdish people in the discourse of Komala testify, above all, to the precarious nature of the emergent national identity in Iranian Kurdistan.

2

KOMALAY JK TO THE REPUBLIC: THE FORMATION OF THE KDPI

Komalay JK had only a brief life: it did not collapse or disintegrate, but at the peak of its power and popularity it was abolished and transformed into the Kurdistan Democratic Party of Iran (KDPI) on 15 August 1945.[1] The declaration of the formation of the KDPI carried 61 signatures by merchants, civil servants, clergy, landowners and tribal leaders demanding regional autonomy within the framework of Iranian Constitutional Law (1906). The declaration, which was published in Kurdish and Persian, located the Kurdish demand in the context of post-war conditions, especially the promises contained in the 'historic Atlantic treaty', asking for an end to national oppression in Iran.[2] 'Why should our [national] rights be trampled on, why do not you allow Kurdistan to become an autonomous province, and through the provincial association specified in the constitutional law to run its own affairs?', the declaration asked. The KDPI is presented as the organization created to attain this national goal. 'The great objective of the party in the present situation' is thus defined in its programme (part 2, clause 4):

> to safeguard the rights of the Kurdish people within the boundaries of the Iranian state ... In Kurdistan democracy

should be fundamentally accessible to the people and they should have the right to take part in the elections for the national consultative assembly [the Majlis] without national and religious discrimination.[3]

The KDPI remained committed to the autonomy project, and its programme remained unchanged under the Republic. This transformation is widely believed to have buried the political project of the Komalay JK, putting an end to its nationalist ideals and reformist programme. But informed opinion on the actual causes of the transformation is sharply divided. Why did the leadership of this popular and expanding organization give up its political project and sign away its right to exist? Was this an astute political move, or capitulation to external political pressures exerted upon it by the Soviet Union?

Mainstream nationalist opinion holds that the fateful transformation was in line with the natural progression of Kurdish history and politics, and that the KDPI espoused the essentials of the political project of the Komalay JK and represented its ideological position. The notable absence of Komala's agrarian populist rhetoric from the discourse of *Kurdistan*, the official organ of the KDPI, along with the exclusion of key members of the central committee (especially its learned chairman Abdul Rahman Zabihi) from the leadership of the new organization, are either dismissed as insignificant or attributed to 'changing circumstances', a catch-all phrase seldom specified in the writings and speeches of the mainstream nationalists. This view, although widespread among the members and supporters of the KDPI, is clearly one-sided. It pays little attention to the political and ideological conditions governing the process of transformation, and still less to the manner in which these conditions determined the political and ideological specificity of its outcome – the KDPI, and subsequently the Republic.[4]

The radical nationalist view, often voiced in populist-Marxist terminology, is different. The dissolution of the Komalay JK is believed to signify the political capitulation of its leadership to Soviet policy, which opposed its radical political project, fearing adverse consequences for Soviet security and strategic interests in the region. The absence of radical populist rhetoric and the marginalization of popular reformist measures in the discourse of *Kurdistan* were designed to ensure the support and co-operation of the tribal leadership, the landowning class and the mercantile bourgeoisie, who were strongly represented in the political and military organizations of the KDPI and the Republic. The transformation of the Komalay JK to the KDPI, it is thus maintained, distorted the nationalist ideal, diverting it from its radical roots and revolutionary path.

This view is central to the contemporary radical left, who offer a variety of Marxist analyses of the rise and demise of the Kurdish Republic.[5] In particular, it is closely associated with those sections of the Kurdish intelligentsia who were grouped around *Komalay Shorishgeri Zahmatkeshani Kurdistani Iran*, a Marxist-Leninist organization with Maoist orientation which surfaced in the political field soon after the Iranian Revolution in 1979, attracting a significant number of educated young Kurds to its ranks and challenging the growing predominance of the newly revived socialist KDPI in the region. It was often invoked to castigate the leadership of the KDPI, to question its revolutionary legitimacy, and criticize its policies as reformist and opportunist, betraying the radical political project and the revolutionary ideals of the nationalist movement. It is still deployed by the populist left to serve this purpose, with or without the customary Marxist terminology.[6]

The main argument of the Marxist-Leninist account of the transformation of the Komalay JK into the KDPI seems to be correct, but only partially. True, the existing evidence suggests that the leadership of the KDPI had effectively abandoned the radical political project of the Komala, both its territorial ethnic nationalism and its agrarian populism, before the creation of the Republic in January 1946. It is also true that such changes in the direction and objectives of the nationalist politics, which reincorporated the Kurdish landowning class, especially the powerful tribal leadership, into the social structure and political and military organizations of the movement, were bound up with Soviet security and strategic interests in the region during and after the Second World War.[7] But while Soviet pressure was indeed a decisive factor driving the nationalist leadership to change the stated aims and aspirations of the movement, this is only one side of the story. The Marxist-Leninist analysis fails to consider the structural conditions of this transformation, which were internal to Kurdish society in Iran. Nor does it take into account the political, economic and institutional requirements of mass political organization and modern popular politics. These conditions, it will be argued, were far more important in defining this fateful transformation than the security and strategic considerations of the Soviet Union. They largely determined not only the conditions of the formation of the KDPI, but also the political form and social character of the Republic. They were, in other words, the *prima causa* of the Republic, defining its rise, development and demise. But before considering the conditions of the formation of the KDPI, I shall briefly focus on the role played by the Soviet Union during this crucial and formative period in the development of Kurdish nationalism in Iran.

Soviet Policy in Kurdistan: Conditions and Strategic Objectives

Arguments about the nature and direction of Soviet policy in Kurdistan from 1941 to 1947 are central to most recent scholarship on the formation and dissolution of the Republic, both Marxist-populist and centre-right nationalist. There is in the core of these analyses a common argument, which blames not only the conservative traditionalism of the KDPI but also the rise and unfortunate demise of the short-lived Kurdish Republic on the cynical and unprincipled pragmatism of Soviet foreign policy in the region during this fateful period.

For the centre-right nationalists, the formation of the KDPI and the creation of the Republic were but part of a larger 'Soviet Game' in the process of a sustained and increasingly violent power politics in which small and stateless nations such as the Kurds were mere pawns, powerless and dispensable. The Soviet policy-makers, it is contended, manipulated Kurdish nationalist aspirations and used them to serve their own regional and global political and strategic objectives. The centre-right nationalist view, which is often heavily coloured by an anti-Marxist ideological bias, blames the Soviet Union for the political opportunism and Machiavellian pragmatism which are seen as characteristic features of the regime, inherent in its political and ideological systems.[8]

The Marxist-populist position, on the other hand, blames Soviet policy for its Stalinist revisionism, for deviating from the 'true' revolutionary Marxist-Leninist line and betraying the popular democratic cause of the nationalist movement in Kurdistan. Underlying the Marxist-populist argument is the idea that the founding of the Komalay JK marked the onset of a 'bourgeois-democratic' national liberation movement in Iranian Kurdistan, which was spreading rapidly before it succumbed to Stalinist betrayal. This argument, it will be shown, rests on a number of unfounded assumptions about the construction of national identity in the Kurdish nationalist movement on the one hand, and the nature and strategic objectives of the Soviet policy in Kurdistan on the other. The Marxist-populist argument cannot be sustained if these assumptions are questioned, on theoretical and empirical grounds.[9]

The Marxist-populist characterization of the Kurdish movement as 'bourgeois-democratic' and national-liberationist is class-essentialist and reductionist. The political identity of the movement is deduced from its social structure, which bears the identity of the assumed dominant class within it, i.e. the emergent national bourgeoisie and the middle strata. This, in turn, is based on the equally reductionist assumption that these social forces espouse nationalism as their class ideology in the process of capitalist development and (in the underdeveloped world) anti-colonial/anti-imperialist struggle. This double reductionism underpins the Marxist-populist argument and is central to its definition of the movement as bourgeois-democratic and national-liberationist.

There is no doubt about the nationalist identity of the movement which began in the Iranian Kurdistan soon after the collapse of the first Pahlavi regime in 1941. It is also true that the urban petty-bourgeoisie and the middle strata played leading roles in the political and organizational formation and development of the movement. But neither the nationalist identity of the movement nor the political position of the Kurdish urban middle classes can be deduced from their class structures and interests. Marxist-populist argument conflates class identity with national identity and deduces the former from the latter, on the assumption that nationalism is the ideology of the democratic bourgeoisie in the historical period of the transition to capitalism and the formation of the nation state.

True, class relations and class identities, as we have seen, play a role in the shifting configuration of political, economic and cultural forces and relations which cut across ethnic relations and specify the inner boundary of national identity. It was seen that the exclusion of the Kurdish landowning class from the territorial nationalist political process and strategy under the Komalay JK had a direct bearing on its nationalist discourse, and hence on the construction of national identity in the discourse of *Nishtiman*. It will also be shown in the following section that the subsequent inclusion of the landowning class in the autonomist nationalist political process by the KDPI resulted in a significant change in the constructions of Kurdish national identity in the discourse of *Kurdistan*. This is because the exclusion of the landowning class from and its inclusion in the nationalist political process were conditions of the existence of two different forms of nationalist politics: territorial nationalism and regional autonomy respectively, each involving a different form of the relationship of the Kurdish 'self' and the Persian 'other'.

This relationship of the 'self' and the 'other', which defines the outer boundaries of Kurdish national identity in Iran, as was seen, is one of identity and difference; ethnic and cultural differences with the 'other'. Ethnic and cultural differences defining the outer boundary of national identity, however, are never given, but are constructed in nationalist discourses. The latter may and indeed do vary in form, but they cannot be reduced to specific class interests or explained by specific class categories, bourgeois or otherwise. Particular configurations of class relations and constellations of class interests in specific political conjunctures do affect the mode of the articulation of ethnic and cultural differences in nationalist discourses, but they are not constitutive of these differences. Nor do they play a decisive role in the construction of ethnic and cultural differences as national differences, the constituent elements of national identity. National differences are constructed in nationalist discourses, which remain constitutive of national identity in general.

For the Marxist-populist position, however, ethnic and cultural differences defining the contours of national identity are trans-historical phenomena. They are given to nationalist discourses, whose conceptual structures are primarily determined by specific class relations and interests, namely those of the national bourgeoisie. Ethnic and cultural relations, therefore, are conceived as mere adjuncts of economic class relations, and their role in the construction of national identity is attributed not to the specificity of the nationalist discourse but to the social structure of the nationalist ideology. In the Marxist-populist discourse, nationalism has no discursive autonomy and national identity is a historical construct generated and sustained by specific class relations; it depends on these relations for its survival.

This general theoretical argument informs much of the Marxist-populist perception of the Soviet policy towards the nationalist movement in Kurdistan during the period under consideration. Soviet policy, signifying the revisionist essence of the Stalinist regime, goes against Marxist-Leninist orthodoxy; it betrays a progressive bourgeois-democratic nationalist movement in favour of preserving the status quo in the emergent bipolar international political order. Although there is no reliable evidence, official policy statement or party declaration representing or pertaining to the Soviet perception of the class character of the nationalist movement in Iranian Kurdistan, the political and ideological thinking behind Soviet policy is not difficult to gauge.

The sheer opportunism of Soviet policy not withstanding, it seems highly unlikely that the Soviet and especially Soviet-Azeri political and military officers who were directly and indirectly involved in policy and decision-making and influenced the course of the events in the region ever treated the Kurdish movement and its subsequent political form as bourgeois-democratic. Ironically, the most likely reason for this refusal could have originated from the very same class-essentialist conception of nationalism that informs the Marxist-populist critique. In fact the Soviet approach and its Marxist-populist critique share the same essentialist and reductionist theoretical and conceptual framework; they are informed by two different essentialist readings of the historical development of Kurdish society in Iran.

From the Soviet point of view, Kurdish society in Iran in the early 1940s was essentially feudal, dominated by tribalism, religion and tradition. It was structurally incapable of producing and sustaining a genuine nationalist movement with a bourgeois-democratic character.[10] This reading of Kurdish politics and society, emphasizing the strong presence of the Kurdish landowning class (especially the tribal leadership) in the political and military organizations of the movement, the conservative outlook of the leadership and their resistance to popular demands for socio-economic reform, and the increasing presence of religion in the official discourse, seems to have been the main reason for the Soviet refusal to treat the Kurdish nationalist movement, and later on the Republic, as bourgeois-democratic, at least on a par with the Azerbaijan movement. International and regional considerations and determinants of the Soviet policy aside, it seems that the Soviet policy and decision-makers, especially those political commissars and field officers with ideological zeal and conviction, were not particularly well disposed to the Kurdish movement and its traditional leadership. However, this point should not be taken to mean that the Soviet policy and decision-makers had a doctrinal approach to the Kurdish movement. For there is little doubt that political pragmatism rather than ideological zeal defined the Soviet approach to the Kurdish movement and the shifting boundaries of the Soviet-Kurdish relationship during this period.

Further, given the essentialism of the Soviet analysis of Kurdish society and its socio-economic structure and political organization, there remains hardly any ground for an appreciation of the emergent national identity in Kurdistan. Like its Marxist-populist critics, the Soviet view, following the official line which was informed by Stalin's conception of nation and nationalism, could not but reduce national identity to the mere effect of social class relations, that is, an attribute of a liberal-democratic bourgeoisie in the early stages of capitalist development. The predominance of feudal relations and tribal forces in the economic and political organization of Kurdish society was thus taken to mean that the movement lacked the necessary structural foundation to qualify as nationalist and bourgeois-democratic.

It is true that the primary objective of Soviet policy in Iran in general, and in Kurdistan and Azerbaijan in particular, was to maintain social order and political stability. Co-operation with those sectors of local population who could help the Soviet command achieve this objective was, therefore, actively sought and nurtured by the Soviet forces stationed in Kurdistan. These were usually powerful local elites, political and intellectual, who for their own pragmatic reasons responded favourably to the Soviet overtures for co-operation. In Kurdistan, as will be seen, the policy of maintaining order and stability led to co-operation primarily with the tribal leadership and the nationalist intelligentsia, which was drawn largely from the ranks of the urban petty-bourgeoisie, traditional and modern.[11]

The tribal leadership mostly heeded the Soviet call, for fear both of the Red Army and of the impending threat of a rapidly spreading radical populist nationalism. The minority of tribal chiefs who had opposed Reza Shah's detribalization and disarmament and suffered the consequences in harsh prison sentences, banishment and loss of landed property and political authority also had strong motives for responding to the call for co-operation.[12] Having returned to their lands and re-established the lost seat of political and economic power, the benefits of Soviet military presence and protection exceeded both the fear of a likely permanent communist presence and radical territorial nationalism, at least temporarily. The nationalist petty-bourgeoisie likewise sought Soviet protection to ward off the omnipresent menace of the Iranian army to the developing nationalist movement and the emergent nationalist political authority. Unlike the mercantile bourgeoisie, the small business and the salaried middle class did not fear the loss of access to the Iranian markets.[13]

The maintenance of order and stability in Kurdistan, therefore, involved a complex balancing act among local social forces whose diverse and contradictory economic and political interests often jeopardized the unstable structure of Soviet policy. In fact, the persistent attempt to maintain an 'unstable balance of compromise', an uneasy working alliance to establish a modus operandi among the Kurdish social and political forces, remained the only invariant of Soviet policy from September 1941 to May 1946, when the Soviet military units withdrew from Kurdish territory for good. The maintenance of the status quo was threatened not only by the variations of a precarious balance of compromise in Kurdistan, but also by the mutations of regional and international variants of the Soviet strategy during and after the war. The logistics and security requirements of Soviet wartime strategy were never fixed or permanent; they varied considerably both in the course of the Second World War and in the early phase of the Cold War and the confrontation with the West.

Soviet policy in Iranian Kurdistan was thus the nodal intersection of internal and external conditions, each with their own variants and determinants, which cannot be reduced to or deduced from a single and uniform set of political and strategic relations and interests. It follows from this observation that Soviet policy in Iranian Kurdistan was neither uniform nor fixed. It varied considerably, assuming different forms in pursuit of a different hierarchy of political and strategic objectives. This point, which is clearly borne out by the existing British and American official documents, is fundamental to the analysis of the Soviet role in the rise and fall of the nationalist movement in Iranian Kurdistan.[14] But, despite its significance, this point is completely overlooked by the protagonists of the Marxist-populist approach. For the Marxist-populist analyses Soviet policy is uniform and fixed, and this assumption lies at the heart of their critical commentary, often at the expense of overlooking the historical specificity of nationalist politics in Kurdistan.

Reading the British and American official documents pertaining to Soviet policy in Iranian Kurdistan, one is immediately struck by a remarkable similarity of perception and analysis. The official reports produced by the British and American diplomats, field officers and counsellors indicate, in no ambiguous terms, that the Soviet Union did not have an autonomous and specified Kurdish policy with fixed determinants, national or regional, least of all a political commitment to the cause of a Kurdish national state. Rather, Soviet policy in the occupied Kurdish territory was closely tied to its overall strategy in the region and reflected the modality of its development since September 1941. Soviet strategy, it is further indicated, varied considerably during the war and after, and this variation signified changes in its security and logistical requirements. But, in so far as the specific case of Kurdish politics was concerned, Soviet policy and decision-making filtered through two sets of relations, associated with its policy towards the Iranian government and the Azerbaijan Republic respectively. To this must be added the regional considerations of the Soviet Union, chiefly her relationship with Turkey, and to a lesser extent the Arab states, especially Iraq; both Turkey and Iraq were sensitive to and concerned with Soviet policy in Iranian Kurdistan, though to varying degrees.[15]

The British and American diplomatic representations in Tehran were at the time clearly aware of the fact that Soviet policy and decision-making regarding occupied Iran was less than uniform or direct, and that the Soviet diplomatic corps in Tehran was restrained by the general political and ideological imperatives of the Communist Party of the Soviet Union (CPSU) in Moscow, which were often geared to wider and more long-term considerations of a global power struggle. This issue was broached by Sir Reader Bullard, the British Minister in Tehran, who thought that 'the main difficulty is that the Soviet political policy in the occupied zone is run by an organization over which the Soviet Minister at Tehran has little influence'.[16] When Sir Anthony Eden took up the issue with Molotov, he was quick to respond to the allegations of political disunity and ideological bias in the process of foreign policy-making during the war, when the exigencies of an anti-fascist alliance with Western powers clearly overrode all other long-term policy considerations: 'The assumption expressed by the British Minister, Sir R.W. Bullard, that Soviet policy in those parts of Iran where Soviet troops are stationed, was being carried out by organizations on which the Soviet Ambassador had very little influence, is without foundation,' he declared.[17] Molotov's denial, however, does not seem to have changed the British perception that the Soviet foreign policy in Azerbaijan was being overseen by specific organizations closely associated with the CPSU.

The British government, whose declared aim was to safeguard the sovereignty and territorial integrity of the Iranian state, was closely monitoring Soviet policy towards the Kurds and their political aspiration to achieve independence from the central government in Tehran. Reports pertaining to the early phase of Soviet occupation suggest that the Soviets did not have a specific 'Kurdish policy' and that their activity on the local level was not guided by a uniform strategy, subversive or conservative. In fact, the British reporting describes the Soviet local political activity as lacking operational autonomy and resource, 'improvizations' strictly subordinated to the logistics of the war effort: to secure the military supply lines which ran through Kurdish territory, mainly along the Iranian-Turkish borders.[18]

The Soviet effort, it is further maintained, was beset by two problems: the unruly tribes in the countryside and the rising tide of nationalism in urban centres.[19] Initially, the Soviets seem to have pursued a policy of friendship and local co-operation with the Kurdish tribes rather obsessively, assigning a secondary importance to the political aspirations and activities of the nationalist forces in Kurdish urban centres. This is because tribal rebellion and rural unrest were perceived as real possibilities in the wake of the collapse of the Pahlavi authority and the return of the hostile landlords and tribal chiefs to their lands. This posed an immediate and serious danger to the maintenance of supply lines in Kurdish territory, which largely passed through tribal lands. Given this priority in Soviet policy, it is therefore not surprising to see that the Soviets took the side of the Kurdish landlords and tribal leaders in the growing rift and impending hostility with the urban nationalist forces which had recently formed the Komalay JK. In fact, the cool reception of the Komalay JK and its territorial nationalist programme by the Soviets and their subsequent efforts to exert pressure on its leadership to incorporate the unfriendly and hostile landlords and tribal leaders into the nationalist political process should be seen in this context.[20]

Of the reasons pertaining to the conduct of Soviet policy in Iranian Kurdistan during the Second World War, British official reports give more weight to regional issues. Regional considerations, especially the crucial wartime relationship with Turkey, it is thus maintained, were of primary importance in the formulation and conduct of policy regarding the Kurds of Iran. There were a number of reasons for this. First, Turkey was perceived as the bulwark against German influence and attempts to disrupt the logistics of the war effort, especially the security of military supply lines to the Russian front. The Soviets wished to secure the goodwill and co-operation of the Turkish government, and for this they had to rely mainly on Britain, which also shared the same policy concern in the region. The Turkish government, however, was suspicious of Soviet activity in Iranian Kurdistan and feared its likely destabilizing effects on the Kurdish region in the south and south-east of the country. This issue is highlighted in a memorandum addressed to J. Maisky by Eden in late June 1942:

> In view of interest expressed by M. Stalin during our conversation at Moscow in encouraging the Turkish government to maintain their position as a bulwark against Germany, I feel I should point out that according to Sir Hugh Knatchbull-Hugessen anxiety over the situation in Persian Kurdistan is at present the chief obstacle to the improvement of Turko-Soviet relations. (FO 248/3321)

The major cause of anxiety for the Turkish government, it transpires in the same memorandum, was the visit made by certain Kurdish public figures to Baku earlier in the same year. In response to Eden, the Soviet government deems it necessary to assure the Turkish government of the non-political and purely 'cultural' nature of the Kurds' visit to Baku. Molotov's prompt 'declarations about the Kurds' only testifies to the importance of Turkey in the Soviet regional strategy:

> Turkish Ambassador added that Molotov's declarations about the Kurds (or Kurdistan) seem to him very sincere, only

false point being 'cultural' visit to Baku. His information being that whatever Soviet authorities might be planning in Azerbaijan they were not supporting Kurdish movement as such. He thought the Turkish government and his colleagues in Tehran had been unduly alarmed. (FO 248/ 410)

Secondly, the likely reaction of the Arab states, especially Iraq, was a matter for concern for the Soviet Union and had to be taken into consideration in the formulation and conduct of policy in Iranian Kurdistan. The relationship with Iraq was further complicated by the British influence and interest. Although the British foreign office was almost certain that the Soviets had no design for an independent Kurdish entity in Iran, it was nonetheless concerned about the likely destabilizing effects of a growing nationalist movement on Iraqi Kurdistan. The Iraqi government was clearly worried about the development of Kurdish nationalism across the border and exerted pressure on its patron to use its influence with Soviets to discourage it, if not curb it, effectively. Needless to say the relationship with Britain, in particular in the early phase of the war and the anti-fascist alliance, was paramount not only in the regional but also in the global considerations of Soviet foreign policy. It easily overrode the local and less significant considerations of Soviet wartime strategy.

But as the war drew to a close and the balance of military forces in the Russian front shifted significantly in favour of the Red Army, the Soviet policy towards the Kurds began to change from pacification to cautious support and encouragement.[21] This shift, it should be noted, did not signify the onset of a new and radical tendency in the Soviet strategy, but rather an early and cautious anticipation of an impending change in the regional and international balance of forces defining the status quo. In this sense, the new policy of guarded support and measured encouragement did not deviate from the general conservative ethos of the Soviet strategy. For the new approach too was intrinsically related to the Soviet attempt to redefine its status in the emerging balance of power, to accommodate its long-term political and strategic objectives in the region. It therefore involved no active political and military commitment to the idea of Kurdish nationalism, still less to the cause of an independent territorial Kurdish state.

The regional autonomy plan nevertheless proved popular and certainly attractive enough to appeal to a cross-section of Kurdish nationalists, especially those with a more conservative political orientation and traditional outlook from within the ranks of the landowning class, mercantile bourgeoisie and urban petty-bourgeoisie, whose attachment to private property and Sunni Islam did not stand in the way of co-operation with a communist regime. Of course, there was also the attraction of the 'Azeri model', to which the Soviets had given considerable support and commitment and which, with the Red Army still on guard, had a fair chance of survival. But, as will be shown in the following section, there were other and more important reasons than Soviet persuasion and manipulation or the populist attraction of the 'Azeri model' for the sudden appeal of the regional autonomy project to the Kurdish nationalists. These reasons were internal to Kurdish society; they were deeply rooted in the historical specificity of the nationalist political process in Iranian Kurdistan.

The project of regional autonomy on which the new Soviet approach was founded required two essential conditions if it were to succeed: first, a modification of the political programme of territorial nationalism and agrarian populist reformism of the Komalay JK, and secondly, the incorporation of the landowning class and tribal leadership in the nationalist political process. The existing evidence suggests that before the end of the war and certainly by early 1944, the focus of Soviet policy had already shifted from the landowning class to the urban nationalist forces. Although with the change in the fortunes of the war and the impending German defeat the tribal leadership had largely lost its significance in Soviet strategy, it was not only a force to be reckoned with; it was certainly the most powerful political force in the Kurdish territory, and almost exclusively in possession of military power. The landowning class, therefore, could not be dispensed with, and its active participation was deemed necessary for the implementation of the Kurdish autonomy project. The creation of a working alliance between the tribal leadership and the urban nationalist forces largely represented by the Komalay JK seems to have been a major objective of Soviet diplomatic activity in Iranian Kurdistan from early 1944 to the declaration of the Republic in January 1946.

US official reports convey a similar message. The main point, reiterated variously, is that the Soviet Union did not have a systematic and uniform policy regarding the developments in Iranian Kurdistan. The primary concern of the Soviet policy initially was to safeguard the military supply lines. In so doing it attempted to pacify and manipulate hostile or potentially hostile tribes which threatened the logistics of the war effort. But this policy did not involve major political and military commitments to the Kurds for fear of disturbing the regional status quo, in which the suppression of Kurdish nationalist aspirations and demands had been an important inter-governmental consideration at least since the Sa'd Abad treaty in 1937. The Kurdish landlords and tribal leaders who had opted for co-operation with the Soviets, however, were not particularly enthused, as they soon realized that an active commitment and aid was not on the Soviet agenda. Mobley, drawing on the American official records, clearly explains the nature and extent of Soviet aid after the war, especially to the tribal leaders. He also indicates that by 1945 the Soviets had succeeded in cultivating some influence among sectors of the tribal leadership, which they subsequently used to help the nationalists. As he writes:

> After the war, the Soviet authorities chose to use their residual influence on behalf of the Kurdish nationalists. They assisted the Komala and later on Kurdish Democratic Party (KDPI) recruiting efforts among the tribes and made

stirring promises of moral and material support to several Kurdish dignitaries. Many of these promises were soon kept ...

But after citing instances of Soviet military, logistical and political support for the Kurdish nationalist movement, he concludes,

> Yet it should be noted that such an outside (USSR) assistance was extremely limited; the Kurdish nationalist movement possessed a momentum of its own and did not depend on the USSR for its inspiration. It had however benefited from the Soviet restraint of the Iranians and would, to its ultimate detriment, reluctantly continue to seek Soviet support against the central government ...[22]

US official reports further show that after the implementation of the autonomy plan, the promised Soviet support for the Republic remained rather minimal, politically and militarily. In so far as the Republic was concerned the continued presence of the Red Army to the north of the Saqqiz-Baneh-Sardasht line was the most significant contribution of the Soviet Union to its survival, for it effectively deterred the Iranian army from entering the Republican jurisdiction and marching towards Mahabad. But the safety of the Red Army and Russian economic, military and cultural aid did not prevent the Republican leadership from rethinking its relationship with the Soviet Union and reassessing the conditions of Soviet commitment to and support for the Kurdish autonomy project. This trend, which grew stronger as the withdrawal of the Soviet military contingents became imminent, also involved a reassessment of the relationship with both the Azeri regime and the central government in Tehran.[23]

US official reporting, it is worth noting, lays much emphasis on the significance of the Azerbaijan Republic in the Kurdish-Soviet relationship. This relationship involved two major issues:

first, the territorial dispute between the Kurdish and Azeri republics over the administration and control of the three towns of Urmiya, Khoi and Salmas; and secondly, the changing relationship between the Azeri Republic and the central government in Tehran, which also included the Tudeh party. These issues were both of paramount importance to the Soviet diplomats in Tehran and policy and decision-makers in Baku and Moscow.[24]

The Conditions of the Formation of the KDPI

Komalay JK was a political association with a nationalist programme which defined its objectives, above all the creation of a national state in a united Kurdistan. These nationalist objectives gave the Komala an inbuilt legitimacy which bolstered its self-image as the vanguard of the struggle, thus overshadowing the crucial issue of the political and institutional requirements of the perceived nationalist strategy: that is, the political and institutional conditions of the existence of the nationalist political process and practice in Greater Kurdistan. Although this issue had direct implications for the legitimacy of the Komalay JK and its call for national unity and popular action, it had not been specified in its programme. At the heart of this issue lay the fundamental questions of political authority and administration in the institutional structure of the Komala, and these in turn concerned the nature of its relationship with its membership and constituency of support in Greater Kurdistan.

In so far as the Komalay JK remained a parochial political-intellectual association and its membership and constituency of support were chiefly confined to the town of Mahabad and its immediate vicinity, the questions of political authority and administration could be easily sidestepped without undermining its legitimacy. But the cosy conditions which had enabled the association to function without addressing these questions did not last long. They soon changed in response to the institutional exigencies of modern mass politics in a traditional/pre-capitalist society.

The nationalist programme of the Komalay JK and its call to action were attractive to the people of Mahabad, and significant numbers from the ranks of the urban petty-bourgeoisie, traditional and modern, and the lower and middle ranks of the mercantile bourgeoisie flocked to the association, to join or to lend support. By mid April 1943, barely six months after its formation, the association had already managed to consolidate its basis in Mahabad and extend its influence south and westward to major urban centres such as Bokan, Baneh, Saqqiz and Sardasht, enlisting some new members and considerable popular support in the area north of the British controlled zone.[25] However, the increase in membership and the development of popular support posed the intractable problem of administration. The Komalay JK, like any other political organization aspiring to democratic politics, mass base and popular support, had to face this crucial issue. It was unavoidable. It could no longer remain as a parochial political association of free individuals. But administration meant formal *authority* and a set of rules and regulations specifying its conditions and means within the association. The introduction of formal authority had grave consequences for the subsequent development of the Komalay JK politically and organizationally.

It was, therefore, the institutional requirements of modern mass politics which led the core members of the Komalay JK to elect a central leadership committee in April 1943. This committee, widely believed to have been led by Abdulrahman Zabihi, signified the emergence of political authority and institutional hierarchy within the association. Informal political relations and personal and familial ties and associations to a considerable extent had to give way or succumb to the emergent hierarchy of command and obedience characteristic of modern political organizations. The Komalay JK was, in other words, in the initial stage of the transition from a semi-clandestine political-intellectual association to a political administration, from a loose political grouping of like-minded individuals to an organized political party. This trend was further intensified towards the end of the year, when the Komalay JK looked poised to burst out of the urban centres, making significant inroads into the rural areas in the north and north-western sectors of the Kurdish territory.[26]

There was thus in early 1944 an increasing pressure on the central committee to define more clearly the institutional structure and the process of the exercise of political authority within the organization, as the increasing membership and the expanding mass base had shifted the locus of legitimacy in the organization from its nationalist ideology to its political practice. The nationalist-populist programme of the Komalay JK, the core of its ideological rhetoric, had by now achieved popular acceptance; it was its politics which was the focus of popular gaze. This development signified yet another step in the direction of modern politics. It seemed as if the fledging nationalist movement was already in the grip of modernity.

But this was not to be. In fact, the issue of political authority and leadership proved to be the Achilles heel of the nationalist movement, dragging it back to the mire of traditional social relations and primordial loyalties. For the shift in the locus of legitimacy, which signified the growing popular democratic character of the movement, also meant that the conditions of political authority were no longer confined to the organization of the party alone. They were also firmly grounded in the social and economic structures and cultural organization of Kurdish society in Iran, which were still predominantly pre-capitalist in character and traditional in ethos. The retarding weight of pre-capitalist relations in the socio-economic structures and cultural organization of political authority easily counterbalanced the 'driving force of modernity'. Popular religion, primordial loyalties and local tradition remained indispensable to political legitimacy in the unfolding nationalist political process.

The emergent leadership of the Komalay JK found it necessary to call on the traditional forces to bolster its political authority in the context of increasing membership, expanding organization and developing mass support. In fact, the stronger and more popular the organization grew the closer it became to the traditional forces and institutions. The Komalay JK's overture to the landowning class and tribal leadership was, therefore, hardly surprising. By early 1944 it had established fairly strong political and institutional relations with sections of the Kurdish landowning class, tribal leadership, mercantile bourgeoisie and religious dignitaries, who declared their commitment to the nationalist project and refrained from overt collaboration with the Iranian political and military authorities. The large landlords and tribal leaders, too, welcomed the Komalay JK's overtures; their fear of its growing popularity among the urban masses easily exceeded their hatred of its agrarian populism.[27]

The Komalay JK's overtures to the Kurdish landlords and tribal leaders and its increasing reliance on the traditional pre-capitalist forces and relations in the urban centres were a stark reminder of the pivotal position of primordial relations and popular religion in the structure of political authority and legitimacy in the Kurdish society. These forces and relations defined the conditions of Komalay JK's political practice, undermining its efforts to consolidate the emergent national identity on modern political grounds. Although Komalay JK succeeded in creating a popular-democratic base for nationalist politics, the pre-capitalist structures of Kurdish society in Iran militated against its efforts to institute modern political authority and administration in its expanding domain. The conceptual distinction between the 'Kurdish people' and the 'Kurdish nation', the subjects of 'nationalist politics' and 'nationalist history' in the discourse of *Nishtiman*, was rapidly losing its political foundation, falling victim to the exigencies of popular political process in a predominantly pre-capitalist society.

The growing gap between the Komalay JK's ideological rhetoric and political practice thus signified the increasing importance of traditional social forces, especially the tribal leadership, in the structure of political authority and administration in the Kurdish community. The political development and territorial expansion of the nationalist movement and the growing need to create an effective organization capable of political and military administration forced the leadership of the Komalay JK to compromise its political programme. The collaboration with the traditional forces was the price paid for the development of the nationalist movement, which set the stage for Ghazi Muhammad's rise to prominence and the subsequent transformation of Komalay JK into the KDPI in August 1945.

The fate of the Komalay JK was a telling example of the perils of modern nationalism in traditional/pre-capitalist social formations. The organization laid the ideological ground for a modern nationalist political process, but could not survive the pressures brought to bear by the political and institutional imperatives of this process. The growing need for a central political authority with a territorial institutional base came into conflict with the parochial organizational structure of the Komalay JK and the semi-political formation of its leadership. The outcome of this process was over-determined by an anomalous historical conjuncture that inadvertently brought together the strategic and security interests of the Soviet state and the economic and political interests of the Kurdish landowning class. The birth of the KDPI and the subsequent adoption of the autonomist political project by its leadership were to be a political 'solution' to the contradiction, defining the parameters of modern nationalist politics in the predominantly pre-capitalist Kurdish society in Iran.

3

THE REPUBLIC: THE FORMATION AND STRUCTURE OF POLITICAL POWER

The Republic that came into being on 22 January 1946 was the product of the same social and political conditions that had led to the formation of its maker, the KDPI, some six months earlier. In fact, during its brief existence the organizational structure of the Republic was constituted by the KDPI. The Republic was as it were the institutional form of the KDPI's political authority, its practical existence, centred on the town of Mahabad but stretching far beyond it to the south and south-western sectors of the Kurdish territory, covering the towns of Bokan, Baneh, Sardasht, as well as smaller urban centres such as Naqadeh and Ushno. The Republic was formed in the safety of the Soviet Zone, where the presence of the Red Army to the north of the Saqqiz-Baneh line was a barrier effectively keeping the Iranian army outside its formal jurisdiction – a factor which, as will be seen, proved significant not only in the formation of the Republic, but also in the political orientation of various social forces towards it. The Republic was centred on the town of Mahabad which, strictly speaking, was outside the Soviet zone (extending from Miandoab to Sardasht).[1]

The fact that the Republic was officially declared in the wake of the second visit by the Kurdish dignitaries to Baku is often taken to support the widespread view that the idea of the

Kurdish Republic was born when the Kurdish delegation met with Bagherov, the president of the Azeri Soviet Republic, in late September 1945. On this occasion Bagherov, representing the official stance of the CPSU, is said to have instructed Ghazi Muhammad to plan to establish an autonomous Kurdish Republic in Western Azerbaijan with the ultimate aim of full independence and secession from Iran. The KDPI in this view was formed as the vehicle of this Soviet-inspired plan, entrusted with the task of accomplishing this mission. This scenario, expressed differently in different political and ideological contexts, is often given credence by referring to the change in the aims and objectives of Soviet foreign policy at the end of 1944 and the beginning of 1945 which, as was seen in the previous chapter, was followed by a change in the Soviet approach towards the Kurdish question in Iran. As the First World War drew to a close and the Soviet Union became confident of victory over fascism, it decided to modify its conservative approach towards the issue and encourage Kurdish nationalism in Iran in the context of the approaching Cold War.

The change in the aims and objectives of the Soviet foreign policy and its approach to the Kurdish question in Iran notwithstanding, however, this scenario is weakened by historical errors and inconsistencies which cast serious doubts on its claim to truth. It has already been pointed out that the KDPI, supposedly the political and organizational means in the new Soviet strategy in Kurdistan, was established on 16 August 1945, that is, before the date of the second visit by the Kurdish delegation to Baku which reportedly took place in late September of that year. Further, there is to my knowledge no record of the negotiations between the Kurdish delegation and their Soviet hosts in Baku, and nothing that would point to a plan to establish an autonomous Kurdish Republic in Iranian Kurdistan as the prelude to an independent Kurdish state in the region. In fact existing accounts of these negotiations, for the most part, depend on other sources, and tend to give unreliable if not implausible explanations. Eagleton, for example, provides a version of the encounter which is most likely to have originated from some members of the Kurdish delegation, presumably the tribal chiefs such as Ghassem Agha Ilkhanizadeh. According to this account, the Kurdish leadership asked Bagherov for help in establishing an independent Kurdish state. In response Bagherov asked Kurds to be patient, stating that although the creation of a united Kurdish state was a general policy objective to which the Soviet Union was committed, at present priority should be given to the Azeri case, and in the meantime, the Kurds should try to realize their aspirations in the juridico-political framework of the autonomous Azeri state in Iran. Eagleton then affirms that the Kurds rejected Bagherov's argument, insisting on their desire for a separate Kurdish state, upon which Bagherov was forced to concede that 'as long as the Soviet Union exists the Kurds will have their independence' (1963, p. 44). Eagleton goes on to argue that in the same meeting Bagherov stated that the Komalay JK was no longer necessary and that it should be closed down and replaced by the KDPI. Hence, in his view, the transformation of the Komalay JK into the KDPI, which allegedly took place in November 1945 (ibid., p. 45).

But this view of the sequence of events (which, as was seen, was also held by Zabihi and Nebaz) is problematic. For if, as the existing evidence suggests, the KDPI was indeed established in mid-August, and thus already in existence before the second Baku visit, then there would have been no need for Bagherov to argue for its creation in the meeting. In this case he might have only demanded the closure of the Komalay JK which had been functioning alongside the newly established KDPI since mid-August; and it would thus have been only the dissolution of the Komalay JK and its incorporation into the organization of the KDPI that was declared by Ghazi in November in Mahabad. But if Eagleton's account is correct and the KDPI was in fact established on Bagherov's orders in November 1945, then it raises the question of the actual reason behind Bagherov's desire to establish a popular political party, given the fact that, according to Eagleton, he was opposed to the creation of an autonomous

Kurdish state. In other words, why should Bagherov propose that the Kurds should form a popular political party to facilitate the creation of an autonomous Kurdish Republic if he was opposed to such a plan in the first place? It seems logical to conclude that if Bagherov did indeed order the creation of the KDPI, it was intended to be an instrument of local Kurdish administration under Azeri rule, that is, to facilitate the administration of Kurdistan as an integral part of the Azeri autonomous state in Iran, as clearly suggested by him to the Kurdish delegation in the meeting in Baku.

This conclusion is corroborated by the reaction of the Soviet authority in Iran to the creation of the Republic. Whether or not the KDPI was established in November, the Soviet reaction to the creation of the Republic shows very clearly that it was never intended as a party representing popular nationalist demand for an autonomous Kurdish government based in Mahabad. Indeed Eagleton is only one among many scholars who registers Soviet dissatisfaction with the declaration of the Republic by the Kurdish nationalists. Ghazi Muhammad and his colleagues in the leadership of the KDPI had already been warned by Pishevari and his Soviet advisers not to embark on the Kurdish autonomy plan, but to remain under the jurisdiction of the Azeri Republic, which was soon to be recognized by the central government in Tehran (1963, pp. 60–1). Soviet and Azeri opposition to the Kurdish nationalist quest for an autonomous government seems to be the official stance agreed upon before the declaration of the Azeri Democratic Republic on 12 November 1945 and subsequent to the second visit of the Kurdish delegation to Baku in the late September of that year. Witness Eagleton's account of the reaction of the Kurdish delegation representing the KDPI at the inauguration of the Azerbaijan National Assembly on 12 November 1945:

> The Kurdish delegation ... soon discovered that they had joined the Assembly 'not as representatives of a separate Kurdistan, but merely as deputies from specific

constituencies, like all others'. They soon became aware that under the new dispensations Kurdistan was to have merely a town council inferior to the provincial council of Azerbaijan. The Kurds proclaimed their dissatisfaction in Mahabad ... (ibid. p. 60).

The Soviet and Azeri opposition to the Kurdish nationalist quest for an autonomous government created a rift in the leadership of the KDPI, a division between the moderates who were prepared to accept the Soviet proposed plan to remain part of the Azeri Republic, and the radicals who wanted to defy the Soviet proposal and declare an autonomous Kurdish Republic with its own jurisdiction centred on Mahabad. The moderates, who had Ghazi Muhammad among them, were in the minority. But the day was reportedly won by the radical nationalists on 17 December, when the people came out in force to support the quest for a separate autonomous government in the Kurdish territory. Eagleton describes this crucial moment in the history of the formation of the Kurdish Republic in the following terms:

> A meeting of the party members was converted into a march on the vestigial remains of Iranian authority in Mahabad, the Department of Justice. The crowd demanded the building should be set on fire; but moderation prevailed and instead the coat of arms was shot from the façade and the Kurdish flag was raised on the roof. (ibid. p. 61)

The extent and strength of popular support for the nationalist quest for an autonomous Republic must have taken the moderates in the leadership of the KDPI, especially Ghazi Muhammad, by surprise. Although it did not put an end to his doubts about the Soviet support, it made him rethink his hesitations about the likely reaction of the powerful tribal lords to the nationalist scheme. The nationalist quest for an autonomous government now had a popular-democratic mandate which could be used to counter-balance the tribal opposition and quell the Azeri Democrat opposition. The Soviet authorities, Ghazi Muhammad thought, could be made to accept the *fait accompli* if they realized that it had the support of the tribal landlords and the tacit acceptance of the Azeri democrats. The Soviet public approval of the Kurdish Republic would have been enough to convince both hostile Azeri democrats and unruly Kurdish tribal leaders to change their attitude from overt opposition to reluctant acceptance. Ghazi Muhammad's calculations proved correct, but only in the short term. For neither the Azeri democrats nor the Kurdish tribal lords saw any reason to respect the popular democratic mandate of the nationalist scheme beyond May 1946, when the Red Army left Kurdistan.

That Ghazi Muhammad had by the late December already decided to defy the Soviet and Azeri opposition and declare an autonomous republic in Kurdistan is clearly indicated by his decision to approach the British Consul in Tabriz to explore the possibility of establishing some kind of official relation between the autonomous Kurdistan of the future and the United Kingdom.[2] The Consul replied in ambiguous terms, carefully avoiding any encouragement of the nationalist cause, much in line with the general direction of British foreign policy in Iran during the period. The British reaction does not seem to have discouraged Ghazi Muhammad and his colleagues in the leadership of the KDPI from seeking international support for the nationalist cause, though often to little or no avail. The idea, however, was to drum up as much support and help as possible before the official declaration of the Republic, thus presenting the Soviet authorities in Tabriz, and Pishevari and his associates in the leadership of the Azerbaijan Democratic Party, with a case which they would find hard to refuse public recognition and approval. The principal power whose goodwill and support the KDPI leadership was eager to secure was the United States of America. They saw the USA as a rising power in the international arena, with increasingly expanding strategic interests in the region, but free of historical, political and economic ties with those countries which ruled parts of the greater Kurdistan and suppressed the Kurds in their sovereign jurisdiction. The early American anti-colonial history, as well as Wilson's 14 points legitimating the doctrine of the rights of the nations to self-determination (which had inspired the imagination of Kurdish nationalists from Shaikh Mahmoud to Khoybun), was still fresh in the national memory. But despite its enthusiasm to secure American support, the Kurdish leadership's overtures to the American diplomatic corps in Azerbaijan and Tehran did not bear fruit (Yassin, 1995; Roosevelt, 1947).

The persistence of the popular support for an autonomous Kurdish government in major urban centres, and the increasing pressure brought to bear by the radical nationalists in the central committee of the KDPI, were instrumental in convincing Ghazi Muhammad and his more moderate associates in the party to go with the current and prepare to defy both Soviet advice and Pishevari's veiled threats. The radical nationalists in the central committee and lower echelons of the party hierarchy were for the most part younger-generation, urban Kurds of petty-bourgeois origin, modern and traditional, with modern school education; many of them were steeped in the liberal and social democratic discourse which marked the advent of the public sphere in Tehran and other major urban centres in Iran following the collapse of Reza Shah's regime. They identified with the nationalist cause, but through liberal and social democratic discourses and practices which helped ground the ethnic dimension of their Kurdish identity in a predominantly modern political context. For the radical nationalists in the KDPI the political and cultural expressions of Kurdish identity were invariably tethered to the ideal of independence and autonomy and their juridical-political framework. A political and intellectual commitment to the idea of Kurdish self-government was central to their self-perception as Kurdish nationalists. This commitment enabled them to navigate through the waves of external political and cultural influences of the time, in particular the Marxism of the Tudeh party and the ethnic-collectivism of the Azeri democrats, to withstand and refuse their increasing influences in the wider political and ideological field. Kurdish nationalists sailed through these powerful political and ideological currents charged with the growing force of their political commitment to the nationalist cause. They continued relentlessly to pursue the nationalist cause of self-government, never ceasing to think it and struggle to realize it.

The nationalists' anxiety about the Soviet and Azeri reaction did not end with the public declaration of the Republic on 22 January 1946. Nor did the disagreements and tensions in the central committee of the KDPI, which continued unabated – especially on issues related to defence, economy and the relationship with the central government – up to the very last moment in the brief but eventful life of the Kurdish Republic. But Ghazi Muhammad's calculations about the Soviet reaction to the declaration of the Republic proved correct in all but one respect. He was right to believe that the Soviet authorities in Tabriz, faced with a *fait accompli*, would have to accept the reality of the Kurdish Republic, albeit with a great deal of reluctance and dissatisfaction, still insisting on unification with if not integration in the Azeri Republic (Eagleton, 1963, pp. 60–1). Ghazi's refusal to accept Pishevari's offer of integration/ unification with the Azeri Republic is reported by the British Consul in Kermanshah to Tehran on 4 February 1946: 'Ghazi forms the Republic and refuses the offer of a local government under the dominance of the Azeri democrats, and the latter accept reluctantly.'[3] The news of the Soviet acceptance of the Kurdish Republic and the Azeri dissatisfaction is relayed on 8 February 1946 by the British Consul General in Tabriz to Tehran in the following terms:

1. Pishevari still hopes to subordinate the Kurdish autonomous government to the Azerbaijan national government, but Ghazi Muhammad demands complete independence. He is unlikely to have done so unless confident of the Russian support.

2. Kurds claim not only Miandoab and Sardasht, but also Western Azerbaijan including Khoi, Maku and Rezaieh. There are indications that Pishevari will give in on Rezaieh but not the other two.[4]

The Soviet acceptance of the reality of the Kurdish Republic did not mean the end of pressure on the KDPI to succumb to Pishevari's plan. In fact it soon became evident to the leadership of the KDPI as well as the Kurdish public that Soviet approval was only tactical: the Soviet authorities in Tabriz accepted the reality of the Kurdish Republic only in order to continue to exert pressure on the Kurdish nationalists to agree to the Azeri plan, that they should become part of the Azeri Republic and live in its domestic jurisdiction under Iranian sovereignty. The Soviet pressure was also accompanied by sweeteners to convince the KDPI and the Kurdish public that they did indeed support the nationalist cause and intended to defend it against external aggression. The arrival of the first batch of Soviet military aid in the form of small firearms and ammunition in the middle of February in Mahabad was meant to serve such a purpose (Izzat, 1987; Emin, 1993; Mobley, 1979; Eagleton, 1963; Yassin, 1995). The Soviet policy achieved its intended objective on 23 April 1946, when the leadership of the KDPI succumbed to Soviet pressure and eventually signed a treaty with the Azeri national government in Tabriz.

The Azeri-Kurdish agreement of 23 April bore the hallmark of Soviet political pragmatism, reflecting their strategic priorities in the wider context of Iranian politics and more specifically their recent agreement with Qawam, the Iranian premier of the time. The Azeri-Kurdish agreement carefully avoided the territorial issue between the two governments; the boundaries of the autonomous Kurdish Republic were left unspecified, ostensibly pending the final unification of the Kurds and the establishment of an independent Kurdish state in the territorial framework of the greater Kurdistan (Mobley, 1979; Eagleton, 1963). But so far as the Kurdish government was concerned the most adverse consequence of the agreement was that it effectively gave a mandate to the Azeri government to represent the Kurds in the course of negotiations for autonomy with the central government. That the Azeri government were to become the voice of the Kurds in autonomy negotiations with the central government in Tehran was an inevitable outcome of the legal status of the Kurdish government. The central government insisted on the validity of the existing administrative division of the country as the appropriate territorial framework for autonomy negotiations. The Kurdish government, unlike the Azeri democrats, had no province to its name; its territory had no administrative-political unity on the official map of the country. The boundaries of the Republic, real or imagined, fell mainly within the domestic jurisdiction of Western Azerbaijan and to a lesser extent Eastern Azerbaijan, administered from Rezaiyeh and Tabriz respectively. Thus while the Azeri democrats claimed autonomy to rule over a territory which already constituted a province with specified legal and administrative boundaries clearly delineated on the map, and could as such obtain juridical-political recognition from the central government to represent the Azeri minority in Iran, the Kurdish nationalists in Mahabad failed to ground their claim to autonomy in such a legal foundation, to secure legal recognition to represent the Kurdish population living in a territory without a single administrative-political centre and delineated boundaries.

In the Iranian Constitution of 1906, which was the point of reference for both Kurdish and Azeri claims to autonomous rule within the territorial boundaries of a sovereign state in Iran, the concept of minority, ethnic and cultural, was not defined on a territorial basis, but was left ambiguous. Instead the term *mahalli*, meaning local, was used, referring primarily to the non-central provincial character of these ethnic and linguistic communities, rather than to any territorially delimited boundaries. The central government's emphasis on the territorial qualification in the autonomy negotiations was only tactical, intended not only to refuse the Kurdish government the right to represent the Kurds but also to create a split in the Kurdish-Azeri front, sowing seeds of distrust and discontent in their ranks. The idea, which is said to have been a brainchild of premier Qawam himself, was an intelligent tactical device, showing an awareness of the growing rift between the Kurdish nationalists and the Azeri democrats, and in particular the latter's reluctance to accept the establishment of an autonomous Kurdish administration in Mahabad and its territorial claims over the three towns of Urmiya, Khoy and Salmas. The Kurdish-Azeri agreement sanctioned by the Soviets revealed not only the weakness of the Kurdish government in the dispute, but also and more importantly its inferior status in Soviet strategic thinking at the time. It was only too logical for the central government to move to exploit these weaknesses and differences and take advantage of the Soviet reservations about the very existence and viability of the Kurdish government.[5]

The Azeri government's opposition to the idea of an autonomous Kurdish Republic and their insistence on representing the Kurds in the process of negotiation with the central government, on the other hand, had undoubtedly been encouraged, if not influenced, by their awareness of Qawam's reluctance to recognize the legitimacy of the Kurdish government. They had clearly realized that the central government's insistence on territorial qualification for regional/provincial representation was basically a tactical ploy to sideline the Kurdish government and deny them political status. In fact the Kurdish government had been caught in the throes of an acute political and diplomatic crisis, resulting from and perpetuated by the overlapping political interests of the central government and the Azeri administration regarding their exclusion from the autonomy negotiations in Tehran. That the negotiations leading to the signing of the Pishevari-Firuz treaty followed the Azeri-Kurdish agreement meant that the central government was certain that its insistence on the territorial qualification, and hence the exclusion of the Kurdish government, had Soviet approval.

The Kurdish Republic had, therefore, been effectively marginalized and subordinated to the Azeri Republic shortly before Pishevari travelled to Tehran to commence the autonomy negotiations with the central government on 28 April 1946. The Pishevari-Firuz treaty signed on 13 June 1946 put an end to the last vestiges of Kurdish influence in the centre. In so far as the Kurdish government was concerned, the Soviet-engineered Kurdish-Azeri agreement of 23 April had paved the way for the Pishevari-Firuz treaty. The Agreement, as they rightly anticipated, marked the onset of a process of internal political decline and external diplomatic capitulation to the central government, culminating in the loss of power and of the capacity to influence the course of events before the eventual demise of the Republic. The Soviets not only silenced the Kurdish nationalists by pulling the rug from under their feet, but also delivered them to Pishevari to be used as a bargaining chip in the political haggling with Qawam's government. The treaty remained silent on the Kurdish demands for the recognition of their rights as citizens of the autonomous Republic. Article 13 of the treaty referred to them as the Kurds living in Azerbaijan and extended the terms of the treaty to them to the point of robbing them of their national identity (Rossow, 1956 and Eagleton, 1963, p. 93). If before 1941 Kurds spoke to the sovereign in the language of the sovereign, they now had to speak to the sovereign in Azeri, which was the officially recognized language of the Azeri parliament, the officially accepted provincial council, and the seat of the Azeri governor general who was to rule the province under the Iranian sovereignty.

Social and Political Structures of the Republic

Throughout its brief existence the Republic remained a predominantly urban administration. It could not extend its popular power base to the country or spread its nationalist message among the mass of the Kurdish peasantry, for reasons specific to its social and political structures. Nor could it extend its authority to all the major urban centres over which it claimed jurisdiction; Urmiya, Khoy and Salmas continued to be administered from Tabriz by the government of Azerbaijan. There remained an acute discrepancy between the 'real' and the 'imagined' boundaries of the Republic, which overshadowed the nationalist claims of its leadership. The nationalist project was seriously undercut by the structural weakness of political authority.

The Republic thus did not have specified geographical boundaries, and its legal jurisdiction depended on its political authority, which was sustained by an articulation of the economic and the military: that is, by taxation and by tribal contingents, though a small corps of regular army also existed.[6] This meant that the exercise of political authority by the leadership, and the range of its efficacy in the Kurdish territory, depended on its capacity on the one hand to levy and collect taxes, and on the other to muster and field military contingents within its domestic jurisdiction when required. These two capacities in turn defined the social basis of political authority in the Republic.

Taxation was the main source of governmental revenue. The Republican administration, civil and military, was paid by tax revenue extracted mainly from the urban population within its jurisdiction. Taxation was accordingly defined as the 'the soul of the nation', on which administration of the governmental affairs depended.[7] Although there is little information about the nature of fiscal policy and the actual tax regime in force in the Republic, the existing evidence, especially the occasional official announcements in *Kurdistan*, suggests that the criteria for decision-making about taxation were largely political. Despite the deepening economic crisis that progressively engulfed the Republic, the authorities seem to have upheld the political criterion, especially with respect to agrarian production and land revenue. In this regard Republican fiscal policy differed little, if at all, from the monarchist policy introduced under Reza Shah. The reason, as will be shown in the following section, was the dominance of the landowning class in the structures of political and economic power in Kurdistan.[8]

The existing evidence, scanty and fragmented as it is, can nevertheless help to outline the organization and structure of taxation in the Republic, though in a rudimentary manner. In the months before the advent of the Republic, the evidence suggests, fiscal policy was decided by the central committee of the KDPI, which had now effectively filled the power vacuum left by the collapse of the Iranian government in September 1941. The leadership of the KDPI appointed a 'Tax Association' or 'Tax Commission', composed of 12 merchants and civil servants from the town of Mahabad, to enact its directives. The Tax Commission was entrusted with the task of collecting income tax for the two years of 1945 and 1946, first in urban centres and then in the countryside.[9] Neither the form of fiscal policy and tax regime adopted by the KDPI nor the actual strategy pursued by the Commission to achieve its policy objectives are known to us in any detail. The public announcement on 16 February 1946 by the director of public finance clearly appeals to a sense of patriotism and national duty to persuade the public to comply with the directives of the party, although financial and juridico-political coercive means to realize policy objectives are not discounted.[10]

With the advent of the Republic, there was an attempt to institutionalize taxation. The Office of Public Finance (*Maliya*) was set up to take charge of fiscal policy and administration. This office, which was institutionally attached to the Ministry of Finance (*Dara'ie*), presided over the work of two Tax Commissions established by presidential edict soon after the declaration of the Republic. These Commissions were entrusted with the arduous task of collecting taxes in urban and rural areas. The urban Commission was composed of merchants, traders and civil servants from Mahabad, while the rural Commission, ostensibly formed at the request of landlords and tribal leaders in the vicinity of Mahabad, represented the landowning class in general.[11]

The Office of Public Finance was formally an independent unit, with powers of decision-making and execution in matters related to fiscal policy and administration. But in practice it was little more than an executive arm of the central committee of the KDPI, whose directives it was expected to carry out.[12] The leadership of the KDPI retained exclusive control over financial affairs of the government, especially fiscal policy and administration, which were so crucial to its survival. A central committee 'Directive Concerning Taxes and Expenditures' dated 21 July 1946 helps to illustrate this point:

> The Central Committee has ordered all governmental offices and external committees everywhere that they should, on a daily basis, render all their income such as tariffs, taxes and excise, in part or in whole, to the local tax office in return for receipt ... It is the duty of the tax office of each locality to pay, at the beginning of every month, the salaries of those governmental employees which have been approved by the central committee. (*Kurdistan*, no. 69, 21 July 1946.)

This intimate relationship between the central committee and the fiscal apparatuses of the government was symptomatic of the structural weakness of the Republican government. In the Republic, the party rather than the government was the locus of power. The central political apparatuses of the KDPI remained at the heart of policy and decision-making, with adverse consequences for the development of a democratic polity and civil society in the Republic, as will be seen in the following section.

The government's capacity to tax rested not so much on its institutional structure as on the active support of the urban population, especially the lower and middle ranks of the mercantile bourgeoisie and the traditional petty-bourgeoisie. Both of these were primarily engaged in forms of economic activity associated with the sphere of exchange and circulation traditionally located in urban bazaars. Their active support was ensured by ideological and political means, ranging from mass mobilization to participation in the administration on the local level.

But the most effective means of ensuring the active support of the popular urban social forces and their participation in the political process was the emergent civil society and developing public sphere, that is, the emergence of a discursive formation which functioned to support popular-democratic politics. The case in point here is the popular-democratic discourses and institutions that came into existence under the Republic. On the conditions which provided for the emergence of this 'free political space' Eagleton writes:

> The Republic was characterized by free economic activity and open political space, freedom of speech, association and the absence of secret police, all standing opposite to the Tabriz government ... Hamid Mazuji, chief of the Kurdish military police, during a year's service arrested only a handful of Ghazi's personal enemies. The Republic was universally popular in Mahabad town and region and was assured of tribal support [in the area] ... [It was] Ghazi's express orders that citizens should not be bothered for their political inclinations ... Ordinary citizens were free to move in and out of the Republic as they wished ... (1963, pp. 100–1)

The urban petty-bourgeoisie and the bulk of the mercantile bourgeoisie were actively involved in the creation of this discursive formation, both on civic and cultural levels, and their subsequent partisan activity helped regenerate political and financial support for the Republican leadership. The urban petty-bourgeoisie was undoubtedly the author of popular-democratic politics in the Republic, politically and intellectually. It was nationalist-populist in orientation, and it demanded the political independence and social reform which were fundamental elements of its political identity. The urban petty-bourgeoisie, traditional and modern, formed the social structure of the emergent public sphere in the Kurdish community, and was the main beneficiary of its political and institutional development.[13]

While the social structure of the Republican government was heterogeneous, made up of an amalgam of landowners, urban petty-bourgeois and mercantile bourgeois elements, the active core of the leadership of the Republic was drawn from the ranks of the urban popular classes.[14] This curious mixture was united by adherence to Kurdish nationalism, the main unifying factor holding together a heterogeneous political elite running the affairs of the government in the name of the Kurdish nation. Although its leading members in the government had very different understandings of Kurdish nationalism and its strategic objectives, they nonetheless publicly professed their commitment to the sovereignty of the Kurdish nation. The same classes also formed the basis of the modern intelligentsia, which was the author of the nationalist discourse and the architect and developmental force of the emergent public sphere in the Kurdish community. The intrinsic link between the political leadership and the modern intelligentsia, consolidated in the organization of the KDPI, and the subsumption of the latter in the institutional structure of the Republic, had important implications for the development of this public sphere, and hence of the nascent civil society. It meant above all that the public sphere, the public location of rational discourse bearing on the nature and the working of political authority, became almost exclusively the field for the expression of 'difference' from the sovereign Persian/Iranian ethnos/nation and ethnic/national identity. The internal differences, conflicts and contradictions in the leadership and within the administration never surfaced in the public sphere. The popular-democratic discourse was for the most part incorporated into the official discourse, whose nationalist contours defined the shifting boundaries of the public sphere. Thus the institutional development of the emergent civil society in the Republic was never matched by a corresponding development in the democratic political process with which it was closely associated.

This apparently paradoxical feature of the Republican government – the contrast between its social structure and modern ideological outlook – has been noted by various commentators. Eagleton (1963) observes that the Republican government displayed an odd combination of social conservatism and political-cultural modernism. This amalgam, odd though it may look in retrospect, was thoroughly in line with the historical reality of nationalist politics in a predominantly traditional society. Jwaideh also offers interesting observations on the social structure and political character of the Republican leadership, in particular the person of Ghazi Muhammad himself. The rise of Ghazi Muhammad to power, Jwaideh argues in typically Weberian language, represented a break with the traditional norms defining the status of the ruling elite and the sources of their domination in Kurdish history. For he was neither a hereditary prince like Badir Khan, nor from the line of Shaikhs and religious orders like Shaikh Ubaidallah, nor had tribal lineage and ancestry like Ismail Agha Shikak. The sources of Ghazi's domination, Jwaideh further argues, were modern, stemming from political party, urban support, modern bureaucracy, and the support of the modern intelligentsia. The presence of the modern means of political domination and rule in the Republic thus leads Jwaideh to argue that Ghazi's rise to power 'was a clear indication that the old social order was in a state of ferment and that the system of polity which it had sustained for centuries was in imminent danger of collapse' (1965, p. 755).

The upper stratum of the mercantile bourgeoisie, the large bazaar merchants, also paid taxes to the Republican administration, but more through necessity than conviction. The main figures in this small but economically powerful sector of urban population were also large and middle landowners, holding both real estate and agricultural land. They feared the Republican leaders and had serious reservations about their aims and intentions, suspecting them of communism. That the Republican leadership received qualified Soviet support (having been invited to Baku twice for negotiation) and was on cordial terms with the neighbouring Republic of Azerbaijan (whose leaders were mostly convinced Marxist-Leninists, some active members of the Third Communist International, the Comintern) was sufficient to confirm the worst fears of those bourgeois landlords. Their financial support was thus ensured only in so far as the Republican leadership was able to enforce its authority and maintain law and order in its 'real' territory, which in turn depended on its military capacity, and hence on its relationship with the tribal leadership. The tribal leaders, who had formed a loose political alliance with the Republican leadership on the basis of a broad autonomist political project, controlled the majority of the rural population, politically and economically.

The landlord-bourgeois families constituted a small but powerful social stratum which may be termed 'urban notables'.[15] They had in their ranks no more than 20 families. The power and influence of the urban notables resulted not only from their superior economic class position but also from their social status in the community. This latter often resulted from factors other than property ownership, e.g. religious authority, education and knowledge, esoteric knowledge, lineage and descent, and moral authority and social influence, at times acquired by marriage to powerful tribal landlords, although in most cases it was also combined with wealth and economic influence. Broadly speaking, social status was the main factor differentiating the urban notables from other members of the mercantile community in Kurdish towns. Shateri and Shafe'ie were two prominent landlord-bourgeois families in Mahabad. Their heads, Haj Salih Shateri and Haji Rahmat Shafe'ie, it was widely believed during and after 1946, maintained covert but active opposition to the Republic and its leadership, in particular the person of Ghazi Muhammad. This opposition, which was at the time common knowledge in the town, especially in nationalist circles, may have stemmed from two sources. First, their personal animosity towards Ghazi Muhammad, a form of personal rivalry with an inter-class communal basis which was widespread in the small but established circle of urban notables with non-tribal landowning roots; and secondly, political opposition to the KDPI, which they suspected of harbouring communism and paving the way for the Soviet domination of the area. The two men, part of the same social circle in the town, were widely considered to be in touch with anti-republican political and social forces within and outside the Kurdish community, including the disgruntled members of the Kurdish tribal leadership, the Iranian government, and also the official and the secret agents of foreign governments, especially Britain, active in Kurdistan and Azerbaijan.[16]

The rural population did not contribute to the coffers of the Kurdish administration in any significant way, since the mass of Kurdish peasantry paid their land rents and other fiscal dues to the landlords in both tribal and non-tribal areas, and had no financial relationship with the Republican administration in the towns. The landlords, who pocketed the bulk of the revenue resulting from agrarian production, on the whole did not pay taxes to the Kurdish administration, any more than they had paid the Pahlavi state before its collapse in September 1941. The tax on agricultural land, predominantly owned by the Kurdish landowning class before 1963, was meagre, an indication of the privileged position of landowners in the social structure of political power under Pahlavi absolutism. The Republican administration had neither the power nor the will to change the prevailing tax regime; it did not want to antagonize the landowning class, on whose active political and military support it depended for survival.

The Tax Commission set up in early February by presidential decree to oversee the administration of fiscal policy in rural areas does not seem to have succeeded in its mission. Although the Commission was ostensibly voluntary, and selected representatives of the landowning class had taken part in the determination of fiscal policy, the third public announcement by the Director of Public Finance in late March indicated that no taxes had yet been paid. Announcement no. 2020, dated 25 March 1946, reads as follows:

> Following decree 2838 of 28.12.1324 by the central committee of the Democratic Party of Kurdistan, we are informing all the village owners for the third time that so far they have not taken the smallest step to help the government by paying the taxes due. Although the meagre tax levied on them by the government was to be paid immediately and fully, they have refused to pay it to the coffers, and still continue refusing and wasting time. Since at present the government has high expenditures and its coffers need money, once again it is making another concession to you by extending the period for payment to 15 of Khaka liva (5 April) ... . It should however be known that if the payment is not made during this period you will be dealt with by the police and the army ... (*Kurdistan*, no. 27, 25 March 1946)[17]

This announcement, signed by Ahmad Ilmie, the Director of Public Finance, though it duly invokes the authority of the KDPI, nonetheless does not seem to have been heeded by the powerful landlords and tribal leaders; a further reminder by him dated early May 1946 confirms that the income tax from the landlords and tribal leaders was still overdue.[18] This sad saga of empty threats and cynical non-compliance seems to have continued to the very end, becoming more pronounced as the Republic plunged deeper into economic and political crisis.

It should be noted, however, that the Kurdish landowning class was by no means a homogeneous social force, and it maintained a less than uniform political and financial relationship with the Republic. The large landlords, predominantly tribal, had been the primary target of Reza Shah's territorial centralism in Kurdistan in the 1930s, and many had suffered major political and military setbacks. They were able to rearm, regroup and reassert their political authority in their traditional areas of influence soon after the collapse of his centralized rule in September 1941. The tribal landlords were thus once again in possession of the military contingents and paid for their upkeep, which traditionally exempted them from paying taxes to the central political authority. The nature and extent of their political and financial support for the Republic varied considerably according to the strength of their nationalist feelings and convictions, which were mediated in turn through a complex network of political and economic relations with the Iranian state.

There was also another factor influencing the attitude of the large landlords, particularly the tribal chiefs, towards the Republic and its predominantly urban leadership. The tribal leadership was the locus of traditional political authority in the Kurdish community at large, but especially in the countryside, stemming from their pivotal position in both economic structure and military organization of the Kurdish community. This gave them a sense of legitimacy and superiority in their conduct with the urban dwellers, who were mostly engaged in trade and commerce or worked as minor or middle-ranking officials in government bureaucracies. This 'tribal bias' proved significant in the relationship between the Kurdish tribal chiefs and the Republican leaders and administrators, who with a few notable exceptions originated from the ranks of the urban petty-bourgeoisie and the bazaar merchants. On the significance of this 'tribal bias', and especially the tribal leaders' resentment of the modern means of domination and rule which ensured Ghazi Muhammad's rise to power, Jwaideh comments: 'Many Kurdish tribal leaders resented the rise of Qazi Muhammad to a position of supreme power by the rather unusual means of party machinery and support of the urban population.' (1965, p. 753) The middle and small landowners were mostly non-tribal in origin, and on the whole possessed stronger nationalist convictions than the tribal landlords. They were more forthcoming in their support for the leadership of the Republic, though this was mostly confined to financial help. The prominent figures among the middle and small landowners could easily identify with the top rank in the Republican leadership, who came from the same social background. However, as smaller non-tribal landlords, they lacked the effective military force to influence the course of events in the Republic or to bolster its authority within its perceived territory.

The Republic's capacity to muster and field military contingents, that is, its effective military power, thus depended primarily on the tribal leadership. The tribal leadership itself, however, was further divided; like the landowning class as a whole, it did not constitute a homogeneous force. Some, who had actively opposed Reza Shah's policy of detribalization and pacification, and suffered torture and incarceration, genuinely supported the Republic, fearing the return of the military dictatorship. The political and cultural repression that accompanied the centralizing functions of the state had effectively politicized this small but powerful fraction of the tribal landowners. Kurdish nationalism was pronounced in their political aspirations when they were detained for opposing the authority of the state; and, when they were eventually released by the new government in Tehran, they were more than eager to give public expression to their nationalist aspirations.[19]

Others, who had submitted to Pahlavi absolutism and had subsequently become part of the political and economic power structure in Iran at large, had a more guarded attitude towards the Kurdish administration.[20] These 'conformist' chiefs, too, mostly lent their support to the Republican leadership, though for entirely opportunistic reasons. They feared political isolation and economic loss, especially in view of the growing threat posed by the development of populist nationalism and the expansion of popular democratic politics in Kurdistan. The majority of the 'conformist' tribal landlords tolerated the moderate leadership, restrained ideological rhetoric and autonomist political pro-gramme of the KDPI. They had, as was seen, mostly joined the party as active members, which subsequently enabled some to enter the Republican administration, holding honorary posts, especially in its military organization. But the policy of the majority of these powerful tribal leaders towards the Republic was wholly opportunistic. There is ample evidence to show that prominent figures among them regularly contacted the central government in Tehran as well as the British and American political officers stationed in Kurdistan and Azerbaijan, seeking advice and guidance concerning their relationship with the Republic. Meanwhile they bided their time, waiting for the eventual collapse of the Kurdish administration and the return of the central government.[21]

The leaders of the Republic, especially its president Ghazi Muhammad, seem to have been aware of the political opportunism of the paramount chiefs, some of whom had sworn allegiance to the Republic and held important posts in the government. Ghazi Muhammad, in his speech inaugurating the independent Kurdistan, refers to tribal conflict and discord not only as an obstacle to achieving the 'national goal of freedom and independence' of the Kurdish Republic, but also the main 'internal danger' threatening its security and survival'. 'It is clear,' he states, 'the Kurdish nation will continue its struggle against the remnants of this danger, internally and externally.'[22] In a speech delivered three months later Ghazi invokes the issue again, referring to the covert but persistent relationship between some elements of tribal leadership and the Iranian government, especially the army commands in Southern Kurdistan. He thus warns the tribal chiefs:

> The government of Kurdistan is very strong today, and it can deal very effectively with those who want to unite with the enemies of the Kurds. But I will not give up the peaceful way as far as possible. If there is no peaceful way left to deal with them, the government of Kurdistan will then rub their heads to the ground with all its might.[23]

But despite Ghazi's warnings, illicit dealings with the Iranian government and the British and American emissaries in the region continued unabated. Witness the news in *Kurdistan* regarding the chiefs of Debokri and Ardalan barely two weeks after Ghazi's warning:

> According to the information that has reached us, Agha Aliyar and Saifallah Khan Ardalan, together with Colonel Pezeshkan, have entered Saqqiz. Their treason against the motherland is now clear to everyone. Since the day the national government of Kurdistan was declared these reactionaries have not refrained from opposing it for one moment. They think in their own naive way that they are busy destroying the powerful government of Kurdistan. (*Kurdistan*, no. 45, 6 June 1946)

But the threatening tone of the article changes significantly towards the end, as the writer tries to persuade the two tribal chiefs to return to the republican/nationalist fold. 'So brothers,' thus he addresses the treasonous chiefs, 'do you not want to give up, even after having been repeatedly forgiven by the government of Kurdistan?'[24] This drastic change of tone, from coercive threat to persuasive reminder, is an indication of the recognition by the Republican leaders of the limits of their powers *vis-à-vis* the landowning class.

From the outset, the leadership of the Republic was certainly aware of the fact that a number of landlords and tribal chiefs were overtly hostile not only to the Republic, but to the very ethos of Kurdish nationalism and independence. Barely a week after the inauguration of the Republic, on 28 January 1946, an article attacking Kurdish collaborators appeared in *Kurdistan*. This article, which names the chief collaborators, is the first explicitly nationalist critique of the hostile landlords and tribal leaders, and implies that their treachery predates the inauguration of the Republic:

It is unfortunate to see that now there are Kurds who not only continue to serve these Persians, who have kept us under their oppressive rule for so long, but who are also openly selling out the Kurdish nation. The dealings of Ali Agha i Amir Asa'd, who has sold out all the Kurds, with the chief of the staff of the Iranian army are known to all of us. It is clear to the people that Mulla Abdulrahman i Surounjadaghi, Muhammad i Faroughi, Hamza i Ghawachi and others are spies and nation sellers. Gharani Agha i Mamash, Muhammad i Abbasi, Alijan Mangur, Abdullah Agha Mangur and a few others are openly trying to sow discord and divide the Kurds ... You damned people, you should be ashamed of yourselves! Wake up before it is too late.[25]

Similarly, following Ghazi Muhammad's veiled reference to tribal discord and opposition in his inaugural speech, Muhammad Hussein Saif Ghazi, the minister of war and deputy commander-in-chief of the armed forces, made a speech in the same ceremony celebrating the declaration of the autonomous Kurdish Republic but also addressing internal discord, opposition and treason. He named a group of 12 men, mostly tribal chiefs with some townsmen included, as hostile elements who refused to recognize the authority of the Republic and its leadership and continued instead to co-operate with their enemies.[26]

The emphatic and sharp tone of this criticism, and the explicit public exposure of specific landlords and tribal chiefs, reflects the confident mood of the KDPI leadership in the early days of the Republic, before the departure of the Red Army from Kurdistan and the conclusion of the autonomy treaty between the Azerbaijan and Tehran governments.[27] But as events took a turn for the worse and more cracks appeared in the already fragile structure of political power in the Republic, the authorities had to modify their position. They were obliged, however reluctantly, to turn a blind eye, and tolerate the covert and at times overt activities of the hostile landlords and tribal leaders. This reluctant tolerance was not entirely tactical, nor did it stem from a trenchant democratic spirit in the Republican administration. Rather it signified once again the bitter recognition by the Kurdish leadership of the pivotal status of the tribal landowners in the structure of political power in the Republic. The survival of the Republic depended largely on their co-operation.

The position of the large landlords in general and the tribal leadership in particular was determined by the predominantly pre-capitalist character of relations of production in the economic structure of Kurdish society in Iran in the 1940s. The predominance of feudal ground rent in agriculture, the lack of a marketable economic surplus large enough to sustain a developed structure of commodity relations and exchange, and the consequent backwardness of trade and commerce and the absence of a uniform regional market, meant that the economic structure of Kurdish society was not able to provide the means and mechanisms necessary for the territorialization of political authority in the Republic. In the absence of capitalist commodity relations, military power was the most extensive mechanism capable of providing for and sustaining territorially centralized rule in the Republic. Military power in the Republic, therefore, amounted to more than an institution for national defence; it was a structural force, which sustained the political organization of authority and determined the range of its efficacy in the territory. The military organization of the Republic defined the crucial difference between the 'real' and 'imagined' boundaries of the Republic. It was vital to its survival.

The military organization of the Kurdish Republic was heterogeneous. It was composed of a regular army and tribal contingents. The regular army, established soon after the formation of the Republic, was small in size and inexperienced in the field. The officer corps as well as the soldiery was drawn primarily from the ranks of the urban petty-bourgeoisie. Their loyalty was to the Republic and its president, and they were represented in the government by the minister of war, who was also their commander-in-chief. The regular army depended for its training chiefly on a tiny group of Kurdish nationalist officers who had deserted the Iraqi army in the 1940s, and for arms and equipment mainly on the Soviet army corps stationed in the territory.[28] The size and military power of the regular forces were insignificant in comparison with the tribal contingents, which were the main force in the military organization of the Republic.[29] Of the four generals who formed the command structure of the military forces of the Republic, one was the commander-in-chief of the regular army; the other three were tribal leaders.[30]

The command structure of the Republican army, which presided over both the regular and tribal contingents, according to Eagleton, was created in March 1946. Theoretically, it was a centralized command bound by a set of rules and regulations which defined its relationship to political authority on the one hand and the rank and file on the other. In practice, however, the military command was unable and unwilling to enforce its authority centrally and without resorting to processes and practices outside the formal organization of the army. This was due primarily to the prominence of the tribal leadership, tribal soldiery and tribal lineage in the military organization of the Republic. The tribal chiefs held unsalaried honorary ranks in the command structure; the tribal soldiery in the service of the Republic were also unsalaried, and their relationship with the army command was at best indirect, working almost invariably through the agency of the tribal chief. This also meant that lineage rather than formal relations defined the status of the tribal soldiery in the organization of the army as well as the nature of their loyalty to the Republic, and with minor exceptions it always overshadowed the Republican nationalist ideology.

Tribal contingents were the main component of the military forces of the Republic. Their number is variously estimated at 10,000–13,000, a sizeable force given the fact that the Iranian military force stationed in Saqqiz and posing a military threat to the Republic did not exceed 5,000 in number. But tribal contingents were traditionally organized into cavalry units, which posed serious military and logistical problems. In strictly military terms, the efficacy of tribal units was geographically very limited; they could not easily be fielded outside the tribal area (that is, beyond a radius of 50–70 kilometres) without local logistical support, a shortcoming which was usually remedied by tribal raids and plunder. Logistical issues also seriously hindered the use of tribal cavalry in modern combat against infantries carrying light arms. Nor was the use of cavalry by any means confined to the tribal forces of the Republic. The bulk of the small regular army of the Republic was also cavalry, as was a sizable section of the Iranian military forces at the time. The persistence of cavalry forces in Iran in general and in Kurdistan in particular signified a wider anomaly at the very heart of the economic and political development of Iran since the late nineteenth century (Eagleton, 1963, pp. 90–3).

The Republican government attempted to remedy the logistical pitfalls of tribal cavalries by providing them with food and ammunition while on the move, thus enabling them to extend the range of their military activities without needing local support. The officers of the regular army were entrusted with this task; as Eagleton notes, 'to each tribal group was assigned an officer whose duties, in addition to the transmission of military instructions, included the provision of adequate food supplies'. The new measures may have helped the military command to overcome 'the most disruptive factor in large-scale tribal movements, the foraging which often led to looting', but only temporarily. For the provision and use of military logistics depended ultimately on the level of development of the productive forces in the economy, in particular in the sphere of agrarian production (Eagleton, 1963, p. 92).

The leadership of the Republic, however, had another force at its disposal that to some extent helped redress the existing imbalance between the tribal and regular forces in its military organization. This was the Barzani force, which had been stationed in the town of Mahabad and its vicinity since 1945.[31] This contingent, estimated at 2,000 to 3,000 men, was led by its chief Mulla Mustafa Barzani, who had fled to Iranian Kurdistan to escape persecution by the Iraqi government, with which he had been in conflict for over a decade. Although the Barzani contingent was organized on tribal lines, and primordial loyalties governed the relationship between the chief and the tribesmen, it operated under different political conditions to those defining the conduct of the Kurdish tribes of Iranian Kurdistan. Mulla Mustafa and his tribal force were outsiders in Iranian Kurdistan, and their continued presence in the area was resented by some of the major local tribes, whose leaders made no secret of their dislike of Barzani. The local tribal leaders, whether for or against the Republic, found Barzani's presence intrusive, disturbing the political and military arrangements on which their perceived notions of the balance of forces and tribal power and privilege in the area rested. For those inside the Republican administration such as Amar Khan and Hama Rashid Khan, Barzani's allegiance to Ghazi Muhammad and his loyalty to the government represented a threat to their status in the military organization of political power in the Republic, often exposing the opportunistic nature of their relationship with the Republic and the person of Ghazi Muhammad. For those such as Bayiz Agha Mangur and Gharani Agha of Mamash and his son Mam Aziz, who stood in opposition to the Republic and were publicly hostile to its president, on the other hand, Barzani and his armed men were not only a bulwark against their efforts to undermine the Republic but also an instrument that Ghazi could use to suppress their opposition and aggression.[32] Nor did the Soviet political officers in the area welcome the Barzanis; they suspected Mulla Mustafa of being a British agent, and feared his cordial relationship with the leadership of the Republic.[33]

The Barzanis thus had to rely on the goodwill and co-operation of the urban population and political forces, namely the KDPI and later on the Kurdish Republic, on whose economic support they largely depended. They could not, therefore, afford not to form a political alliance with the leadership of the Republic, and to take an active interest in its survival, given that their relationship with the Iranian government was less than friendly, and the prospect of a safe return to their tribal homeland in Iraqi Kurdistan in the near future was bleak.[34] The leadership of the Republic, especially Ghazi Muhammad, could and did rely on the support and co-operation of the Barzanis, who proved more effective than the standing army, and were occasionally decisive in local military conflicts, especially when a local tribal leader refused to join forces with the Kurdish government.

The planned military operation by the Republican government to take over Sardasht is a prime example of tribal discord. The heads of Harki and Shikak tribes refused to comply with Ghazi's request to co-operate with the Republic in the attack on Sardasht. The British Consul in Kermanshah wrote to Tehran about the incident:

> Ghazi Muhammad wished to involve the Shikak and Herki Kurds in the attack on Sardasht and their leaders were brought to Mahabad but demanded Shahin Dehz and Miandoab as the price of their co-operation. Ghazi Muhammad did not agree to this and Shikak and Herki Kurds did not, therefore, join in the attack. (FO 371/3625)

Similar discord in the command structure emerged when the government appealed to Hama Rashid Khan of Bana for military help. In this case Ghazi Muhammad eventually seems to have won the day with the help of Mulla Mustafa and his armed contingents. The discord in the command structure of the Republican army, and the opposition expressed by hostile, uncooperative and impassive tribal leaders such as Amar Khan, Zero Beg and Hama Rashid Khan, undoubtedly loomed large in the military calculations and decision-making of the Iranian military command in the region. General Homayuni, the head of the Iranian forces, clearly capitalized on the continued discord and conflict in the Republican command structure, as he knew very clearly his forces, estimated at 2,500 men by the British consul in Kermanshah, would be unlikely to withstand the Republican military forces if the tribal contingents, the regular armed units and the Barzani forces were united under a single command: 'General Homauni seemed confident of his ability to cope with the situation unless Ghazi Muhammad, Hama Rashid and Mulla Mustafa combine their forces for a southward move in which case there might be serious trouble.'[35]

The local tribal forces did not constitute a standing military unit with a uniform command structure, but rather a highly disparate force, diverse in origin and organization, maintained, controlled and fielded by their respective chiefs, to whom alone they owed allegiance. In principle, tribal contingents could be provided at the request of the president of the Republic, but in practice this depended on the political position of the chief, which, as has been seen, itself depended on the complex network of short and long-term political and economic interests defining his changing relationship with the Iranian government. Inter-tribal rivalry, an endemic feature of tribalism in Kurdistan, was also important in this respect. Rival tribal leaders associated with the Republic often acted against each other, vying for position, or refused to work together in joint military operations, thus bringing them to a halt.[36]

Though heterogeneous and disunited, these local tribal forces nonetheless clearly outnumbered and out-gunned the combined force of the standing army and the Barzani contingents. They were the dominant force in the military structure of the Republic. This accounted for both the military weakness of the Republic and its dependence on the good will of the tribal leadership. The conditions of military weakness and dependency continued to reinforce each other, with adverse structural consequences for the territorialization and consolidation of political power in the Republic.

The preponderance of military power in the structure of political authority thus ensured the autonomy of the tribal leadership in the Republic. The leadership of the Republic had to recognize this autonomy (albeit in a *de facto* manner) and try to come to terms with its political consequences; but they did so at a high price. For the conditions that ensured the political autonomy of the tribal landlords also subverted the conditions of modern political sovereignty in the Republic. The Kurdish Republic was a modern political structure sustained by traditional relations. The pre-capitalist social and economic relations had already forced its nationalist leadership to compromise the essential condition of the modern national identity. The autonomist political project, formally pursued by the Republican leadership, was more a basis for this compromise, articulating modern and traditional forces, than a mere conservative response to the prevailing geopolitical conditions. It failed to secure the conditions necessary for the consolidation of the nascent national identity. The Kurdish national identity remained fragile, although it continued to assert itself in every instance of the conflict between modernity and tradition that marked the rise and demise of the Republic. It was at the heart of the ambiguities and anomalies that characterized the political discourse and practice of its leadership.

4

AMBIGUITIES AND ANOMALIES IN THE DISCOURSE OF THE REPUBLIC

In the course of its brief legal existence, the KDPI published 113 issues of *Kurdistan*, of which 83 have survived the vicissitudes of time.[1] These surviving issues are unevenly spread across the crucial period from the formation to the destruction of the Kurdish Republic. The discourse of *Kurdistan* is heterogeneous in both form and character, showing the diverse political and cultural influences on the intellectual formation of its authors and contributors. Contributions by local authors, mostly members of the KDPI and hence of the Republican government, whether dealing with domestic political, cultural and socio-economic issues or just with local civic problems, demonstrate the persistent influence of Persian culture and language. Although written in Kurdish, the prose lacks a uniform style; it borrows extensively from Persian in its vocabulary, mode of expression and writing, all of which tend to follow the current order in modern Persian – a condition symptomatic of the political and cultural immaturity of the nationalist intelligentsia during this period.

The influence of Persian on the writing and mode of presentation is evident especially in descriptive articles, which are often trying to elaborate a nationalist view of the position of the Kurds in contemporary Iranian history and politics, or making a case for the creation of the Republic as an expression of the civic and democratic rights of the Kurds. The early nationalist discourse often lacks a conceptual vocabulary other than an emotional appeal to ethical-political notions and natural rights theory. [2] The influence of Persian fades into the background, however, in contributions which are more abstract in character and focus on more substantive social, economic and political issues, especially those which attempt to deploy some form of general theoretical and conceptual language. These contributions, which are generally marked by the influence of Soviet Marxism and Marxist categories, are for the most part authored by Kurds from Iraq, as well as including a smaller number of translations into Kurdish of articles written by Azeri democrats.[3] Kurdish prose in these latter contributions, which make their appearance gradually after July 1946, is more uniform in style and more akin to that which subsequently became the dominant literary mode of writing. Later issues in general thus show a marked difference in style, as the writing of the local Kurdish intelligentsia is increasingly influenced by the changing political and ideological conditions in Iran and Kurdistan at large.[4]

The substantive writings in the surviving issues of *Kurdistan*, leader comments and features as well as interviews, bear the mark of the ambiguities and anomalies that characterized the painful development of Kurdish national identity during this crucial period. However, this development, as we have seen, did not signify a crystallization of Kurdish nationalism and national identity in Iran, but rather its self-redefinition, which involved a new self-perception. This new self-perception was precipitated by the developments that specified the dissolution of the Komalay JK, the formation of the KDPI and the subsequent creation of the Republic. The fundamental feature of these developments, as was seen, was the crisis of political authority that came to grip the nationalist movement soon after its inception in 1942.

The discursive construction and representations of this new self-perception were marked by a silence about the 'origin' of these developments. There is in the discourse of *Kurdistan* a silence, a closure, on the subject of Komalay JK and its place in the formation and development of nationalist history and politics. This silence amounts not so much to exclusion or denial as to forced amnesia, an attempt to suppress Komalay JK in the national memory, or, at best, to treat the process of its formation and development as the pre-history of the creation of the KDPI and constitution of the Republic, a pre-history which lacks discursive autonomy and finds meaning only when history is read backwards. In fact, references to the founding members of Komalay JK and their political activity, scarce as they are, are only intended to highlight their subsequent positions and actions in the Republic and in Republican politics. Their integration into the organizational structures of the KDPI and subsequently the Republic is also the assimilation of their political histories into the history of the KDPI and the Republic. In the discourse of *Kurdistan* the Republic is the route through which Komalay JK and its founders enter national history and acquire political identity. They have no history or identity prior to the formation of the Republic.[5]

The silence of *Kurdistan* on the rise and demise of Komalay JK, the attempt to suppress its history and identity in the national memory, are symptomatic of the conditions in which the KDPI and the Kurdish Republic came into existence. These conditions were defined by the crisis of political authority and a new configuration of internal and external forces and relations, whose active presence in the political and cultural process influenced not only the development of the nationalist political project, but also the metamorphoses and the contours of the nascent national identity. The nationalist political project of Komalay JK and the concept of Kurdish national identity entailed in the discourse of *Nishtiman* were thus modified, redefined and reconstructed to suit the new conditions.

It was noted in Chapter 1 that the discourse of *Nishtiman* entailed a concept of Kurdish national identity whose inner core and outer shell were defined by two distinct notions of the Kurdish nation, political and historical respectively. The political concept of the Kurdish nation was conceived as a social community internally differentiated into social classes and strata, with diverse and contradictory political, economic and cultural interests, which cut across ethnic relations. This concept as such signified the subject of nationalist politics, informing the agrarian populism that underpinned Komala's moral critique of Kurdish society, and in particular of the landowning class, which was thus excluded from the ranks of the Kurdish nation. The Kurdish nation as a historical category, on the other hand, was conceived as an ethnic community unified by a common history, language and tradition, including all Kurds living in Greater Kurdistan. This ethnic notion, repeatedly historicized in the discourse of *Nishtiman*, signified a uniform sovereign entity, which informed Komalay JK's nationalist project and its vision of national history. It defined the contours of Kurdish national identity *vis-à-vis* its 'other', the uniform Iranian identity constructed in the official discourse of the first Pahlavi state.

The perceived conceptual difference between Komala's agrarian populist rhetoric and its ethnic nationalist discourse, and the corresponding conceptions of the Kurdish nation specified in the discourse of *Nishtiman*, clearly pointed to the strategic issue of political power and authority in the formation of Kurdish national identity. In fact, the strategic issue of political power was never detached from the specific position of the landowning class and tribal leadership in nationalist discourse. Their simultaneous inclusion in and exclusion from the definitions of the nation was central not only to Komala's self-perception, but also, and more importantly, to its position regarding the identity of the 'other', the Iranian state and the central political authority in Tehran. This point became increasingly manifest in the subsequent course of events, as the crisis of political power and territorialization of authority unfolded to grip the nationalist movement in its infancy.

Unlike Komala, the KDPI was formed with the support and blessing of the landowning class and the majority of powerful tribal leaders, who found it easy to rally around an autonomist political programme which had in part been designed to incorporate them into the political process.[6] The incorporation of the landowning class and tribal leadership into the political process also had the active support of the Soviet Union which, for reasons of self-interest, discouraged territorial ethnic nationalism in favour of an autonomist political programme. These developments had important consequences for the constructions of the conceptions of Kurdish nation and national identity in the discourse of *Kurdistan*.

As was noted in Chapter 3, the moral critical categories, especially the moral concepts of exploitation, oppression and justice, so frequently deployed in the discourse of *Nishtiman*, are strikingly absent from the discourse of *Kurdistan*. *Nishtiman*'s moral critique of the socio-economic conditions of existence of the Kurdish landowning class, and of their exploitation of the peasantry, incessant greed and exorbitant rents, is replaced by a rather qualified political criticism which emphasizes their relationship with political authority in the Republic, and their support for and devotion to the defence of the Republic and its ideals. The political critique of the Kurdish landowning class is selective in form and subjective in character; it does not focus on tribalism or the political organization of tribal power, but on the conduct of individual tribal leaders who do not co-operate with the Republican government in instances of military confrontation with the Iranian armed forces stationed in Kurdish territory, and who are seen to be biding their time for the eventual defeat of the Republic and the return of the central government.

This displacement of the moral critique of the economic position of the landowning class in favour of a subjective and qualified political critique of selected elements of the tribal leadership in the discourse of *Kurdistan* is hardly surprising, given the pivotal position of this class in the economic and military organizations of political power in the Republic. However, while this was the main reason, it was by no means the sole motive for the change of attitude towards the landowning class. There were other political and ideological factors contributing to this change, both internal and external.

The internal factors were diverse, but they resulted mainly from the political and cultural specificity of the Kurdish community of the time. Religion and tradition constituted major elements in the ideological formation and outlook of the Republican leadership which, with some notable exceptions, was drawn from the ranks of the urban mercantile bourgeoisie and petty-bourgeoisie, old and new. The mercantile bourgeoisie and traditional petty-bourgeoisie of the Kurdish bazaars and marketplaces were largely lacking in cultural and economic autonomy. Historically, Kurdish urban centres were the sites of the political and administrative power of the Kurdish landowning class, primarily the tribal leadership, who had also dominated the urban cultural scene for at least three centuries. The prolonged political and cultural dominance of the landowning class and tribal leadership was never separate from their economic supremacy in the Kurdish community. The two were articulated in the structure of pre-capitalist agrarian relations, which reproduced and sustained the dominance of the country over Kurdish towns and hence the hegemony of the landowning class and tribal leadership in Kurdish political and economic life. The Kurdish mercantile bourgeoisie and urban petty-bourgeoisie, engaged in traditional forms of economic activity, were both dependent on agrarian production and exchange for their economic production.[7]

The major external force behind the change in the attitude of *Kurdistan* towards the landowning class was the Soviet Union, which, as has been seen, initially played an important role in the formation of the KDPI and the republican leadership, and especially in the incorporation of the tribal leadership in the nationalist political process, albeit purely for reasons of self-interest. The fear of a Soviet military presence in Kurdistan and the weakness of the Iranian army, on the other hand, were decisive in softening the overtly hostile attitude of the large landlords and tribal chiefs towards the nationalist forces. But the relationship between the Soviet political and military authorities and the Kurdish landowning class was never cordial or warm. It was for the most part defined by mutual suspicion and mistrust, which grew stronger as the negotiations between the Republican leadership and the Iranian government failed, and the prospect of an autonomous Kurdistan began to fade in the light of mounting Anglo-American pressure on the Soviet Union to withdraw her military force from Iran.

The change in the mode of criticism of the landowning class and the tribal leadership apparent in the discourse of *Kurdistan* thus signifies an attempt to redefine the position of these groups in nationalist discourse, and to affirm their status within the nation and the nationalist political process. The qualified political critique of large landlords and tribal leaders unwilling to co-operate with the republican authorities is always couched in broad nationalist terms, appealing to their sense of duty to the nation and the motherland. The discourse of *Kurdistan* therefore entails an ethnic-nationalist conception of the nation, whereby Kurdish ethnicity operates not only as the criterion of inclusion and exclusion defining the boundaries of the nation, but also as the sole ideological organizing principle of political authority and legitimacy in the Republic.[8] The leadership of the Republic often invoked this concept when addressing internal discord and opposition, appealing to the authority of the Kurdish nation, although at times it was also invoked in order to assert the national-democratic nature of its authority and the legitimacy of its demands *vis-à-vis* the Iranian government. The invocation of the concept and its role in the representation of authority in the discourse of *Kurdistan* depended on the prevailing political conditions in the Republic.

This ethnic-nationalist conception of the Kurdish nation was not only the silent voice of authority, which spoke in critical political conditions, but also the origin of the uniform national history ever-present in the discourse of *Kurdistan*. It did not, therefore, only represent political authority or legitimize its discourse and practice; it also historicized it. For political authority represented the national will, which was thus perceived as the source of national history, imparting meaning into an uninterrupted process of struggle for freedom and independence.[9]

The tactical invocation of this ethnic-nationalist concept, the appeal to the authority of the nation to legitimize the practice of the republican government, is not without its problems. For, more often than not, this tactical invocation takes place in the context of a regional autonomist discourse, the political requirements of which are clearly incompatible with an ethnic-nationalist political project. The autonomist discourse repeatedly delimits the boundaries of the nation, effectively confining it to the Kurdish territory in Iran. Further, allusions to the concept of the Kurdish nation in this context are immediately undercut by a shift of emphasis in the discourse from the political to the cultural. In fact, the concept of nation associated with the autonomist political project in the discourse of *Kurdistan* is akin to the notion of 'ethnie' or 'ethnos', clearly devoid of its juridico-political connotations in the modern nationalist discourse. This is evident in the writings and especially utterances of the Kurdish leaders, in particular Ghazi Muhammad, prompted by the quest for regional autonomy and the subsequent negotiations with the Iranian Government.[10] In such cases not only the political sovereignty of the Kurdish nation but also its discursive autonomy is denied, as the republican leaders are at pains to emphasize their intention of remaining an integral part of the sovereign Iranian nation, and respecting the territorial integrity of the Iranian state.

The Kurdish autonomist discourse is informed by a specific reading of the Iranian Constitution that emphasizes political pluralism, decentralization of power, provincial and local administrative and cultural autonomy, and respect for religious and ethnic difference. The implementation of the Constitution, this reading suggests, presupposes a fairly developed civil society to ensure the democratic political process in a multi-ethnic and multi-cultural nation state in Iran. In other words, in Kurdish autonomist discourse the juridico-political recognition and protection of ethnic and religious difference by the state is the essential condition of existence for a genuine and lasting democratic political process.

In fact, in the discourse of *Kurdistan* the quest for regional autonomy is unambiguously linked with the need to revive the democratic political process in Iran, as stipulated in the Constitutional Law of 1906. It is presented as a democratic measure, a device for decentralization of power, constitutionally sanctioned ever since the advent of popular sovereign rule in 1905. The Kurdish leadership frequently refers to the *Anjumanhayeh Iyalati v Velayati* (the Provincial and District Councils), stipulated in the Constitution to empower the provinces to self-govern, as the appropriate institutional framework for the realization of its demands. The Kurdish quest for regional autonomy is often tantamount to the quest to revive Provincial and District Councils; it is presented as a democratic 'Iranian' demand for the revival of the decentralized administration that had been suppressed by the Pahlavi dictatorship. The underlying assumption here is that Iran is a multi-ethnic (multi-national) and multi-cultural society, and that this ethnic and cultural diversity is recognized and sanctioned by the Constitution, which stipulates appropriate democratic processes and practices for its free expression. Ghazi Muhammad, speaking as the leader of the KDPI in a press conference held in Mahabad two weeks before the declaration of the Republic, specifies the nature of Kurdish demands in the following terms: 'we demand the implementation of the Constitutional Law from the Iranian Government; we want to be autonomous under the Iranian flag, and we have already obtained this autonomy'. Responding to a question regarding the programme of the KDPI, he elaborates, 'the Provincial and District Council for Kurdistan, as stipulated in the Constitutional Law, should be established at once to administer and supervise all social and governmental affairs'.[11]

The Iranian Constitution of 1906 remained central to the politics of regional autonomy in the discourse of *Kurdistan*. The quest to establish the Provincial and District Councils with full administrative powers in Kurdistan defined the position of the Kurdish leadership in the unsuccessful autonomy negotiations with the Iranian government throughout the brief existence of the Republic. This, as was noted earlier, enabled the Kurdish leadership to present its demand for regional autonomy as a legitimate popular democratic right central to democratic governance in Iran as a whole. The popular-democratic presentation of the politics of regional autonomy as such often marginalized Kurdish ethnicity and ethnic/national difference in the discourse of *Kurdistan*. Early statements of the Kurdish position clearly play down 'ethnic differences' with Persians; they are subordinated to the necessity of a common Iranian cause, the struggle for democracy in Iran. Thus Ghazi Muhammad, addressing a public meeting in Mahabad shortly after the declaration of the Republic, argues:

> The dictatorial apparatus in Tehran ... for the reasons that I have explained has not yet understood the affairs of the Kurds properly. Otherwise [it would have understood that] even after achieving our full independence, we would wish to make it clear to the central government and also show to the world that the Kurds have not done these things in order to deny their brotherhood with the Persians, or to be proved not to be Iranians, but rather to oppose the dictatorial apparatus [in Tehran] ... Otherwise if freedom could be established in Iran there is no reason why all those who live in Iran could not hold hands in brotherhood.[12]

Muhammad Hussein Saif Ghazi, the minister of war, who headed the Kurdish delegation in the autonomy negotiations with the central government in Tehran, states in the same meeting: 'After much discussion and dispute and a few days of negotiation with reference to lies and empty words of the

Constitutional Law, we did not reach an agreement ... it has become clear to me that according to the Tehran government the Constitutional Law means trampling on the rights of the nation, binding the hands and feet of the nation ... for them Iran is only Tehran.'[13]

References to the Constitutional Law as the juridico-political frame in which to solve the Kurdish question become more frequent after the Soviet withdrawal and the Firouz-Pishevari autonomy agreement signed on 13 June 1946. This was in part due to the fact that the 1906 Constitution, in particular the Provincial and District Councils stipulated in it, formed the juridico-political basis for the autonomy agreement between the Tehran and Tabriz governments. The agreement, which had the support of the Soviet Union and the endorsement of the Tudeh party, effectively tied the question of Kurdish regional autonomy to Azeri self-rule, denying it political and territorial autonomy.

These two events both had adverse effects on the morale of the Kurdish leadership, and on its resolve to forge ahead with the proposed regional autonomy plan unilaterally. Given the circumstances, it had no option but to change its position and work towards a more restricted notion of administrative and cultural autonomy within the framework of the Firouz-Pishevari agreement. In the opinion of the Kurdish leadership, this change of position did not only amount to the loss of political autonomy *vis-à-vis* Tehran, but also to the loss of territory to the autonomous Azeri government, which had long claimed authority over a significant part of its designated national territory. It nonetheless moved, rather reluctantly, to explain and justify the change in policy to a public likely to question its merits. A leading article in *Kurdistan* entitled 'The Kurdish Question' thus reads as follows:

Let us consider the Kurdish Question. Dear readers, as you know, the Kurdish Question is a frightening thing in the context of world politics. For this reason our great leader with his wise policy has tied the affairs of Kurdistan to the affairs of Azerbaijan. And in so doing we have not lost but gained, since the Azeri nation like the Kurdish nation was suffering under the sway of colonialism and Reza Khan's dictatorship ... For this reason our wise beloved leader not only has not seen any reason to avoid such a policy, but also has considered it necessary for [the resolution of] the Kurdish Question. (*Kurdistan*, no. 60 [20 June 1946])

The article goes on to argue that if the Constitutional Law is made to conform with democratic principles and applied to Iran as a whole, that is, irrespective of the ethnic origin of the citizens, the case for Kurdish opposition will cease to exist:

Thus far our misfortune has only been this, that we have not studied in our own language. Strangers were sent to become our rulers, and this was not in conformity with the Constitutional Law and the principles of democracy. If, however, Constitutional Law is honestly and uniformly applied throughout Iran, it would mean that both in Kirmanshah and Senna education will be in Kurdish, and the Provincial and District Councils will be elected by the nation in a direct democratic way, and will also choose their leaders themselves. (ibid.)

And it concludes: 'The Azerbaijan-Tehran agreement does not include the Azeri nation alone, but also the Kurds; even the Armenian and Assyrians are included in this ... If we look at the Kurdish Question in Iranian Kurdistan from this point of view, it will easily become clear that the hardship of so many years [of struggle] has not been wasted, and we have achieved our objective.'[14]

Kurdistan here clearly argues not only for the implementation of the 1906 Constitution but also, and more significantly, for the democratization of the political process in Iran, involving decentralization of power and redistribution of the political and administrative functions of the state. Although the argument reiterates the need for the creation of the Provincial and District Councils, it is nonetheless clear that the demand for the recognition of the Kurdish rights involves more than political and administrative decentralization. In fact, implicit in the argument for the uniform and indiscriminate implementation of the Constitutional Law is the demand for the de-ethnification of the concept of citizenship entailed in it, although, as the concluding chapter will show, this demand was never directly articulated in the discourse of the Republic.

The discourse of *Kurdistan* shows an acute awareness of the essentially undemocratic character of the concept of citizenship informing the Constitutional Law of 1906. Modern Iranian citizenship, which was introduced to define the relationship of the citizens and the state in constitutional Iran, as was seen in Chapter 1, was essentially defined by elements of the 'sovereign', Persian, ethnicity, thus effectively excluding the other non-Persian ethnic relations from the definition of the conditions of citizenship. In other words, the sovereign ethnicity as such defined the common national identity of the citizens as Iranians, and specified the conditions of their access to the rights of citizenship stipulated in the Constitutional Law. The rights of citizenship which empowered Iranian citizens *vis-à-vis* the constitutional state thus by definition presupposed the denial of non-Persian ethnic identities in the national political and legal spheres.

This undemocratic streak, which ran through the Constitutional Law, also specified the conditions governing the distribution of political and administrative power; the proposed decentralization and delegation of power to the provinces did not follow national and ethnic lines, nor did the provision of local administrative autonomy in the form of the Provincial and District Councils involve a recognition of the multi-national or even multi-ethnic nature of Iranian society. The Constitution of 1906 excluded all political, administrative and cultural processes and practices deemed incompatible with or threatening to national identity, defined in terms of the sovereign Persian ethnicity. This is because the Constitution had already established a direct and fixed relationship between Iranian national sovereignty and Persian ethnicity, at the expense of other ethnicities and national identities. In this sense, therefore, the quest for the creation of the Provincial and District Councils to serve as a juridico-political frame for Kurdish regional autonomy had to be coupled with the demand for democratization of the Constitutional Law, the essence of which was the change in the conditions of citizenship. The concept of 'Iranian citizenship' entailed in the Constitution of 1906 had to be 'de-ethnified'; it had to be decoupled from Persian ethnicity, if it was to recognize and respect the multi-ethnic and multi-cultural formation of Iranian society and polity.

This by implication meant that the Kurdish leadership was aware that the Azeri democrats were simply asking too much of the Iranian Constitutional Law, and that the Provisional and District Councils as such could not provide a viable juridico-political basis for a genuine regional autonomy of the kind stipulated in the political programme of the KDPI. The point, however, was that although the Pishevari-Firouz agreement had secured a degree of recognition for Azeri demands, it was unable to provide a juridico-political framework for the expression of Azeri national identity. The political and institutional arrangements that were to be put in place in Azerbaijan amounted to a degree of cultural and administrative autonomy that did not threaten or infringe the discursive and political primacy of the Iranian identity defined by the constituent elements of Persian ethnicity.

So far as the Kurdish administration was concerned, the Pishevari-Firouz agreement signified its growing inability to assert its authority in the course of negotiations with the central government. The central government had succeeded, despite political discord and military weakness, in decoupling Azeri and Kurdish issues on the national Iranian level, effectively isolating the Kurdish leadership. The Kurdish question had not been swept aside, but rather denied political autonomy; it had been treated as an ethnic issue, to be dealt with in the domestic jurisdiction of the Azeri government. The Kurds were thus seen as part of the population of Azerbaijan, with different ethnicity but subject to the political and cultural arrangements stipulated in the Agreement.

Thus Clause 13 of the Pishevari-Firouz agreement stated that 'the [central] government agrees that Kurds residing in Azerbaijan may enjoy the privileges of this agreement'. Ghazi Muhammad hailed the agreement as a victory for the Kurds, stating that 'they have in this clause recognized our existence and confessed to our legitimacy, but we want all of Kurdistan to enjoy these privileges and the freedom which will soon be established by the Kurds throughout Iran'.[15] But evidently the agreement was far from being a victory for the Kurds. Ghazi was well aware of the fact that it denied Kurdish identity, and that its extension to Kurdistan as a whole, unlikely as it was, still would not amount to the recognition of the Kurdish rights and demands. The 'Tehran-Tabriz' agreement was a severe blow. A creeping despair and a sense of helplessness had already gripped the Kurdish leadership.

The Iranian government, which had now succeeded in isolating the Kurdish leadership, hardened its position in autonomy negotiations, with the intention of exploiting the mounting differences between the Kurdish and Azeri administrations over territorial and political issues. In response, the Kurdish leadership made a feeble attempt to shift the political ground by asserting the national rather than the regional identity of the Republic as the principle guiding the leadership and its political practice. The Republic, asserted Ghazi Muhammad, was a national government:

Again you yourself know that in the beginning we did not ask for separation from Iran at all, and our only aim was [to obtain] our freedom and to safeguard democracy [in Iran]. But in the beginning the Iranian authorities not only failed

97

to respond to our demands, but also ridiculed them. So we were compelled to establish our national government and test our strength against theirs, and when they pushed [their forces] forward against us we pushed ours against them. Now they are prepared to pull back, we too are prepared to pull back; now they have come forth to help us, we too will reciprocate, and respect them.[16]

Despite the apparent severity of this assertion, Ghazi Muhammad clearly leaves the door open for the resumption of the autonomy negotiations with Qawam's government, indicating that regional autonomy remains the strategic objective of the Kurdish administration. This apparent shift of ground, and the subsequent references to the national identity of the Republic, should not therefore be read as a policy statement, but rather as a measured warning to the central government to heed Kurdish demands for regional autonomy.

Such warnings, uncompromising as they may have sounded, clearly rang hollow against the background of the new developments in the political and military situation in Kurdistan and in Iran at large. Distrusting the Pishevari-Firouz autonomy agreement and dismayed by the conduct of the tribal leadership in the aftermath of the Soviet withdrawal, Ghazi Muhammad was clearly aware of the growing weakness of the Republic *vis-à-vis* the Iranian government. He soon realized that he had been left with no option but to fall back on the earlier position, a position that in his own admission had already been ridiculed and rejected by the Iranian government. The Kurdish administration thus renewed its demands for regional autonomy in the framework of the Iranian Constitution, but from a much weaker position.[17]

The autonomist discourse became more pronounced in *Kurdistan* in the aftermath of the Tabriz-Tehran and Tabriz-Mahabad agreements, as prospects for a political agreement with the Iranian government became daily more remote. The cultural concept of the Kurdish nation was further subordinated to the political exigencies of the rising constitutionalist discourse, which reiterated the unity and sovereignty of the Iranian nation and the territorial integrity of Iran. Various articles celebrating the 41st anniversary of the Constitutional revolution clearly testify to this point. They repeatedly reaffirm the status of the Kurds as part of the Iranian nation and Kurdistan as part of the sovereign state of Iran in order to establish and justify the primacy of the autonomist political project, and its unity and compatibility with the democratic precepts of the Iranian Constitution.[18] The concepts of Kurdish nation and Kurdish national identity lose their discursive autonomy, and ethnic-nationalist precepts are largely marginalized in the constitutionalist/autonomist discourse. Kurdish nationalist precepts are invoked only to serve general rhetorical rather than concrete political aims.

Autonomist and nationalist concepts of the Kurdish nation and national identity continue to appear in the discourse of *Kurdistan*, however, though in an uneven manner. Their persistence signifies an anomalous field of discourse operating in the widening gap between the political practice and the political rhetoric of the Republic. For the two concepts of nation and national identity are not only incompatible, but also, and more importantly, involve two different perceptions of the Persian 'other'. The wider nationalist concept, alluding to self-determination and independence, defines the boundaries of the Kurdish nation by ethnic relations. Ethnic differences thus not only supersede the existing socio-economic and political differences within the Kurdish nation, but also firmly and unambiguously set it apart from its Persian 'other'. This is because here ethnic differences are constructed in nationalist discourses that, in effect, privilege them, transforming them into irreconcilable differences, culturally determined historical contradictions. The ethno-nationalist differences as such can and to some extent do function as a demarcation line between the Kurdish 'self' and the Persian 'other' and are potentially capable of defining the contours of Kurdish national identity, in much the same manner as they had done in the discourse of *Nishtiman*. But the efficacy of ethno-nationalist differences in defining the contours of Kurdish national identity in the discourse of *Kurdistan* is seriously undermined by the political and discursive conditions of the autonomist project increasingly defining the agenda of the Republican administration.

This anomalous discursive field continues to expand in the gap between political practice and political rhetoric as the discursive boundaries between Kurdish and sovereign Iranian identities begin to crumble. Writings and utterances demanding independence and self-determination for the Kurds living in Greater Kurdistan or within the framework of Iranian sovereignty, infrequent as they are, become more rhetorical, assuming the form of declarative statements with neither ideological grounding nor political support. This further undermines the specific ideological role that ethnic-nationalist discourse played in the definition of the inner core of Kurdish identity. The Republican leadership's appeal to the common Kurdish ethnicity comes to fall on deaf ears, in the face of the increasingly acute political and economic differences and contradictions which were tearing the community apart internally. The nationalist constructions of ethnic difference which specified the boundaries of the Kurdish national identity *vis-à-vis* the Persian 'other' had lost their significance in the mire of this persistent discursive anomaly. Detached from nationalist discourse, Kurdish ethnicity had lost its political import, signifying no more than a cultural construct grounded in myth. Little wonder, therefore, that in the discourse of *Kurdistan* Kurdish national identity is either conflated with ethnic identity or directly reduced to it; at times the two are almost indistinguishable.

Another discourse in the surviving issues of *Kurdistan*, though heterogeneous and rudimentary, signifies important political and cultural trends, which come to influence the outlook of the nationalist intelligentsia in the 1940s and indeed for the decades to come. This new discourse, which becomes more pronounced after July 1946, is an incipient anti-imperialism, attempting to locate the Kurdish movement in general and the Republic in particular in the context of the post-war anti-colonial and national liberationist struggles in the colonial world. The appearance of this anti-imperialist discourse signifies the rising influence of Soviet communism on the Kurdish leadership and the nationalist intelligentsia in the post-war period. But this influence, characteristically filtered through the medium of regional communist parties and associated national and local organizations (the Tudeh Party of Iran, the Democratic Party of Iranian Azerbaijan and the Communist Party of Iraq), is haphazard and for the most part rhetorical rather than systematic. For example, the official Soviet-communist conceptions of imperialism and of anti-imperialist bourgeois-democratic liberation movements, derived from Lenin's writings, are entirely absent from the discourse of *Kurdistan*, as is the Soviet approach to the national question formulated by Stalin. There is no indication of a systematic and doctrinaire reading of Marxism, Soviet or otherwise, in the discourse of *Kurdistan*.[19] The exceptions to this are a few contributions by 'outsiders', usually Kurdish and non-Kurdish members of communist parties and organizations in Iran and Iraq, who were clearly influenced by Soviet Marxism and adhered to its doctrinal principles.

This incipient anti-imperialist/national liberationist discourse is heterogeneous in form and character. The main, if not the only, unifying factor in these contributions is the Soviet scheme for international political relations and the global balance of forces in the post-war period, which was rapidly popularized by communist parties worldwide, providing the conceptual frame of communist strategic thought and practice in the decades to come. These articles are premised on an early outline of the division of the globe into imperialist and anti-imperialist camps, represented by the US and the USSR respectively, and the necessity of siding with the latter against the former; a perception which subsequently became the hallmark of international communist thinking, informing the political analyses of communist parties and organizations worldwide, including the Tudeh party in Iran.

The Soviet scheme, as is well known, was an elaboration and redefinition of an older conception of global politics which had its political and theoretical roots in the discourse of the Third Communist International (Comintern) in the early 1920s. Theoretically, so far as nationalism in the colonial world was concerned, the Soviet scheme sought justification in Lenin's writings on imperialism, which, by articulating vertical relations of class exploitation in the horizontal chain of imperialist domination, seemed to have resolved the longstanding contradiction between class and national relations and identities.[20] The concept of imperialism as such provided the necessary economic foundation for the national question in the colonial setting, and anti-imperialist struggle legitimized the popular-democratic discourse and practice of national self-determination and independence in class terms, albeit on the political level. The surge of anti-imperialist movements in the colonial world in the post-war period gave a tremendous boost to the Soviet scheme, which already enjoyed an immense popularity in the colonial world after the pivotal role played by the Soviet Union in the decisive victory over fascism.

The Soviet scheme now represented the political stance of a superpower, whose global interests were defined in terms of antagonism to imperialism and its regional allies. This specific ideological feature of the scheme, along with its declared support for the national self-determination of subordinate peoples, made it particularly attractive to the latter, easy to identify with even in the absence of a doctrinaire allegiance to its Marxist-Leninist ideological formation. This was certainly the case in the Republic, although the 'populist' and overwhelmingly non-doctrinaire attitude was by no means uniform, varying widely among the nationalist intelligentsia.[21] The leadership of the Republic – particularly Ghazi Muhammad himself – often uses the language of anti-colonialism, but usually in a veiled or indirect manner. For example, in a speech delivered in late July 1946, Ghazi Muhammad assigns an anti-colonial character to the Kurdish movement by making a veiled but pointed reference to the rise of the national liberation movements in the colonial world:

> Kurds only want their own rights; they want to study in their own language, to benefit from the resources of their own land and become owners of buildings and factories. Kurds do not want to take the land of any other nation. We consider ourselves part of the light that is now shining in the world. We cannot close our eyes in daylight and sit in the darkness.[22]

The younger generation of active Kurdish nationalists, often holding secondary positions in the Republican administration, are less discreet in associating anti-colonialist movements with the political stance of the Soviet Union, although in this case, too, their allegiance to Soviet policy remains largely 'non-ideological'.[23] More doctrinaire expositions of the emergent political outlook, as was pointed out, emanate from the 'outsiders', whose contributions, at times translated from Arabic or Persian, show clearly the influence of Soviet Marxism.[24]

Anti-imperialist discourse in *Kurdistan*, then, is often imbued with Marxist class categories, deployed to aid political analysis. But class relations and contradictions are almost invariably linked with the central issue of colonialism which, in effect, serves to locate the Kurdish movement in the context of national liberation struggles, assigning to it an anti-imperialist character.[25] The incipient anti-imperialist discourse, crystallized in the vocabulary of the Soviet schema, is the nodal intersection of the nationalist and Marxist categories. In fact, in the discourse of *Kurdistan* Marxism is unambiguously identified with the political position of the Soviet Union, and Marxist class categories lose their explanatory power outside the conceptual framework of the Soviet ideological schema. The ideological identification of Marxism with communism and of the latter with the discourse and practice of the Soviet regime in most general terms is the hallmark of the position of the younger generation of Kurdish nationalists in the Republic. In their contributions, the Marxist character of class categories is almost never mentioned. Nor is there any reference to Marxism or Marxism-Leninism as a specific philosophical and political discourse. Rather, its ideological significance and political relevance to Kurdish society is almost invariably derived from its identification with the Soviet regime, its achievements, and above all the thoughts and practice of its leader Stalin. This mode of approach, which is generally in tune with the increasingly radical-democratic stance of the younger generation of the Kurdish nationalists, becomes more vocal and evident after July 1946. The post-July issues more frequently contain articles deploying the language of class analysis, characteristically ending with lofty praises for the Soviet regime and its 'great' leader, at times defined as the saviour of the human race! Marxist class categories in themselves, however, have no discursive autonomy and are never used to define or explain policy or programmes of action in the Republic, national-democratic or populist and social-reformist.

A brief comparison with the discourse of *Nishtiman* may help throw light on the specific status of Marxist class categories in the discourse of *Kurdistan*. The former, though marked by the absence of Marxist class categories, clearly contained an element of populist social reformism which gave it a distinctly radical cutting edge. In the case of the latter, by contrast, the explanatory power of Marxist class categories was undermined by the absence of a radical social-reformist programme capable of providing a concrete political basis for its anti-imperialist and national-democratic discourse. The exigencies of the territorialization of political authority in the Republic and the consequent reliance on the military and political support of the landowning class sapped the life out of the national-democratic and liberationist discourse of *Kurdistan*. It was effectively reduced to a populist political rhetoric, heavily coloured by the religious outlook of its authors and practitioners.[26]

The emergent anti-imperialist discourse, however rudimentary, entailed a new configuration of social and political
relations and forces, a new perception of friend and foe on
the global level, whose identities were defined in terms of their
real or assumed relationship with imperialism. In this sense,
therefore, it seemed that the emergent anti-imperialist discourse
could provide a new political ground for the redefinition of
Kurdish national identity. For, although still in rudimentary
form, it did not hesitate to redefine the relationship between
the Kurdish people and the Iranian state by placing the latter
firmly in the imperialist camp, in the camp of the new global
'other'. But the people-imperialist contradiction, which defined
the boundaries of the self and the other in the context of the
new global politics, could not provide the theoretical basis
necessary for the redefinition of Kurdish national identity. This
is because the definition of the contradiction in the Iranian
context presupposed a clear conceptual and political distinction
between the people/nation and the state/government. The
Iranian people/nation was further conceived and represented as
a constituent element of the anti-imperialist bloc, a politically
homogeneous force, internally differentiated by ethnic relations.
These relations, which defined the boundaries of the Persian
and Kurdish communities within the Iranian nation, were
further subordinated to the exigencies of the people-imperialist
contradictions. It seemed, therefore, that in the anti-imperialist
discourse the relationship between the Kurdish and Persian
communities could only be defined in purely ethnic terms, in
terms of a relationship between minority and majority ethnic
communities seemingly sharing a common political destiny: to
establish a popular democratic state in Iran.

This mode of representation of the relationship between
the two communities is central to the nascent anti-imperialist
discourse in *Kurdistan*. The point, however, is that the conceptualization of the relationship between the Kurdish and
Persian communities in the anti-imperialist discourse seriously
obscures the actual nature of the relations of identity and

difference between them, thus shifting the contours of the relationship between the Kurdish self and the Persian other from political to purely cultural terrain. In the emergent anti-imperialist discourse, the Kurds have no political identity, national or otherwise. Their identity is defined in purely ethno-cultural terms.

The political discourse of the Republic was secular; references to political authority and legitimacy were invariably grounded in national rights and civil and democratic liberties suppressed and denied by the state, though religion occupied a significant place in the outlook of the nationalist intelligentsia. The influence of religion was more prominent in the political rhetoric of the Republic, in the personal and semi-official statements, leader and positional articles, so often used by the nationalist intelligentsia to address the nation, reiterating their commitment to the struggle for the recognition of national rights and civic and democratic liberties and denouncing the state for centuries of national oppression and denial. The religious and ethical principles and precepts of Islam were also invoked to warn, threaten, condemn and denounce the internal collaborators, informers and real or potential traitors. The prominence of religion in the discourse of the republic as such signified not only the force of traditionalism in the political organization of the society, but also the weakness of the fledgling secular political culture in Kurdish society under the Republic.

The entrenched religious outlook and traditionalism of the nationalist intelligentsia in the Republic was undoubtedly an important factor contributing to the weakness and marginalization of radical social-reformist tendencies in the discourse of *Kurdistan*. Although the religion of the nationalist intelligentsia was by no means political, it has an active and at times imposing presence in the discourse of *Kurdistan*. Quranic verses and prophetic tradition are often cited, and religious notions, imagery and ethical precepts regularly invoked to serve populist political ends, and above all to legitimate authority and to appeal for unity. There are at times clear indications

106

that recourse to Islam by the Republican leadership, the older generation with traditional education and more pronounced religious convictions as well as the younger generation of the nationalist intelligentsia with modern education and outlook, is often meant to underpin and bolster the nationalist message for a deeply religious and largely illiterate community, not quite adept with the complexities of a modern ideology with secular notions of political authority, legitimacy, loyalty and citizenship and participation. In this sense, therefore, they should be viewed for the most part as calculated responses to what may be termed the structural weakness of a nascent nationalist movement struggling for survival against great odds in a predominantly traditional rural community. In this respect see, for example, the KDPI's command regarding Ghazi Muhammad's instructions on the purpose and content of the Friday *khutba'* (Friday sermon) to Mulla Hussein Majdie, the leader of Friday prayers in Mahabad. Ghazi, the party command indicates, instructs the leader of the Friday prayers to focus on the following issues in his sermon: 'struggle against superstition, respect for law and religion, construction of health centres and hospitals, effect of security on the progress of the motherland, ancient Kurdish civilisation, self-confidence and the importance of national military service and its necessity, how should women be in society, preparing kindergartens, how to prevent eye disease, spirit of chivalry, national unity ...'.[27] In general, however, the political use of religion is not programmatic so much as ad hoc, signifying the popular rather than political approach of the nationalist intelligentsia to religion. Some in the higher echelon of the republican leadership had had a traditional *madrasa* education, where the study of the *fiqh* and the *shari'a* were part of the curricula, and a few were trained clergy, but religion never played any role in the articulation and expression of their political positions, which remained thoroughly secular. In fact the idea that religion can play a political role in the political organization of the society remained alien to the discourse of the republic.

This argument, however, cannot be extended to the juridical processes of the government. The judiciary did not constitute an autonomous sphere in the institutional structure of the republican government, but rather was an adjunct of the party machinery and was treated as such. Juridical rules and processes emanated from the ruling party and were carried out by the government; and Islam in general and the *shari'a* in particular carried a significant weight in the KDPI's approach to legal issues. The Penal Code formulated by the central committee of the KDPI for the Ministry of War (edicts 1607 and 250201) testifies to the influence of *shari'a*. In article 2, for example, on drunken behaviour and lewd conduct, the punishment is set out as follows: '10 to 30 days of imprisonment with hard labour and 50 to 200 lashes, no more than 50 lashes to be applied each time'.[28] It is nonetheless interesting to note that the leadership of the KDPI at the same time had a critical and uncompromising attitude towards some of the social traditions commonly practised in the Kurdish community. A case in point here is the practice of *jin be jine* (exchange of sisters in marriage): the practice was banned by the party for being socially harmful, while at the same time there is an official silence on the practice of polygamy in Kurdistan. Although the party's silence on polygamy may have been prompted by political expediency rather than religious conviction, there is ample evidence in the discourse of the Republic to suggest that it maintained a differential attitude towards religious rules and teachings on the one hand and social tradition and common law principles on the other. The former were treated as beyond criticism or reproach.

Recourse to religion, whether political or juridical, especially when it was used to legitimate the conduct of the government or the status of Ghazi Muhammad, thus represented not so much the depth of the religious convictions of the nascent political class as their political and ideological immaturity. This immaturity, which carried the mark of centuries of economic backwardness, political parochialism and cultural isolation, was hardly self-inflicted. Nor was their consciousness of their political immaturity, which dawned upon them when they encountered the task of running a modern political administration in a predominantly illiterate society steeped in religion and tradition. They were men with a dream who wanted to liberate their nation from domination and repression by the other, to lay the foundations for a new political order to protect its existence and promote its interests. Now they had come to realize the bitter truth, that although they may have been free to choose their mission, they had no say in the nature of the circumstances in which they had to strive to accomplish it. Their nationalist dream and their project to realize it both fell victim to the politics of consolidation of power in the modern nation state in a period of acute 'national' crisis. It was the exigencies of political power in the modern state which made it necessary to co-opt the Kurdish tribal leadership and the landowning class into the power structure which maintained and bolstered the otherwise tenuous link between the state and its claim to represent a uniform nation. That the survival of the very idea of a modern nation state claiming modern sovereignty and legitimacy in Iran necessarily required an active support for the traditional pre-capitalist forces and relations in Kurdistan is a paradox which was at the core of the specific formation of modernity in Iran.[29]

The military organization of political power had already broken down under the weight of this paradox before the Republic fell on 15 December 1946, barely 11 months into its turbulent existence. The tribal landlords, on whom the republic depended for its defence, had already begun deserting the Republic as the Azeri democrats abandoned their defences in Zanjan and the Iranian army continued marching towards Tabriz on 10 December. Some, like the Shikak and Harki leaders, joined the Iranian military operation, mopping up the countryside around the towns of Urmiya and Tabriz in anticipation of the return of the old order. Others, like the Mangur and Mamash aghas, joined welcoming parties, renewing their allegiances to the monarchy

109

and offering their services to the commander of the advancing Iranian army on the way to Mahabad.[30] The tribal landlords who had sworn allegiance to the Republic now, after the fall of Tabriz on 13 December, threw caution to the wind, blowing their monarchist trumpets out in the open. They were actively repositioning themselves in the political field in anticipation of playing a part in the restoration of the monarchist order in Kurdistan. Their intention was to safeguard their power and status and further their privileges in the process of political transformation.

The War Council, the highest military office in the Republican administration, meeting on 5 December to review the military situation mainly in response to the news regarding the imminent military action by the central government to retake Azerbaijan and Kurdistan, pledged resistance to repulse and destroy the invasion. But the War Council disintegrated and the bulk of its active military force deserted the government before the Iranian troops set out to reconquer Kurdistan. This swift change of allegiance hardly needed any justification on the part of the perpetrators, political or ethical. For tribal landlordism was historically replete with opportunism, and sailing with the wind was the *modus operandi* of tribal politics. Lineage, primordial loyalty and parochial mentality, which are the stuff of tribal politics, could not by definition accommodate the processes and practices associated with modern political identities such as the people and the nation. Nor did this quick shift in allegiance by the tribal leadership take Ghazi Muhammad and his nationalist associates in the government and the party by surprise. They had long realized at their own peril that the power and status of tribal landlordism in Kurdistan was the product of the very same historical processes and practices which had defined their opposition to the modern state and official nationalism in Iran. This historical relationship between the power and status of tribal landlordism in Kurdistan and the development of the modern state in Iran meant that the so-called paradox of modernity was grounded not only in the economic structure and political organization of Pahlavi absolutism but also in the very core of political power in the Republic.

Iranian modernity, and more specifically the political and cultural processes and practices of the construction of a uniform nation and national identity by an absolutist state, had made landlordism indispensable to the persistence of the structures of power and domination in both the Iranian state and the Kurdish Republic. The pre-capitalist agrarian relations in Iran and the logistics of military power in the Kurdish Republic both required and ensured, though in different ways, the active representation of the landowning class in the organization of political power. The position of the landowning class was unassailable for as long as this paradox continued to define the relationship between the economic and political forces and relations in the complex structures of power and domination in both entities. The republican administration, the nationalists in the leadership of the party and the government were aware of this paradox, but perhaps never realized its real significance before the news of the re-conquest of Tabriz reached Mahabad on 13 December. Now the tribal soldiery, the sword which was meant to defend the Kurdish Republic, was being held by the state; and its cutting edge was directed menacingly at Ghazi and his comrades in Mahabad.

Ghazi Muhammad must have been mindful of this paradox and its final manifestations when he set out to meet the commander of the Iranian army on 15 December 1946. The fateful meeting took place in the vicinity of Miandoab, and Ghazi Muhammad surrendered to General Homayuni on the condition that Kurdish cities and their population would be spared the violence and bloodshed perpetrated in the neighbouring Azeri Republic, whose leadership for the most part had already fled to the Soviet Union.[31] The eyewitness accounts of the fall of Tabriz to the conquering Iranian army pointed to a human catastrophe in the making whose shockwaves were rapidly spreading to Kurdish towns in the Republican jurisdiction. The Kurdish townspeople, but above all the people of Mahabad,

111

the seat of Republican power and the stronghold of Kurdish rebellion against the power and domination of the state, were gripped by the fear of reprisals by a triumphant army which had been humiliated by its own weakness and inability to assert its authority in the Kurdish territory since September 1941.

Ghazi Muhammad's surrender to the Iranian army under the bemused gaze of the Kurdish collaborators, and his subsequent trial and execution in Mahabad, was the event in which the paradox of modernity was played out in full force. His public execution was the grand finale of this great event. Captured by the lens of a private photographer, the picture shows the slender figure of a man on the gallows: it is the figure of a man who died for a modern secular cause, clad in the traditional attire of Kurdish clergymen. It was the force of this paradox which took his head up on to the gallows. The irony, alas, was lost on the next generation of Kurdish nationalists, who chose to tread in his path.

Conclusions: The Kurds and the Reasons of the State

This study has examined the formation and development of Kurdish national identity in modern Iran. Kurdish national identity in Iran, it was argued, is fundamentally modern. Its genesis was the relationship of self and other established between Kurdish and Iranian national identity. The constituent elements of Iranian national identity were formed in the Constitutional period, and subsequently welded together by the processes and practices of state formation and consolidation of power under Pahlavi absolutism during 1925–41. The sovereign difference was thus the constitutive of Kurdish national identity, culminating in the formation of the Kurdish Republic in 1946. The Republic was, therefore, both the site and the object of significations of Kurdish national identity in the political field for a brief period in post-Second World War Iran.

The relationship between Kurdish otherness and Iranian national identity, mediated by political power, is an invariant of the theoretical framework of this study. But mindful of the deceptive charm of essentialist readings of political power as well as of the pitfalls of historicist conceptualizations of national identity, this study has attempted to ground its account of the genesis of Kurdish national identity in a theorization of difference and an appreciation of its constitutive effects on

113

the shifting boundaries of Kurdish otherness. The discursive primacy of difference in the theorization of the relationship of self and other means that the genesis of Kurdish national identity does not signify a uniform origin; it only points to a beginning, an emergent identity which is divided by politics and culture inside and outside. This divided relationship of self and other has been present in every instance of recognition and denial, rebellion and suppression, which has marked the development of the Kurdish community in Iran since 1942. It is continuously inscribed and reinscribed in new systems of difference and signification, inaugurating new discursive and political processes and practices governing the changing relationship between the Kurdish community and the state in modern Iran.

The process of the formation of Kurdish identity was underpinned by the historical transformation of the Kurdish community from a predominantly linguistic community before the Constitutional Revolution of 1905 to a chiefly ethnic community under Pahlavi absolutism in the 1930s. This crucial transformation was set in motion by the modern state in Iran and was inextricably tied to its efforts to create a centralized political, juridical and administrative structure and construct a uniform Iranian national identity. The historical relationship between the development of the modern state and the changing structures of the Kurdish community was the principal force in the dynamics of the Kurdish nationalist movement which was born in 1941–2 in the town of Mahabad and continued to spread in the region in the following years.

The dynamic of the Kurdish nationalist movement was relational; it was grounded in the relations of forces in the political field represented in terms of the differential effects of sovereign/juridical power on the shifting boundaries of the Kurdish community. Sovereign power was, therefore, perceived as the 'constitutive outside' of the Kurdish community, which in the course of their encounters defined the changes in the boundary separating that community from the wider non-

Kurdish community outside it. In this sense the transformation from a linguistic-cultural to an ethnic-linguistic community was defined by the modality of the development of sovereign power, which was also at the same time the modality of the development of sovereign difference and its changing relationship with its Kurdish other. This means that the dynamics of the Kurdish nationalist movement cannot be explained by reducing it to its conditions of formation in history, recent or distant – that is, to the first 'original' encounter between Iranian sovereign power and the Kurdish community, a discursive strategy common to historicist readings of national identity. The reference to the constitutive role of sovereign difference and its changing significations in different episodes of its cultural, political and military encounters with the Kurdish community is also necessary to avoid essentialist conceptions of sovereign power as a unitary structure of domination identified with the state and expressed in terms of its juridical effects. I shall return to this issue later on in this chapter.

Although the constituent elements of a uniform Iranian national identity had already been codified in the Constitutional Law of 1906, they nonetheless lacked power of signification and efficacy in the political and juridical processes of the state. The articles of the Constitution pertaining to the identity of the new 'national' sovereign were ineffectual; they were unable to constitute a formal political process with ethnic, linguistic or religious boundaries to exclude 'difference', to 'ban' it, to expel it from the political field. Identities which remained different from the new national sovereign continued to float in the political field, often as constellations of power and privilege firmly anchored in the decentralized structure of pre-modern political power. Nor was there a political urgency to exclude and suppress the non-sovereign difference. The new national sovereign was yet to encounter its non-sovereign 'other' in the political and juridical process of government. Although twin-born with the new national sovereign, the fledgling non-sovereign other was hardly conscious of its new status in the evolving national political field. This lack of consciousness of the self as the other of the new sovereign was clearly reflected in the striking political immaturity of the Kurds in the Constitutional era, an anomaly expressing the glaring political backwardness and cultural isolation of the Kurdish community at the turn of the century.

Thus, although the Constitution had announced the advent of a new sovereign, it was a new sovereign only in name. The Constitutional government, the executor of the sovereign will, lacked the power to enforce the unitary will attributed to the sovereign by the Constitution within the territorial limits of the country. This lack, which so woefully undercut the political efficacy of the sovereign will in the 'national' political field, was a growing anomaly in the structural formation of the juridical power, persistently reproducing the existing disjunction between law and power. This anomaly was expressed most vividly in the tribulations of the sovereign identity, when its very existence was threatened by a *coup d'état* led by the deposed Qajar monarch backed by Tsarist power in 1908. The constitutional state survived the counter-revolution, and Tehran was re-conquered by the Constitutionalist forces a year later, but the structural weakness of sovereign power persisted through the First World War and continued well into the 1920s.

The rise of Pahlavi absolutism was the culmination of the crisis of juridical/sovereign power in the constitutional state. The events which culminated in the *coup d'état* of 1921 had already widened the existing disjunction in the structure of the juridical power, expanding the distance separating it from its constitutionally ascribed objectives. Thus, although the identity of the new sovereign had been largely codified as law, this law was still very much 'outside itself', to use Derrida's expression, and the 'force' required to animate it, to ensure its significatory powers in the national-territorial political and juridical fields, was yet to be created. Political power was still grounded on old foundations, largely averse to the rational juridical processes and practices required to enact formal law (Derrida 1992).

The fateful years between the Constitutional revolution and the rise of Pahlavi absolutism were marked by the crisis of political power in Iran. The constitutional state failed to consolidate its existing foundations in the centre, and its centralizing functions seldom reached the outlying fields of power in the provinces. The functional autonomy of the provinces was perpetuated by the underdevelopment of economic forces and relations which on the one hand assigned a dominant role to military power in the consolidation of the state, and on the other undermined its efficacy by a combination of logistical inefficiency and technological backwardness. This complex and paradoxical articulation of the economic and the military in the structure of political power continued under Pahlavi absolutism. It defined the dynamics of the force which ended the disjunction between power and law, thus enabling sovereign/juridical power to signify, to produce effects as a structure of domination and rule whose public expressions were identified with the will of the absolutist ruler. The advent of Pahlavi absolutism was the resolution of the crisis of juridical power, and as such it presupposed the redeployment of Constitutional/national sovereignty on new economic-military foundations. The Pahlavi monarch was now the absolutist sovereign and his decisions were not only tantamount to law but were in most cases law above all laws. This redeployment of sovereignty fundamentally transformed the national political field, and hence also the political and cultural grounds on which the Kurds encountered power.

The consolidation of state power under Reza Shah was achieved by boosting large landownership while destroying the military organization of landlords' power, especially the military organization of the tribal landlords who were the main targets of his centralizing military measures. The politics of territorial centralism which brought the Iranian countryside under state control had the consent of the large landowners, who were represented strongly in the legislature and held prominent positions in the executive apparatuses of the redeployed absolutism. In fact this redeployed absolutism was the large landlords' regime: concentration of agrarian property and high monopoly prices on agricultural produce, especially cash crops, formed the basis of an active alliance with the absolutist monarchy. The absolutist state had subdued tribal opposition and reintegrated large landowners into the political power structure before it embarked on a policy of modernization from the above. Land registration and the emergence of a market with specified legal boundaries for the purchase and sale of agrarian property, and hence the introduction of modern private property in land under pre-capitalist relations of production and appropriation, was the basis of the landowners' regime and the foundation of state power. This regime not only ensured the power and privilege of the landowning class but also enabled the Pahlavi monarchy to bring the countryside under military control and domination.

The drive for modernization which followed the military processes of consolidation of the state also bore the mark of the social structure of political power. The modernization which was initiated and carried out from above by the absolutist regime was characteristically authoritarian and conservative in ethos. It laid the institutional foundations for a modern state structure but ignored the issue of political power, its character and limits, which had been the major objective of the constitutionalist movement three decades earlier. The persistence of a centralized power structure closely controlled by an absolutist sovereign, who increasingly defied all constitutional limits on power, meant that the process of modernization had only a very tenuous relationship with civil society. The authoritarian power underpinning the process of modernization progressively encroached on civil society, rolling back its frontiers almost to its bare limits in the pre-Constitutional era. The vibrant but still malleable core of this fragile civil society was a fledgling modern urban middle class with a secular education and a rational outlook, committed to modernization and progress on European lines. The relationship of the modern middle class to the state was defined in two ways. It provided the absolutist state with a modernizing elite to staff and direct its executive and juridical apparatuses on the one hand, and it bolstered the ranks of a secular opposition to the absolutist sovereign in the political and cultural fields on the other. It was highly differentiated politically and ideologically.

Although the modern middle class lacked a high degree of structural cohesion and social homogeneity, the most significant divisions in their ranks were political, relating to their varying relationships with the absolutist state, and especially with the person of the sovereign. The affinity of the governmental elite with the absolutist state and their uneasy relationship with the person of the sovereign, like the opposition of the middle-class dissenters in society at large to his despotic rule, was political and ideological rather than economic. Although the relationship with the sovereign was the foremost means of access to economic power and privilege, the governmental elite supported absolutism mainly for political and cultural reasons. To be more precise, it shared the absolutist sovereign's vision of a modern, secular and rationally organized social and political order and his apparent dislike of tradition, superstition and obscurantist religious authority, even though his modernism did not extend to a respect for civil and democratic rights and liberties. The fact that the sovereign was decidedly hostile to any notion of individual, civil and democratic rights and liberties, and opposed popular participation and democratic government, did not seem to bother the new political elite, at least not before they fell from grace and lost their power and privilege. The modern identification of progress with centralized secular order was central to their conviction that the loss of individual liberties and democratic rights, and submission to authoritarian rule, was a small price to pay for a modernizing absolutism that was capable of maintaining order and stability and was committed to social and economic progress in a unified country.

This conviction, however, was not shared by the middle-class dissenters outside the governmental processes and institutions, who for the most part remained loyal to the ideals of the Constitutional revolution. Although their numbers were in decline during the late 1930s, when secularist policies and Western educational and cultural measures had become the public face of sovereign power, these dissenters remained committed to the fundamental conviction that absolute power was by definition unconstitutional, and in contravention of the principle of popular sovereignty and the democratic rights and liberties of the Iranian subject-citizens, however loosely these rights and liberties may have been defined in the Constitution. But the voice of opposition and dissent was successfully suppressed or went unheard by the sovereign, who relentlessly forged ahead with the centralization of state power that was now increasingly identified with his personal domain. That the civil and democratic opposition to absolutism remained confined to political and intellectual circles and severely constrained by the juridical and extra-juridical practices of the state was symptomatic of the political and cultural conditions of the existence of the secular middle class under Pahlavi absolutism. An underdeveloped civil society haemorrhaging in the clutches of the absolutist sovereign and a suppressed and muzzled public sphere were in no way equipped to furnish the secular middle-class dissenters with the means to ground, organize and disseminate their opposition to the sovereign. Their opposition remained local and parochial at best.

Given the predominance of the landowning class in the social structure of political power, the noted prominence of the modern middle class in the institutional structure of the state signifies a duality in the form and character of political power under Pahlavi absolutism. This apparent duality in the character and form of political power, if scrutinized theoretically, may go some way to explain the functional autonomy of the state under absolutism, which has been frequently observed but little explained by recent scholars. This theoretical insight into the nature of political power under absolutism we owe to Marx (*Capital*, vol. I, 1965, pt 28). The import of this conceptual distinction for the analysis of political power notwithstanding, it is not sufficient to explain the crucial process of the transformation of power to domination under Pahlavi absolutism – that is to say, the manner in which power is used to secure domination and enforce subordination and subjugation to ensure political order and rule. This issue, as we have seen, is of pivotal importance for the analysis of the relationship between the sovereign power and the Kurds under Pahlavi absolutism, defining the conditions of the transformation of the Kurdish community from a linguistic to an ethnic community which, in effect, was the condition of the possibility of Kurdish identity.

A consideration of this issue raised the question of the Kurds' encounter with sovereign power, power above all powers. Unlike the Qajar state in the first two decades of the twentieth century, the sovereign power in Pahlavi Iran was not only the locus of decision-making, but also had the capacity to enforce its decisions within and outside the constitutional political process, that is, the capacity to make decisions and enforce them either by means of law and through the formal juridical processes or by means of violence deployed by the coercive and security apparatuses of the state. But in Pahlavi Iran absolutist power was seldom bound by law, and the use of violence to enforce decision was seldom sanctioned by the Constitution, which was repeatedly violated or overlooked, if not effectively suspended, by the monarch during his reign. This meant that the use of violence was almost always extra-juridical, sanctioned not by legal norms pertaining to the constitution of the state but by the will of the absolutist ruler, a situation closely resembling Carl Schmitt's concept of the 'state of exception' (Schmitt, 1986). Although in Schmitt's discourse the sovereign decision to suspend the constitution of the state is always prompted by political crisis and disorder threatening the foundations of the state, the situation obtaining under Pahlavi rule was marked by the absence of such a crisis. The effective suspension of the Constitution and persistence of extra-juridical violence in the absence of political crisis only meant the persistence of the state of exception under absolutism.

In the case of Pahlavi absolutism, the juridical presupposition of sovereign decision did not obtain. The absolutist ruler did not need to suspend the constitution in order to use violence to enforce his decisions. He had already effectively abolished it by excluding it from the political process. This had two important consequences for the characterization of the state and the political under Pahlavi absolutism. First, the effective abrogation of the constitution meant that there were no juridical norms to distinguish between the exceptional and normal situations in the polity, and hence no criteria to differentiate juridical from extra-juridical use of violence by the sovereign. Secondly, the effective absence of constitutional legal norms meant that there was no juridical criterion to distinguish between sovereign power and the person of the sovereign; a situation characteristic of martial law and dictatorship. This means the absolutist monarch in Iran was not the embodiment of sovereign power, but he was the sovereign power *par excellence*.

In Pahlavi Iran, nowhere were the defining features of sovereign power played out more vividly and forcefully than in Kurdistan. In Kurdistan, order signified domination. Instances of order were moments of domination grounded in denial and suppression. Order presupposed subjugation of the Kurdish community by the state, and this in effect meant that the subjugation of the Kurdish community was the condition of possibility of domination, and that the mechanisms which secured the subjugation of the Kurds to sovereign power also ensured the transformation of that power into domination. In the language of contemporary theory, the Kurdish community was not only the object but also the subject of sovereign power – the nodal intersection of domination and subordination which underpinned the sovereign order in Kurdistan.

The argument that sovereign order was the effect of sovereign domination places the focus of the investigation on the means and conditions of subjugation of the Kurdish community under Pahlavi rule. The sovereign deployed both juridical and extra-juridical means to secure subjugation, but the outcome was always the same: the denial and suppression of Kurdish community and identity, which in turn was never without Kurdish opposition, resistance and struggle. Thus the axis of domination-order always rested on the possibility of subjugation, and the latter depended on the violence embedded in the binary opposition between denial-suppression and opposition-resistance. The fact that the two poles of this opposition were mutually exclusive meant that they stood in a relationship of antagonism to one another. The antagonism formed the core of a dialectics of denial and resistance driven by violence, a violence born of this antagonism and which in turn perpetuated it when it was articulated in the juridical and extra-juridical means and mechanisms deployed by the sovereign to secure order.

The means and mechanisms deployed to ensure sovereign domination, juridical or extra-juridical, were always embedded in the centralizing functions of the absolutist state and geared to the strategic objective of laying a modern infra-structure for the state. In this sense, therefore, the politics of territorial centralism, relentlessly pursued by the absolutist state throughout the 1930s, grounded sovereign domination in the project of authoritarian modernization, and the subjugation of the Kurdish community to sovereign power became the *sine qua non* of the modern project of 'mastery' displayed in the political field. Although mastery of the political forces in the Kurdish community was part of a wider project of consolidation of power tethered to the 'reasons of the state', the political rationale of this project was dissolved in violence when sovereign power began targeting cultural and linguistic difference in Kurdistan.

In Kurdistan, the early phase of consolidation of state power ended with the integration of tribal landlordism into the structure of the absolutist state, and the political pacification of the countryside. The processes and practices which ensured the redeployment of state power on large landed property targeted the political organization of the landlords' power in the Kurdish countryside. The mastery of the political field did not target cultural and linguistic difference, which had no power of signification in a political and cultural field dominated by lineage and primordial relations. However, the conditions of subjugation of the Kurdish community changed substantially after the consolidation of the landlords' regime. The redeployed state, backed by large landed property, embarked on a project of modernization whose primary objective was to create a modern institutional structure for political power. The advent of a centralized civil and military administration, along with the introduction of apparatuses of population and property registration and fiscal administration, universal male conscription and universal secular education, were aspects of the project of authoritarian modernization which, as we have seen, led to the creation of a modern salaried middle class in Kurdish urban centres. Sectors of this modern class soon became the mainstay of Kurdish nationalism when the strategies and means of domination deployed by sovereign power began targeting Kurdish ethnicity and language.

The development of modern governmental processes and practices signified a shift in the strategic locus and objectives of sovereign power in Kurdistan. The locus of sovereign power shifted to urban centres and the conditions of domination required processes and practices which targeted ethnic, cultural and linguistic difference. The suppression and denial of ethnic, linguistic and cultural difference, sanctioned by sovereign power as law, were in turn the conditions of conduct of sovereign power in Kurdistan. The sovereign stood in the dialectical intersection of this double articulation of domination and subjugation, which in effect meant that the mastery of the political field now required not only the military subjugation of the Kurdish community but also the juridical-political denial of Kurdish ethnicity and language.

The sovereign power which reproduced this double articulation of domination and subordination in the juridico-political and cultural processes and practices of the state was the constitutive of the Kurdish ethnic community. It precipitated and ensured the transformation of the Kurdish community from a cultural-linguistic community to an ethnic community by targeting and suppressing ethnic and linguistic difference. Kurdish ethnicity displaced Kurdish language and Sunni religion as the defining element of communal identity, setting it apart from the Persian and Azeri Shi'i communities. This, however, should not be taken to mean that the Kurdish ethnic community was an invention or fabrication of sovereign power under absolutism, but rather that Kurdish ethnicity did not operate as a political principle (a means of differentiation and self-recognition through the other) in the process of a developing opposition to the suppression and denial of cultural and linguistic difference at the level of the community. The suppression and denial of cultural and linguistic difference now practised by the sovereign as state policy, grounded in law and backed by the juridical discourse of 'national' legitimacy, gave a sense of communal political legitimacy to Kurdish ethnicity and its discursive representations in the growing opposition and resistance to the policy of suppression and denial. This politicization of Kurdish ethnicity and its discursive representations as a principle of legitimacy of the opposition to the sovereign on the communal level was of crucial importance in the formation of Kurdish national identity in Iranian Kurdistan in the following years.

In fact, it was the politicization of Kurdish ethnicity and its representation as a principle of communal political legitimacy in the growing opposition to the sovereign power in the 1930s that laid the ground for the formation of Kurdish national identity in the early 1940s. For it firmly grounded the struggle for Kurdish ethnic and linguistic rights in the intersection of the dialectics of denial and resistance perpetuated by the sovereign violence, a development clearly signified by the discourse of the Komalay JK in the early 1940s. In the discursive representation of the encounter between the Kurds and the sovereign, this politicized ethnicity became the constitutive outside of the sovereign identity, the linchpin of the differences which defined the identity of the sovereign power and its political and cultural significations, ensuring the subjugation of the Kurdish community. The sovereign discourses and practices which were deployed to secure and reproduce sovereign domination at the same time suppressed ethnic and linguistic difference, thus ensuring the otherness of the Kurd. In this sense, therefore, sovereign domination presupposed the otherness of the Kurd in the political and cultural fields.

The political and cultural processes and practices which ensured the politicization of Kurdish ethnicity and language at the same time transformed the boundaries of Kurdish community, redefining it on new foundations. The concept of identity in difference deployed in this study referred to the constitutive role of difference in the construction of sovereign and Kurdish identities. But Persian and Kurdish ethnicities, the constitutive differences of Kurdish and Iranian identities respectively, were positioned in a relationship of denial-recognition, suppression-resistance by political and cultural processes and practices which were deployed by the sovereign power to secure domination in the Kurdish community. The fact that the political and cultural significations of Persian ethnicity and language depended on the subjugation of the Kurdish community to the sovereign power meant that the constitutive outside Kurdish identity and the subjugation of Kurdish ethnicity were both effects of sovereign power. They were both consequences of discourses and practices which ensured the transformation of sovereign power to domination in Kurdistan.

The fact that sovereign power was constitutive of both Kurdish identity and community meant that they shared the same inner core, which shaped their development in the course of an increasingly complex interrelationship with sovereign identity in the years to come. The Kurdish middle class, including the salaried middle strata, was not only the main force of opposition to the sovereign identity but also provided the backbone of the civil society which emerged in Kurdistan after the collapse of Pahlavi absolutism. The flourishing of Kurdish identity and its expression, in terms of both the national rights of the citizens of a distinct national entity called Kurdistan and the civil-democratic rights of the non-sovereign citizens of Iran, were consequences of this double articulation of two different conceptions of Kurdish community in nationalist discourse after September 1941. That is, a conception of Kurdish community as an integral part of a distinct Kurdish national entity termed the greater Kurdistan co-existed with a notion of Kurdish as an ethnic-linguistic community, an integral part of a juridico-political entity in the state of Iran. These two conceptions of Kurdish community presuppose two different notions of rights – national and civic-democratic – and two different processes of realization, articulated differently in the constructions of Kurdish identity in nationalist discourse.

A consideration of this issue raises the pivotal question of the relationship between the constructions of national identity and democratic and civic rights and their political conditions of possibility in the nationalist discourse. The discourse of Komalay JK, it was demonstrated, entailed a conception of national rights grounded in the democratic doctrine of the right of nations to self-determination. It was directly associated with a conception of Kurdish national identity whose conditions of realization, for the most part, were located in the wider Kurdish community in the Greater Kurdistan, outside the territorial reaches of Iranian Kurdistan. Although the political rhetoric of Komala reiterated its commitment to the realization of national rights of self-determination as a matter of nationalist programmatic principle, its political and cultural discourse and practice were, with minor exceptions, fundamentally regional, focusing on issues associated with the consolidation and expansion of its authority in Iranian Kurdistan. They fell far short of providing a concrete foundation for a nationalist programme geared to the realization of Kurdish national rights in the Kurdish community in greater Kurdistan. The growing gap between the nationalist rhetoric and the political and cultural practice of the organization only radicalized its agrarian populism, pushing it towards a more romantic terrain of national rights, mapped out by ethnic and cultural difference in search of nationalist political foundations.

This rhetorical romantic terrain of national rights was also present in the discourse of the KDPI, though it was often operating alongside a discourse of ethnic/regional rights of self-government loosely associated with the representation of non-sovereign identity in the Constitution. The relationship of non-sovereign identity to the concept of citizenship in the 1906 Constitution, as we have seen, was in turn established through the concept of the ethnic and linguistic minority, with a strictly local/regional foundation. But just as in the discourse of the Komalay JK, here too the rhetoric of national rights associated with the democratic doctrine of self-determination was devoid of political foundations to ground it, and the discourse and practice of the KDPI were unable to establish it on concrete political foundations. The rhetoric of national rights remained ungrounded in the discourse of the KDPI, vacillating in the expanding space between romantic nationalism and political populism during the brief existence of the Republic. This rhetorical instability was a clear affirmation of the fundamentally political character of national rights, a stark reminder of their dependence on power, and of the fact that power not only grounds national rights in the nationalist discourse but also animates them, giving them the force of signification and efficacy to produce effects in the political field. Power is the soul of national rights, without which they will remain exterior to themselves, a voice that does not speak, a force which does not signify. This exteriority of the rights to themselves, their abject silence in the political field, highlights the significance of power both as constitutive and as the driving force of national rights in the political field. It also shows that power is the agency connecting rights and identity in the nationalist political field, both ethnic and national.

The discourse of rights associated with the conception of citizenship, through the medium of the concept of the local ethnic and linguistic minority in the Iranian Constitution of 1906, was, on the other hand, fundamentally different, in character and in application. Although the non-sovereign identity had been buried under layers of cultural generalizations associated with sovereign identity, the political and juridical presuppositions of the concept of local ethnic and linguistic minority were clear enough to highlight its basic features, expressed in terms of the constituent elements of the proposed Provincial and District Councils in the Constitution. The concept of local ethnic and linguistic minority in this sense was the negative determination of the political relationship between dominant/Persian ethnicity and language and sovereign power in the Constitution. This relationship, as we have seen, was not only instrumental in transforming Persian identity into Iranian national identity, but at the same time defined the juridical and political conditions of existence of the Iranian subject-citizen in the Constitution. In other words, subject-citizenship rights were mediated through Persian ethnicity, language and history, and Twelver Shi'ism – relations which were the primary non-juridical conditions of access to rights defined in the Constitution. This meant that the Provincial and District Councils, the only means for the expression of non-sovereign ethnic and linguistic rights in the Constitution, were a corollary of the concept of subject-citizen defined in terms of the constituent elements of the dominant/Persian ethnicity, language and history. They were both constituted by sovereign power, complementing one another in the structure of Iranian national identity in the Constitution.

The consideration of the discursive relationship between sovereign power and the dominant/Persian ethnicity and language highlights not only the ethnic identity of the concept of the Iranian subject-citizen but also its institutional relationship to the Provincial and District Councils. It shows that these councils, which were meant to respond to the needs of 'local and provincial ethnic-linguistic minorities' in the country, were in fact a condition of the existence of the concept of citizenship defined in terms of predominance of Persian ethnicity and language. They were not only related, but in fact presupposed each other, politically and legally. In this sense, therefore, the concept of 'ethnic minority' which underpinned the very idea of the Provincial and District Councils in the Constitution was a discursive adjunct of the ethnic concept of Iranian subject-citizen. It was a product of the linkage between the concept of national identity and Persian ethnicity and as such was deployed to respond to and compensate for the striking absence of ethnic, linguistic, cultural and regional difference in the definitions of the concept of the Iranian subject-citizen in the constitution. This absence, it was seen, turned to an outright denial under Pahlavi absolutism when sovereign power used force to restructure and perpetuate the crucial linkage between Iranian sovereignty and Persian ethnicity. The political commitment of sovereign power to the ethnic/Persian concept of Iranian national identity, and its violent suppression and denial of all non-sovereign ethnicities, languages and cultures, however, did not put an end to the use of the concept of ethnic minority in the official and semi-official discourse. The concept continued to be used as a means of exercising sovereign power over the non-sovereign, signifying his expulsion from the domain of rights and his inclusion in the domain of power where violence rather than law reigned. It was a clear signification of the concept of the 'juridical ban' (to paraphrase Jean-Luc Nancy) imposed on the non-sovereign, for it excluded the non-sovereign from the domain of civic and democratic rights of citizenship by including him in the domain of sovereign violence (Nancy, 1991).

It is true that the Kurdish leadership in 1946 showed no awareness of the conditions and consequences of their quest for the implementation of the Constitution. To them the argument for establishing the Provincial and District Council in Kurdistan, which frequently featured in the discourse of the Republic in the second half of 1946, was but a step in the direction of the restoration of the civil and democratic rights of ethnic and linguistic minorities. The adverse juridical-political effects of the concept of ethnic minority on the representation of Kurdish identity and its exclusion from the constitutional political field were not known to them. Nor were they at all aware of the political effects of the discursive relationship between sovereign power and Persian ethnicity, and hence the Persian-ethnic definition of the sovereign identity, on the democratic claims of the 1906 Constitution. Such issues were, to put it simply, beyond their political and cultural vision at the time. To the Kurdish leadership, democracy was a sacred political ideal to be revered, and the shortcomings of the Constitution, especially those regarding the status of the non-sovereign subject-citizens, could not be attributed to the theoretical and philosophical construction of this political ideal.

But the Kurdish leaders were by no means alone in their reverence for this narrow and, theoretically speaking, essentialist conception of democracy and popular rule. Nor was the KDPI the only political organization in the democratic opposition entertaining an optimistic quest for the restoration and implementation of the Constitution. On the contrary, this narrow essentialist conception of democracy was widely shared by the Iranian opposition throughout the Pahlavi rule and beyond. They were (and still are) never short of admiration for the 1906 Constitution as a genuinely democratic document, demanding its implementation in the turbulent years following the collapse of Reza Shah's absolutism right up to the Iranian Revolution of 1979. Three decades of theocratic repression and the destruction of civic and democratic liberties under the auspices of the *welayat-e faqih* have failed to awaken the Iranian opposition to the harmful deficiencies of this essentialist conception of democracy and the associated forms of pluralism and citizenship. Ignorant of its consequences, they are still pining for a democratic rule constitutionally grounded in the constitutional linkage between Persian ethnicity, language and culture. The Iranian democratic opposition of all shapes and hues is still fundamentally averse to the appreciation of difference in the political and cultural process.

In fact it is no exaggeration to say that throughout the 53 years of Pahlavi rule, the democratic demand for constitutional government and political pluralism never included a call to recognize and respect non-sovereign difference, identities and rights, barring odd statements of respect for religious difference which, given the constitutional status of Twelver Shi'ism as the official religion of the country, amounted to no more than a scanty concession to the Sunni Muslim or non-Muslim communities. Nor did they note, let alone criticize or reject, the ethnic constructions of the sovereign identity and subject-citizenship in the Constitution in their call for the restoration of the Constitution. The political and juridical consequences of the discursive primacy of Persian ethnicity and language in its effect on the definition of Iranian/national sovereignty in the Constitution was (and still is) totally lost on the protagonists of democratic rule in the ranks of Iranian opposition of all political and ideological persuasions, ranging from centre right to socialist left. The democratic forces in the political field in 1946 shared this unreserved reverence for and uncritical commitment to the 1906 Constitution, most demanding its implementation and placing it in their party political programme if not the political agenda. For example, the Tudeh Party's Soviet-Marxist critique of the social class nature of democracy, the formal character of democratic rule and its intrinsic relationship with capitalist exploitation and bourgeois domination, frequently voiced in the discourse of the party organ *Mardom* throughout the five decades of Pahlavi rule, never extended to the Constitution, its anomalies and inconsistencies. The Tudeh Party remained committed to the spirit and letter of the 1906 Constitution throughout its political existence before the Iranian Revolution in 1979.

The Kurdish leadership in 1946, it seems, was sincerely hoping for support for its demand for the implementation of the Constitution from the left and centre-left forces in the political field in Iran. They could see no plausible reason for the refusal of the government and opposition to support the implementation of minority rights entailed in the constitutional provision for the Provincial and District Councils. Little wonder, therefore, that the Kurdish leadership was surprised and dismayed when they saw that their demand for the implementation of minority rights already enshrined in the Constitution was rejected by the government. The public expression of this dismay was compounded by a sense of private despair and even grief when in the aftermath of the failure of autonomy negotiations in Tehran they witnessed the brutal misrepresentation of their positions and the vulgarization of their democratic quest for the recognition of their constitutional rights in the press run by or identified with the opposition forces.

The misrepresentation of the Kurdish question was by no means new or unprecedented; it had a history going back to Shaikh Ubaidollah's movement in 1880–2 and Semko's rebellion in the early decades of the twentieth century. In the final phase of the existence of the Kurdish Republic, however, when the Kurdish struggle for the realization of their constitutional rights had a direct bearing on the claims of the Iranian regime to democracy, and more importantly on the democratic credentials of the Persian opposition to the central government, the misrepresentation of the Kurdish struggle and its strategic objectives presupposed different historical and discursive conditions. The discursive forms used to misrepresent the Kurdish question, and especially the Republic and its origins and objectives, signified the predominance of a different conception of political rationality in the political field; a new conception of the reasons of the state and state security reverberating in the discourse of the regime and the democratic opposition alike. The matrix of rationality underpinning the new forms of conduct of sovereign power continued to define the misrepresentation of the non-sovereign other and their history, politics and culture well into the post-Cold War era, albeit in different forms.

In the past, Kurdish rebellions were often provoked by the government's drive for centralization and the imposition of direct rule and control over Kurdish territory, the recognized domains of declining Kurdish principalities or tribal lands held by powerful Kurdish chieftains. The aim of these rebellions was to safeguard the administrative and fiscal autonomy of the Kurdish principalities, and later, in the early twentieth century, to protect tribal territory, land and its revenue, on which the power and privilege of the tribal leadership depended, within a decentralized pre-capitalist state structure. The traditional Kurdish opposition to the state in the pre-Republican period seldom, if ever, invoked the authority of the Kurdish people and their identity and rights to claim legitimacy in a struggle which remained essentially regional in ethos. The rationality of the Kurdish movements in the pre-Second World War period was grounded in tribal lineage and large land ownership, whose centripetal tendencies targeted a state which lacked political and military unity. The absence of a modern sovereign power in the centre on the one hand, and the lack of a uniform ethnic identity in the Kurdish community on the other, meant above all that Kurdish rebellions, however strong, were only specific forms of bargaining for regional/local autonomy and influence. They did not target the political unity of the sovereign power, nor did they question or threaten its identity.

Twenty-five years of territorial centralism and authoritarian modernization under Pahlavi rule changed the structure and working of power in Iran. The constitution of a modern state deriving its unity from the sovereign will expressed in the juridical unity of the state meant that the working of power required new forms of rationality and mechanisms of domination and rule. Political calculation and decision-making were more often than not guided by the reasons of the state, compounded by an exaggerated view of national security and balance of power, grounded in the strategic and ideological requirements of the Cold War. The important point in this respect was the presence in the official discourse of the new national sovereign, the real or assumed aims and intentions of which constituted the matrix of rationality underlying the reasons of the state in the national political field. This meant that in the juridico-political framework of the nation state all conceptions of reasons of the state were identical with notions of national interest. This identity was an effect of the redefinition of the reasons of the state with reference to the concept of national sovereignty and the underlying official nationalist discourse.

This identification of the reasons of the state and national interest in the juridico-political framework of the nation state had far-reaching consequences for the misrepresentation of the Kurdish question in post-war Iran. For the persistence of the ethnic definition of the identity of sovereign power, variously noted in this study, meant that the modern state in Iran entailed a conception of national interest which was ethnically defined, and that the associated conception of the reasons of the state presupposed forms of rationality and rational political calculation and decision-making which by definition excluded identities at odds with dominant ethnic-Persian identity. This ethnic definition of national interest and reasons of state not only helped to misrepresent the Kurdish question as a foreign-inspired and foreign-led conspiracy against the sovereignty and integrity of the nation state, but also at the same provided for a discursive alliance between the central government and the democratic opposition against the Republican Kurdish aims and aspirations in the course of negotiations and after. The crucial linkage uniting the two was their commitment to ethnic Persian nationalism. They both shared an ethnic conception of nationalism already grounded in the Constitution, the privileged document of democratic struggle in modern Iranian history. Democracy in constitutional Iran, as in all multi-national and multi-ethnic societies, was a victim of its own commitment to ethnicity and ethnic identity. The conception of popular sovereignty, the bedrock of all modern theories of democracy and democratic rule, did not fare well when it was measured against the reasons of the state and the requirements of national security. The democratic doctrine of popular sovereignty and its juridical-political representation proved to be no more than an empty gesture, a statement of an ethical commitment to the people as the highest authority and source of legitimacy, but lacking foundation and force in the political field. The ethnic foundations of political rationality in the nation state robbed essentialist conceptions of democratic pluralism of its political efficacy, turning it into a monument to the unfulfilled aspirations of failed political regimes.

What were the lessons of the Republic, for the Kurds and for democratic politics in Iran in general? The collapse of the Kurdish Republic and the military conquest of the territory were followed by the reimposition of sovereign power and sovereign identity. State power not only reinstated the authority of the sovereign but also reimposed his identity on the vanquished. Kurdish identity, language and culture were suppressed with unprecedented force and vehemence. But the fact that the reimposition of sovereign power and identity in Kurdistan presupposed the violent suppression of Kurdish identity and language, along with the specific technologies of power deployed to achieve this double objective (especially in the field of security and surveillance and management of population), was symptomatic of the transformation of Iranian society and polity since the Constitutional revolution. It showed above all that the Iranian state, despite being gripped by periodic crises of authority, had gone some way in the process of becoming a modern apparatus of domination and rule. It also showed that the Kurdish question in Iran was no longer an expression of discontent by a minority on the cultural periphery of Iranian politics, but was rather its silent centre, constantly pulsating, questioning the political unity and ethnic identity of the sovereign power. It also showed that it is the political formation of suppressed difference which traverses every avenue in the increasingly complex labyrinth of power in modern Iran, from its formation in the early twentieth century to the present.

In fact, the formation and persistence of the Kurdish question in Iran since the collapse of the Republic is a resounding critique of the prevailing essentialist theories of democracy variously conceived and presented by the Iranian intelligentsia, secular and Islamist, as alternatives to the current theocratic-military dictatorship. For the persistence of the non-sovereign difference undermines all democratic claims to pluralism which in one way or another presuppose identity as presence, which do not recognize or respect difference at the core of non-sovereign identities. It shows that difference is the condition of possibility of genuine pluralism, defining its range of efficacy as well as its limits in the democratic political process. The democratic recognition of difference and the civic and democratic rights thereof are essential if democracy is to overcome the fundamental political, juridical and cultural problems arising from the ethnic definition of sovereign power and identity in a multi-national and multi-cultural society such as Iran. Republican democracy modelled on essentialist theories of democracy *à la* France is simply no answer to the political, juridical and cultural problems sustaining and reproducing the Kurdish question in Iran. The Kurdish question will persist as long as the theoretical and juridico-political relationship that firmly ties sovereign identity to the dominant ethnicity and culture is not broken. Breaking this link, ending this ominous relationship alone can show the way to a democratic solution to the Kurdish question in Iran.

To the Kurds, on the other hand, the collapse of the Republic offers more than just a historical lesson. For them it is not only an event that has taken place in the past, but also one that is living in the present, animating not only memories but also the discourses and practices that shape the present. Through this event they think about their past, encounter their present and imagine their future. The Republic is a sign under which they live their lives as resistance and struggle. And this struggle and resistance is the common thread that goes through their lives, giving unity to their community and coherence to their history. The persistence of their struggle is the expression of their unfulfilled desire for freedom. The narrative of the struggle as unfulfilled desire for freedom asserts the necessity of power to freedom. It indicates that power is the stuff of freedom, that freedom can only be achieved by historical practices infused with power. It is only the present condition of the Kurds, the denial and suppression of their identity, that gives meaning to their quest for freedom. For freedom arises out of this oppositional relationship, and is as such always infused with power. Freedom does not arise in the absence of power. The Kurds should not allow the truth of this lesson to pass them by again. They must empower themselves if they want to be heard in a democratic Iran.

NOTES

Chapter 1

1   This view seems to have been first expressed by Basil Nikitine, a keen observer of developments in Iranian Kurdistan; see his influential *Les Kurdes* (Paris, 1956). It was later restated by Wadie Jwaideh with some authority in his unpublished but influential doctoral dissertation, 'The Kurdish Nationalist Movement: Its Origins and Development' (Syracuse University, 1960), which was published posthumously under the same title by Syracuse University in 2006. Jwaideh has been the main source for subsequent statements of the position. See, for example, Robert Olson, *The Emergence of Kurdish Nationalism 1880–1925* (Austin: University of Texas Press, 1989). Among Kurdish scholars the origin of the nationalist movement in Iran is also frequently attributed to Shaikh Ubaidollah's movement. See, for example, Abdul Rahman Ghassemlou, *Kurdistan and the Kurds* (Prague: Czechoslovak Academy of Science, 1965); Kamal Mazhar Ahmad, *Kurdistan le Salekani Shari Yekami Jihani da* (Stockholm, 1990).

2   The concept 'discursive formation' here is used in the Foucauldian sense; it refers to specific discourses and their non-discursive conditions of possibility, that is, the institutions, processes and practice which support and sustain them. In the context of the Kurdish Republic it refers to the emergence of national-democratic discourse and the set of popular-democratic institutions, processes and practices which were created to support it and enhance its

development. See various works of Foucault, esp. 'Orders of Discourse', in *Social Science Information*, vol. 10, no. 2, 1977; *The Order of Things* (London, 1974); *The Archaeology of Knowledge* (London, 1972).

3   For an earlier English translation of the text of the 1906 Constitution see E. Browne, *The Persian Revolution of 1905–09* (Cambridge, 1910). On the Constitution of 1906 and the Supplementary Constitutional Law of 1907 see the following: L. Lockhart, 'The Constitutional Laws of Persia: An Outline of Their Origins and Development', *Middle East Journal*, vol. 8, no. 4 (1959); S. Amirarjomand, 'The Constitutional Law', in Ehsan Yarshater, *Encyclopaedia Iranica*, vol. 6 (Costa Mesa, 1993); M. Bayat, *Iran's First Constitutional Revolution: Shi'ism and the Constitutional Revolution of 1905–09* (London, 1991); M. Adl, *Huquq-e Asasi ya Osul-e Mashrutiyyat* (Tehran, 1327/1948).

4   The 1906 Constitution and its Supplementary Constitutional Law, however, recognized regional and local diversity in the country and attempted to respond to it. But the *Anjomanha-yeh Welayati ve Iyalati* (Provincial and District Councils, also translated as Provincial and District Associations, Provincial and Local Associations), which were introduced to meet this need, were in fact administrative units which derived their authority from the centre. The downward flow of authority from the political centre to provincial and local administration militated against the very notion of regional territorial autonomy on which this perceived solution to cultural, ethnic and linguistic diversity depended. These associations presupposed a decentralized political administration without which they could not function or survive. This was borne out by the course of Iranian history during 1906–79. The Provincial and District Councils were constitutional devices, much admired and often invoked by regional opposition to the state under various governments, but never implemented to fulfil their intended objectives. Successive governments refused to implement them, fearing loss of authority and control. They had fallen victim to the centralizing drive of the authoritarian modernization which followed the demise of the Constitutional movement and its fundamental achievement, the Constitutional state, after 1912. See Browne, op. cit.; E. Abrahamian, *Iran Between Two Revolutions* (Princeton,

1982); N. Keddie, *Roots of Revolution* (Yale, 1981). For a discussion of this issue in the regional context of the Autonomist movement in Azerbaijan see the interesting work of Touraj Atabaki, *Azerbaijan: Ethnicity and the Struggle for Power in Iran* (London, 2000). As will be seen, the Anjomans were also important in the later phase of protracted regional autonomy negotiations between the leadership of the Kurdish Republic and the central government in 1946, discussed in the final chapter of this study.

5   It is widely believed that Shaikh Ubaidollah was the first fully-fledged Kurdish nationalist, espousing the idea of a united Kurdish nation inhabiting a united and independent Kurdistan. This view is generally supported by reference to the Shaikh's much-quoted letter in July 1880 to Clayton, the British vice-consul in Baskale, in which he refers to 'the Kurdish *nation* as a people apart', and declares, 'We want our affairs to be in our hands' (my italics; see Olson, op. cit., p. 2). The British vice-consul was inclined to believe that the Shaikh had 'a comprehensive plan for uniting all the Kurds in an independent state under himself' (Clayton to Trotter, Van, 27 October 1880; Turkey, no. 5, 1891, p. 33; quoted in Jwaideh, op. cit., p. 225. See also G. Curzon, *Persia and the Persian Question*, London, 1892.) Whether or not Shaikh Ubaidollah can be seen as the pioneer of modern Kurdish nationalism depends largely on one's conceptions of nation, national identity and nationalism. On different conceptions of the Kurdish nation and nationalism see my essay, 'Genealogies of the Kurds: Nations and National Identity in Kurdish Historical Writing', in A. Vali (ed.): *Essays on the Origins of Kurdish Nationalism* (Costa Mesa: Mazda Publications, 2003).

6   Amir Hassanpour's *Language and Nationalism in Kurdistan* (San Francisco: Mellen Research University Press, 1992), the best-documented and most comprehensive work on the emergence and development of literary and political discourse in Kurdistan, affirms this point.

7   Nationalist historical discourse claims significant Kurdish participation in nationalist and democratic politics of the time, though opinions on the primary causes of such participation vary widely. Abdul Jabbar Muhammad Jabbari argues that the populations of major urban centres in Kurdistan were actively involved in the Constitutional movement and formed revolutionary

associations in Saujbulaq (Mahabad, since 1935), Saqqiz and Senna during 1905–11. He further maintains that Ja'afar Agha i Shikak, Semko's older brother, campaigned for Kurdish autonomy in the framework of a constitutional state in Iran; see his *Mejuy Roznamaguri Kurdi* (Kirkuk, 1970), p. 136. However, he provides no evidence to substantiate these claims. Ghassemlou also registers widespread Kurdish involvement in revolutionary politics during the Constitutional period, citing the formation of the *Anjumans* (revolutionary associations) in major urban centres such as Saujbulaq, Senna, Saqqiz and Kirmanshah as well as Ja'afar Agha's autonomist rebellion around Urmiya. Ghassemlou's account is more detailed than Jabbari's. He states that the Saujbulaq *Anjuman* was led by Ghazi Fattah, grand-uncle of Ghazi Muhammad, the president of the Kurdish Republic, who was subsequently murdered by the Tsarist army occupying the city in 1915; and that the Kirmanshah revolutionaries formed as many as ten *Anjumans* in the town. Despite this detail, Ghassemlou fails to provide any evidence to support his argument (Ghassemlou, op. cit. p. 44). Jwaideh supports Ghassemlou's point about Ghazi Fattah's participation in the Constitutional movement and subsequent death at the hands of the Tsarist army in Saujbulaq (op. cit., pp. 757–8); but neither of the two sources he cites in confirmation refer to documentary evidence on this particular point (B. Nikitine, *Les Kurdes*, Paris, 1956, p. 36; and a Persian text by N. Pesyan, *Marg Bud va Bazaghasht ham Bud*, Tehran, 1947, p. 152).

8   The active participation of the Kurdish tribal chieftains in counter-revolutionary politics is documented extensively in the histories of the Constitutional period. See, for example, A. Kasravi, *Tarikh-e Mashruteh-ye Iran* (Tehran: Amir Kabir, 1961), and M. Malekzadeh, *Tarikh-e Enqilab-e Mashrutiyat-e Iran* (Tehran: Amir Kabir, 1949), 5 vols. It is most recently documented by David McDowall in his *A Modern History of Kurds* (London: I.B.Tauris, 1994).

9   Although some major Kurdish families, such as Ardalan, Debokri and Fayzollabogi, did indeed derive their authority in part from well-established links with centres of political power in Tabriz, Isfahan and Tehran, their prominence in the regional power structure which nurtured and sustained such links in the first place was a direct consequence of their position within the principality or tribal

confederacy. Kurdish principalities were essentially confederate political structures underpinned by tribal military power, while the tribal confederacies were mainly based on lineage. The commentary by Walter Smart, British Consul in Tabriz in 1910, is an invaluable source on the political and financial administration of Kurdistan in the Constitutional period, especially on the relationship between the central government and the Kurdish landowning class and tribal chiefs. See F.O. 371/953, Smart to Barclay (Tabriz, 3 January 1910); Barclay to Gray (Tehran, 23 January 1910, encl. no. 1. See also G. Curzon, op. cit. vol. 2, pp. 470–2, p. 492. Curzon too refers to the loose ties between the central government in Tehran and the Kurdish province. He also maintains that the Kurdish tribes held land in return for the provision of military service, and that the central government had in the past actively encouraged tribalism against the Kurdish principalities. Both sources are cited in McDowall, op. cit.

10 On this point see Hassanpour, op. cit. Hassanpour's detailed study of literary and cultural developments in different parts of Kurdistan provides a good basis for comparative studies of cultural and intellectual developments since 1918 in Kurdish territory in Iraq, Iran and Turkey.

11 The complex relationship between tribal lineage and the organizational structure of political authority is discussed by Friedrich Barth and Martin van Bruinessen in some detail; see F. Barth, *Principles of Social Organisation in Southern Kurdistan* (Oslo, 1953); M. van Bruinessen, *Agha, Shaikh and State: The Social and Political Structures of Kurdistan* (London: Zed Press, 1992). C.J. Rich's book, *Narrative of a Residence in Koordistan* (London, 1836), 2 vols, is an invaluable source for the earlier part of the nineteenth century, especially on the relationship between the tribes and the Kurdish principalities and their administrative and political organization.

12 For this issue see A.K.S. Lambton, *Landlord and Peasant in Iran* (London: Oxford University Press, 1953), and my work *Pre-Capitalist Iran: A Theoretical History* (London: I.B.Tauris, 1993), esp. chap. 7.

13 Although the exact ratio of the tribal to non-tribal population in Kurdistan during this period is not known to us, the existing evidence

suggests that a sizeable proportion of the Kurdish population was non-tribal (Barth, op. cit., van Bruinessen, op. cit.). However, this study focuses primarily on the tribal population. This is because, as noted already, the tribal organization formed the most cohesive and effective structure for political authority. The tribal leaders easily extended their power and influence to non-tribal population in towns and in the countryside. The socio-economic structures of the non-tribal community generally lacked a matching political organization. The vague and often disputed status of some princely families such as the Ardalans does not undermine the prominence of the tribes in the organization of political authority in Kurdistan. See note 9 above.

14 The forced destruction of the Kurdish principalities was under way before the Safavid rise to power, and gained momentum after the battle of Chaldiran in 1514. See J.E. Woods, *Aqqoyunlu: Clan, Confederation, Empire: A Study in 15th/9th Century Turko-Iranian Politics* (Minneapolis/Chicago: Biblioteca Islamica), 1976; A. Allouche, *The Origins and Development of the Ottoman-Safavid Conflict (906–962/1500–1555)* (Berlin: Klaus Schwarz Werlag, 1983). For the relationship between the Safavid state and the Kurds see the important (though rather scattered) commentary in Eskandar Beg Monshi, *History of Shah Abbas the Great*, trans. R.M. Savory (Boulder: West View Press, 1978), 2 vols. Informed sources on the political structure and institutional organization of the principalities in Iranian Kurdistan are scarce. Of the available sources, however, the following contain detailed historical commentary: Mah Sharaf Khanom Ghaderi (Mastooreh Kurdistani), *Tarikh-e Ardalan* (Tehran, 1343 [1964/5]); Shaikh Muhammad Mardukh, *Tarikh-e Kurdistan* (Tehran: Elmi, 1346 [1967/8]); Mirza Shokrollah Sanandaji, *Tohfeh-e Naseri: dar Tarikh va Goghrafiayeh Kurdistan*, ed. H. Tabibi (Tehran: Amir Kabir, 1366 [1987/88]). These sources, especially Ghaderi and Sanandaji, are concerned with the Ardalan principality, and its rise, development and demise under Qajar rule. Sanandaji's work is particularly interesting in this respect, since he attributes the demise of the principality in the last phase of Nasir al-Din Shah's reign not so much to adverse pressure from the centre as to the increasing internal political and administrative decay in the principality

itself. For general commentary on the political and administrative structure of Kurdish principalities see van Bruinessen, op. cit., and Rich, op. cit.

15 For a detailed theoretical account of the structure of political authority and the relationship between the tribal confederacy and the state in Iran see Vali, 1993, chap. 5, esp. pp. 155–61; van Bruinessen, op. cit., chaps 2 and 3; and R. Tapper (ed.), *The Conflict of Tribe and the State in Iran and Afghanistan* (London: Croom Helm, 1983), esp. van Bruinessen's article in this collection, 'Kurdish Tribes and the State of Iran: The Case of Simko's Revolt'.

16 See sources cited in note 8 above.

17 The concept of passive revolution is used by Gramsci to explain the historical specificity of the 'bourgeois revolution' in Italy, by highlighting its dissimilarities to the French Revolution, the classical bourgeois revolution in Marxist discourse. Gramsci's definition focuses on the conditions of the revolutionary seizure of power by the bourgeoisie and the subsequent processes and practices deployed by the bourgeois forces in the political field to transform class domination into expansive hegemonic rule in society. He views the Risorgimento (the movement for national liberation culminating in the unification of Italy in 1860–1) as a missed historical opportunity to make a genuine bourgeois revolution of the kind exemplified by the Jacobins in the French revolution, which would have laid the foundations for popular democracy in Italy. This missed opportunity had dire consequences for Italian political culture, culminating in the rise of fascism to power in 1922. The key point here is the form and outcome of the victory of the bourgeoisie. Gramsci's concept of passive revolution signifies an aborted revolution, or a revolution which is conservative and restorative in its aims and objectives. In other words, it refers to a revolutionary process in which the nascent bourgeois group comes to power without rupturing the social fabric, but rather adapting to and gradually modifying it. In general terms, the parallels with the Iranian constitutional revolution are hard to miss, though not so much in form as in outcome: an urban popular movement which seized power but after failing to establish its hegemony relinquished its democratic objectives, opting to share power with

the landowning class in a new power bloc which underpinned Pahlavi absolutism. On this see relevant sections of *Selections from the Prison Notebooks* (London, 1971), and for an intelligent reading of Gramsci's writings see C. Buci-Glucksmann, *Gramsci and the State* (London, 1980).

18 The destructive effects of the First World War on Kurdistan are discussed in detail in Ahmad, op. cit. See also the relevant sections in Jwaideh, op. cit.

19 For example, both Kasravi, an Iranian opponent of Kurdish nationalism, and Ghassemlou, a proponent, characterize Semko as a Kurdish nationalist, and credit him with the idea of creating an independent Kurdish state. For Kasravi, however, modern nationalism, Kurdish or otherwise, is a term of abuse signifying a long-standing European conspiracy to destroy the Orient; to call Semko a nationalist is thus in line with his otherwise negative assessment of the movement as tribal, brigandist and destructive. Ghassemlou, conversely, in a typically nationalist vein, overlooks the tribal and destructive character of the movement, and makes no attempt to evaluate its strategic objectives and achievements. See A. Kasravi, *Tarikh-e Hijdah Saleh-ye Azerbaijan*, 2 vols (Tehran: Amir Kabir, 1967), vol. 2, pp. 830–1; A.R. Ghassemlou, 1965, pp. 72–3. For a detailed historical account of Semko and his movement written from a nationalist point of view see M.R. Hawar, *Semko: Ismail Aghay Shokak u Bzutnaway Netewayati Kurd* (London, 1997). For a balanced and dispassionate account of Semko's movement see Martin van Bruinessen's article, 'Kurdish Tribes', in Richard Tapper (ed.), 1983.

20 Author's conversation in the early 1970s in Tabriz with Mulla Ahmad Ghizilji (Turjanizadeh), editor of *Roj i Kurd* during 1919–26 in Urmiya, and subsequently professor of the Faculty of Letters in the University of Tabriz, until his death in the early 1980s. For further information about this newspaper see Hassanpour, op. cit., Jabbari, op. cit., J. Khaznadar, *Rabari Rojnamagari Kurdi* (1973), and Hawar, 1997.

21 For the rise to power of the traditional and conservative forces and their subsequent representation in and control of the state apparatuses, see E. Abrahamian, *Iran Between Two Revolutions* (Princeton, 1982); H. Katouzian, *The Political Economy of Modern*

Iran (London: Macmillan, 1981); N. Keddie, *Roots of Revolution* (1981). For a comprehensive study of the changing social composition of the Iranian Majlis see Z. Shaji'i, *Nemayandegan-e Majlis-e Showra-ye Melli dar Bist-u-yek Dawreh-yei Qanunguzari* (Tehran: Tehran University Press, 1965).

22 On this issue see Vali, 1993, chap. 7 and Conclusion.

23 Extracts from Foroughi's confidential correspondence are published in *Yaghma*, vol. 3, no. 7 (1329/1950), and vol. 2, no. 8 (1337/1958); both are cited with commentary in Hassanpour, op. cit.

24 For the text of this decree and its implementation in Kurdistan, see Hassanpour, op. cit.

25 For a range of views on the formation, development and demise of the Komalay JK, and its social structure, ideological stance and political strategy, see the following: H. Arfa, *The Kurds: An Historical and Political Study* (London: Oxford University Press, 1966); W. Eagleton, *The Kurdish Republic of 1946* (London: Oxford University Press, 1963); A. Roosevelt, 'The Kurdish Republic of Mahabad', *Middle East Journal*, vol. 1, no. 3 (July 1947); N.M. Emin, *Hokoumati Kurdistan* (Utrecht: KIB, 1993); J. Nebez, *Gowari Nishtiman: Zimani Hali Komali J. K.* (Stockholm: Azad Verlag, 1985); S.M. Samadi, *Negahi Deegar be Komala i J. K.* (Mahabad, 1984); A. Shamzini, *Julaneway Rezgari Nishtimani Kurdistan* (Sentry Lekolinaway Stratejie Kurdistan, Sulaimani, 1998), pp. 230–40. For more recent studies of the conditions of the formation and the development of the Komalay JK see H. Gohary, *Komala-I Jiyanawey Kurdistan* (Stockholm, 1999); Ali' Karimi, *Jiyan u Beserhati Abdulrahmani Zabihi 'Mamosta Ulema'* [Abdulrahman Zabihi: His Life and Fortunes] (Goteborg: Zagros Media, 1999), esp. pp. 62–142.

26 From July 1943 to May 1944 nine issues of *Nishtiman* were published. Six issues are reprinted in Nebez, op. cit. Nebez should be commended for making this invaluable resource available to researchers of modern Kurdish history and politics. I am grateful to Hassan Ghazi for making issues 7–9, published together, available to me.

27 For the Komala's response to such charges, see *Nishtiman* nos. 5 and 6. These charges seem to have been precipitated by the publication of articles in praise of the October Revolution and

of Lenin. The constitution of the Komala envisaged Islam as the official religion of the future independent Kurdish state (Clause 7, printed in *Nishtiman*, no. 6). It also argued for the necessity of secular legislation conforming to the principles of Islam.

28 Nebez in his introduction to *Nishtiman* rightly refers to this point, indicating that the Komala was not a Marxist-Leninist organization and did not have a hidden communist agenda behind its popular-democratic programme for the creation of a free and independent Kurdish state. However, he fails to identify the Komala's populist social programme or to explore its relationship with the organization's nationalist ideology. The constant encounter between populism and nationalism and their articulation in the Komala's political and ideological discourse proved essential for the construction of a modern Kurdish national identity in the Kurdish territory in Iran.

29 See *Nishtiman*, no. 1, in Nebez, op. cit. The homeland envisaged by the Komala is Greater Kurdistan; for the Kurdish question, it argues in an article entitled 'Taran-Angara' (Tehran-Ankara), *Nishtiman*, nos. 3–4, pp. 30–3, had ceased to be a local question since 1919, when General Sharif Pasha submitted his well-known proposals to the peace conference at Versailles. Subsequently, the Kurdish question had become an international question which could no longer be ignored.

30 *Nishtiman*, no. 1, in Nebez, op. cit.

31 Nebez notes this fundamental shift of emphasis in the Komala's proposed strategy, but he fails to see its social and political significance. For Nebez, the rejection of the armed struggle in favour of the civil-democratic road to independence is a break with the tradition of the classical Kurdish leadership, signifying the influence of foreign ideologies emanating from the Soviet Union and from Great Britain, whose support the Komala was striving to secure (op. cit., pp. 34–5).

Chapter 2

1 There is disagreement among scholars as to the precise date of the formation of the KDPI. Jamal Nebez, for example, disputes the date

given here, although it is sanctioned by official party publications; he states, citing Zabihi, that the KDPI was in fact established on 15 November 1945 (Nebez, 1985, p. 67). William Eagleton also states that the transformation of the Komalay JK to the KDPI was officially declared by Ghazi in November 1945 in Mahabad (Eagleton, op. cit., p. 57). In an article published in *Gzing*, a Kurdish-language journal published in Stockholm, I had erred about the date of the establishment of the KDPI and the dissolution of the Komalay JK, giving a third date different from both those stated above (*Gzing*, no. 13, 1997, pp. 31–8). Ali Karimi, a member of the editorial board of this journal, at the time rightly questioned my account; referring to a statement published in the first issue of *Kurdistan* (December 1945), he stated that the date in question was indeed mid-November (*Gzing*, no. 14, 1997, pp. 23–9). Accepting Zabihi's authority, I decided to rethink my earlier position, and in a paper presented to a conference celebrating the 60th anniversary of the Kurdistan Republic held in February 2005 in Erbil, I too opted for the later date. But I was corrected by a long-time member of the KDPI in the audience, who produced what seemed to be irrefutable evidence in the shape of a publicity sheet, printed in Mahabad around mid-August, announcing the official inauguration of the KDPI by Ghazi Muhammad on 15 August 1945. The evidence thus seems to indicate that the official version is accurate and that the KDPI was indeed founded in mid-August in Mahabad. The date suggested by Zabihi, Nebez and Eagleton may well refer to the official dissolution of the Komalay JK, in which case the formation of the KDPI may have preceded the official dissolution of the Komala by three months. It is also possible that there was a gap of three months between the founding of the KDPI in mid-August and its official inauguration in mid-November. I am grateful to this friend, who wished to remain anonymous, for correcting my error.

2   In fact the reference should correctly be not to the Atlantic Treaty but to the Atlantic Charter, the basic principles of which were discussed at the Yalta Conference of 4–11 February 1945 by the allied leaders Roosevelt, Stalin and Churchill. This conference subsequently called for the meeting of the United Nations in San Francisco on 25 April 1945 to discuss and prepare the Charter for an organization thus called The United Nations.

3   Cited in Mahmoud Mulla Izzat, 1984, pp. 74–7.

4   This view is espoused primarily by the KDPI, and enunciated in its official discourse and semi-official discourse as well as bi-partisan nationalist writing, within and outside Iran, since the advent of the party (A.R. Ghassemlou, *Chil Sal Khabat la Penawi Azadi: Kurtayek la Mejuy Hizbi Democrati Kurdustani Iran*, vol. I, 1988; Ghani Blorian's memoirs, *Alekok*, Stockholm, 1997; Hamed Gohary, *Komala-i Jiyanawey Kurdistan*, Stockholm, 1999). The official and semi-official publications of the KDP Iraq follow suit, treating the replacement of the Komalay JK by the KDPI as a natural event in the historical process of the development of Kurdish nationalism in Iran. More will be said about this eventful transformation and its discursive and non-discursive consequences in the final chapter of this study.

5   See, for example, Amir Hassanpour's argument: 'The successor to the K. JK, the Democratic Party of Kurdistan (of Iran), was able to establish the Kurdish Republic under the favourable conditions of the post-Second World War years. However the leaders of the Republic not only toned down the anti-feudal campaign, but also tried to win the support of the traditional chiefs by putting them in positions of power. This was bound to be a temporary compromise. Many of the traditional chiefs acted against the Republic both prior to and during the central government's offensive in order to overthrow the autonomist state.' (Hassanpour, 1992, p. 59). He reiterates this argument variously in his subsequent writings related to this subject (see, for example, his 'Introduction' to Ali Karimi's book on Zabihi).

6   The affirmation of the revolutionary character of the Komalay JK and its subsequent deformation by Ghazi Muhammad and his Soviet backers is central to the KSZKI's (*Komalay Shorishgeri Zahmatkeshani Kurdistani Iran* 'The Revolutionary Society of the Toilers of Iranian Kurdistan') attempts to define its own revolutionary identity, an identity which presupposes a negation of the KDPI, its history and politics, and its claim to represent the Kurdish masses in Iranian Kurdistan. The leadership of the KSZKI often presents a trajectory of the revolutionary tradition in Iranian Kurdistan which begins with the Komalay JK and ends with KSZKI. It is interesting to note that the political evolution

of the KSZKI and the various splits that it has suffered since its inception in 1978–9 have not affected the representation of its revolutionary identity. The glorification of the Komalay JK and vilification of the KDPI are invariant in their attempts to define the historical formation of their revolutionary identity. The KSZKI to date has failed to produce a history of its own formation and development, for reasons which do not seem to be immediately known to its founders.

7   The idea that the suppression of the Komalay JK and its replacement by the KDPI was essentially a Soviet plot to further its own regional/ global interests is by no means confined to the radical Marxist-populist left; it is also held by those who view the formation and dissolution of the Kurdish Republic in the context of the Cold War between the USSR and the West. See, for example, the works of Roosevelt (1947) and Eagleton (1963). For Noshirwan Emin, on the other hand, the relationship of the republican leadership with the Soviet Union formed the dynamics of the political process, accounting for its swift downfall. Emin scarcely pays any attention to the internal socio-economic and political conditions and their pivotal role in determining the character and outcome of the movement in that historical conjuncture; see Emin (1993). In his study of the rise and fall of the Kurdish Republic, Borhanedin Yassin provides a better-informed and more balanced view of the inter-relationship between the 'internal' and 'external' conditions. This relationship, he asserts, filtered through a dialectics of modernity and tradition, the nexus of which was the Republican administration. Yassin rightly points out that during the fateful period of 1941–7 the Soviet Union did not have an 'autonomous' or uniform policy towards the Kurds in Iran. Although Yassin avoids the sweeping and unhelpful political generalizations of Hassanpour (1992) and Emin, his analysis remains firmly in the confines of an 'empiricist' historiography, the methodological exigencies of which militate against the attempts to go beyond the 'facts'. He therefore fails to specify the conditions of the existence and the dynamics of his dialectics of modernity and tradition, reducing it to a mere assertion; see Yassin (1995).

8   This position is found most frequently among the present and former members of the KDPI, in the leadership and in the

rank and file; see, for example, A.R. Ghassemlou, *Kurdistan and the Kurds* (London, 1980). Here Ghassemlou mentions the Komalay JK only in passing, as a minor stage in the process of nationalist struggle leading to the formation of the KDPI and the establishment of the Republic. In a later work on the history of the KDPI, he treats the issue in greater detail, attributing the demise of the Komalay JK to its failure to create a popular political base (1988). But there are also many outside the party who hold such a view, voiced more often in relation to the cause of the decline and collapse of the Republic. Mahmoud Mulla Izzat's study of the rise and fall of the Kurdish Republic also maintains such a view, though in a somewhat different manner. Following the essentialist tradition whereby nationalist history is seen as an uninterrupted process, he pays no attention to the political and social conditions governing the dissolution of the Komalay JK and the formation of the KDPI. See his *Komary Milly Mehabad* (Stockholm, 1984).

9 This position is best expounded by Amir Hassanpour; see his various writings, especially his 'Nationalist Movements in Azerbaijan and Kurdistan 1941–6 in John Fron (ed.), *Iran, a Century of Revolution: Social Movements in Iran* (Minneapolis, 1994). He subsequently reiterates the main features of his argument in his articles in *Gzing*, no. 13, 1996 and no. 15, 1997 and his introduction to Ali' Karimi (ed.), *Jiyan u Beserhati Abdulrahmani Zabihi 'Mamosta Ulema'* [Abdulrahman Zabihi: His Life and Fortunes] (Goteborg, 1999).

10 On this see the Soviet document discussed by Amir Hassanpour in *Gzing*, no. 13 (1997). The document suggests very clearly that the Soviet authorities, including and especially Stalin, had a specifically social class-based understanding of the Kurdish movement, and did not hesitate to ignore its urban character and reduce its political and cultural complexities to the political and economic interests of the Kurdish tribal landlords, a class which for the most part opposed the nationalist movement and eventually joined forces with the central government to destroy it. Hassanpour, who shares the theoretical premises of this class analysis of Kurdish nationalism and nationalist movements, nonetheless takes this official Soviet characterization to be the mark of the Stalinist betrayal of the Kurdish movement in Iran during

1941–6 because it fails to recognize the movement's distinctive bourgeois nationalist character.

11 For this see Bullard's report to the Foreign Office regarding the Soviet aims and objectives in Kurdistan in early December 1941. Bullard, who served as the British minister in Tehran during this critical period, clearly confirms Soviet caution and lack of interest in the Kurdish movement. The central point in his report is that the Soviets do not intend to disturb the status quo in Iranian Kurdistan or in the region at large. He writes: 'I believe however that it is not correct to say that the Soviet authorities are encouraging an autonomous Kurdish movement. I have even heard of instances where they assisted the Iranian Government against the Kurds.' In the same dispatch Bullard clearly indicates that Kurdish autonomist aspirations and unrest did exist in the final years of Reza Shah's rule, before the occupation of the country by the British and the Soviet armies in September 1941. The occupation and the collapse of the central government further encouraged the Kurds to raise their voices and complain about their conditions more frequently and freely than before. Bullard argues that the mistreatment of the minorities should be addressed if Iran is to be held as a buffer state successfully. He writes: 'If we are to retain Persia as a buffer state, the central government must be strong, though that does not mean that we should be indifferent to their treatment of minorities, if only because discontent among the minorities would result in a weakening of the buffer state.' (FO 248/1405)

12 For a detailed description of the state-tribe relations in Kurdistan under Reza Shah see the correspondence in FO 248/1400 (1937). This correspondence is exceptionally detailed, containing informed commentary on the social, economic and political impact of the policy of territorial centralism on Kurdish tribal land during the last few crucial years leading to the collapse of Reza Shah's rule. Tribal opposition to Reza Shah's policies is clearly noted in a number of correspondences in this file; see dispatches and reports by R.W. Urquhart, British consul in Tabriz, to the British Embassy in Tehran, esp. report dated 18 June 1937. For further information on the Kurdish tribes, changes in the political structure and organization of tribal power under the Pahlavi rule during the 1920s and 1930s, and especially

the political status and aims of tribal leaders who resisted Reza Shah's policies in Kurdistan and were subsequently imprisoned or banished see the following: FO 371/ 3858, 4147, 4192, 4930, 5067, 6347, 6348, 6434, 6442, 7781, 7802, 7803, 7805, 7806, 7807, 7808, 7826, 7827, 7835, 7844, 9009, 9010, 9018, 10097, 10098, 10124, 10158, 10833, 10841, 10842, 11484, 11491, 12264, 12265, 12288, 12291, 13027, 13760, 13781, 16063, 16076, 17912, 17915, 18987, 20037, 23261. On this issue also see Eagleton, 1963; van Bruinessen, 1983; Hassanpour, 1992; McDowall, 1996. For the socio-economic conditions, political position and the conduct of the Kurdish tribal leaders and their attitude towards the British-Soviet occupation as well as to the central government in Tehran see the following: FO 248/1224, 1225, 1226, 1246, 1278, 1331, 1400, 1405 1410, and FO 371/1965, 2125, 2361, 2422, 2799, 3195, 3316, 3481, 4076, 5068, 6342, 6389, 6670, 6751, 6846, 6954, 6967, 6994, 7129, 7227, 7251, 7499, 8292, 8432, 8463.

13 Jwaideh, in my opinion, overemphasizes the importance of the markets, and does not take into account the fact that the Kurdish mercantile community to which he refers was not a uniform socio-economic entity. A considerable section of this community was still involved in exchange relations with regional and local markets. There were hardly any merchants in Mahabad who had a sustained and growing economic relationship with markets beyond Azerbaijan and Hamedan. This was also true of other Kurdish towns in the area such as Bokan and Saqqiz. In Mahabad there were a few merchant families, e.g. the Tajirbashi family, which had business with Ottoman Turkey and Tsarist Russia in the early twentieth century, but after the Bolshevik Revolution in 1917 and the founding of the Republic of Turkey in 1923 they had either disappeared or fragmented into smaller and less wealthy businesses engaged in local and regional markets. Jwaideh, 1965. On this also see Samadi, 1997, and for the general conditions of commodity production, exchange and trade in Iran as well as the Kurdish regions during this period see M.L. Entner, *Russo-Persian Commercial Relations 1828–1914* (Florida, 1965), and C. Issawi, *The Economic History of Iran 1800–1914* (Chicago, 1971). M.K. Fateh, *The Economic Position of Persia* (London, 1926).

14 The British diplomatic dispatches and reports for the period cover the Soviet strategic interests in Iranian Kurdistan fairly extensively, commenting on the nature and the development of the Soviet relations with Kurdish nationalist forces, and regularly appraising their political aims and objectives regarding the project of an autonomous Kurdistan in the framework of Iranian sovereignty. The conservative character of the Soviet foreign policy before 1944 and the change in its aims and objectives in the months approaching the end of the war are clearly noted in the following: FO 371/ 7674, 8156, 5068, 38421, 4322, 1019, 1215, 4322, 4911, 1679, 2864, 1311, 1476, 5979, 3625, 1507, 1941, 2003, 1940, 2268, 3094, 5270. For US views and interpretation see also Lieutenant Richard A. Mobley, 'A Study of Relations between the Mahabad Republic and the Azerbaijan Democrat Republic: The Turbulent Alliance and Its Impact upon the Mahabad Republic of 1946', seminar paper submitted in partial fulfilment of the requirements for the course on 'Modernization in the Islamic World' at Georgetown University, Washington DC (May 1979). Mobley's paper is particularly significant for its use of the US official records for the period. See OSS, 'The Tribal Problems in Iran's Domestic and Foreign Policy', R&A 2707 (15 March 1945), Diplomatic History Branch, National Archives, pp. 23–30; for a discussion of the regional pattern and the local political limits of the Soviet wartime policy towards the Kurds see sources cited in Mobley (1979, pp. 19–20). I am grateful to Hassan Ghazi for bringing this excellent source to my attention and providing me with a copy. This issue will be variously taken up in the following chapters of this study.

15 On this see the following Foreign Office files: FO 371/ 27155, 27215, 31388. For the evidence of the American public records on this issue see the relevant sections of Yassin, 1995, esp. chaps 4 and 5; also Mobley (1979).

16 See FO 248/1410.

17 See FO 248/3322.

18 A Confidential Report, 'The Kurdish Problem', prepared by the Research Department of the British Foreign Office on 22 March 1946, observes, 'In the months immediately following the entry of British and Russian troops, the policy of both governments was

conditioned by the presence of the Kurds on both sides of the Turkish frontier. We have always been fully conscious of Turkish susceptibilities on the Kurdish question and deliberately refereed from any interference in the affairs of Persia which might have been interpreted as an encouragement to Pan-Kurdishness or as an incitement to the Kurds of Turkey.' The report continues to define the Russian policy as follows: 'The Russians, on the other hand, were for sometime obsessed with the anxiety to have friendly tribes on the frontier between Azerbaijan and Turkey in the event of the military situation deteriorating, although their motives seem to have been somewhat confused and the policy gave the impression of being an improvization ... The improvements in the military situation and the clear perception of the facts (which led the Russians to realise the danger from turbulent tribes to the supply lines across Persia) resulted in a change in attitude and by the end of 1942 they were trying to keep the Kurdish tribes quiet and holding the balance between them and Persian authorities.' On the Kurds' response to the Russian policy, the Report states, 'The Kurds were correspondingly disappointed; they had felt that the Russians had acquiesced up to a point in sponsoring the movement towards Kurdish unity (implying freedom from Persian government interference), and had then drawn back.' See FO 371/52702.

19 The Soviets, the British Foreign Office documents show, continued to court the Kurdish tribal leaders up until 1944, when the tide of the war had decisively turned against the German army and the Red Army was on the offensive; see the Confidential Report cited in note 16 above, p. 5.

20 The leadership of the Komalay JK, principally its chairman Abdulrahman Zabihi, was in direct contact with the Soviet authorities in Tabriz, regularly informing them of developments in Kurdistan, both in major towns and in the countryside. Zabihi's letters (seven in total, written in Azeri during 1944–5) to the Soviet counsel in Tabriz, unearthed by Rahim Saif Ghazi in the 1980s in the Baku state archives, are attempts to secure Soviet support for the Komala, drawing his attention to its programme and activities, and to its pro-Soviet stance in Kurdish and Iranian political arenas. It is interesting to note that Zabihi shows a considerable degree

of pragmatism in relation to the Kurdish tribal landlords, clearly treating them as a heterogeneous political force pursuing mainly pragmatic political objectives. In a letter dated 11 September 1944 he emphasizes the imminent danger of Iranian military activities in the region in an attempt to convince the Soviet counsel to lend support to Hama Rashid Khan, a tribal landlord of the Bana region, who according to Zabihi intends to counter the likely Iranian military advances in the area. In the same letter, Zabihi warns the counsel of the danger posed to the Soviet interests in the region by the Kurdish tribal leaders working secretly with the Iranian government. In another letter dated 5 October 1944 the collaborating tribal leaders are named: Qarani Agha Mamash, Abdullah Agha Mangur, Bayiz Agha Gewirk and Ghazi Muhammad. The inclusion of Ghazi Muhammad as a tribal lord in the list is another indication of Zabihi's political pragmatism, especially given their political and personal relationship in the following two years in Mahabad. The letter, and the three main collaborators reported by Zabihi, signal aspects of a political future which was to come after the creation of the Republic. The main theme and tone of Zabihi's letter were frequently echoed by Ghazi Muhammad himself in the pages of *Kurdistan,* warning the people of the danger of treason by the tribal leaders on whom the Republic depended for its defence. Zabihi's letters were published by B. Lavin in *Hawar,* no. 2 (1997), and subsequently reprinted in Hamid Gohery (1999). I am grateful to Ali Karimi for bringing these letters to my attention and sending me a copy of *Hawar* in April 1998. It is interesting to note here that the above-mentioned British Confidential Report also refers to Komala's approach to the Russian authorities around the same time that Zabihi attempted to contact them. The report, however, indicates that 'the Russians seem to have had some difficulty in reconciling the competition for membership between that party and the Jiana Kurd society'. The term 'party' here presumably refers to the KDPI, in which case the said competition for membership must have been during the brief period of mid-August to mid-November 1945 when it overlapped with the Komalay JK.

21 Evidence concerning the gradual change in the Soviet policy from non-intervention to tacit and at times active support for Kurdish nationalist aspirations after 1944 can be found in the Foreign Office

documents concerning the period; see, for example, sources cited in notes 12–15 above. The Soviet attempts to initiate and develop contacts with the Kurdish notables both urban and rural, directly and through the Azeri Republic, should be seen in this context. But despite this change in policy towards the end of the war, the British authorities were confident that the Soviets did not have a specific policy to establish a Kurdish state anywhere in the Middle East. Witness comments by an official of the British Embassy in Moscow as late as 19 June 1946 on the FO Confidential Report discussed above (note 16): 'We have the general impression that the Russians do not intend in the Middle East to make what might be called "the French mistake" of supporting minorities against the majority population in cases where there is any hope of winning over the majority, except as a … temporary measure.' He then goes on to comment on the specific case of Iran: 'If the Russians can call the tune in Tehran, Kurdish autonomy in Persia will probably cease to be a serious headache for the Persian government … while there is no direct evidence of Soviet support for any larger scheme for Kurdish independence, the Russians have somehow continued to spread the impression among many Kurds that they would at least look favourably on such aspirations.' British Embassy Moscow, FO 371/52702. Perhaps it will not be quite so unrealistic to see the Russian invitation of the Kurdish dignitaries to visit Baku in this context.

22 Mobley, 1979, p. 20.

23 On this see Yassin (1995); Eagleton (1963); Roosevelt (1947).

24 See relevant sections of Mobley's detailed discussion of this issue esp. chap. 3 and the Conclusion (1979, pp. 54–86, 88–92).

25 See Zabihi's letters discussed in note 18 above, informing the Soviet counsel in Tabriz about the Komalay JK, its aims, influence and activities in Kurdistan. He boasts political influence and support and increasing membership in an expanding territory as far afield as Sulaimaniya and Sardasht, Bana. Further British evidence of Komala's expanding influence is found in FO 371/52702.

26 For the creation of this committee and the subsequent drive towards the transformation of the Komalay JK to a modern political organization with a wider territorial base and larger membership see relevant sections of Karimi (1999) and Gohery (1999, esp. pp.

20–52). They both refer to these developments at various points in their narratives but in quite different ways, and without exploring their immediate causes and long-term consequences.

27 The warming of the relationship between Komalay JK and the less conservative tribal landlords and the urban notables has already been variously noted in the British Foreign Office documents cited in the preceding notes. Secondary literature is also telling on this; see, for example, Eagleton (1963) and Roosevelt (1947). In discursive terms Komala's rapprochement with the sectors of tribal landlords at the same time required a shift in its representation of the landowning class from a homogeneous reactionary bloc to a more heterogeneous and differentiated political force, including different factions holding different political positions. Early signs of this change of approach to the landowning class may be seen in Zabihi's correspondence with the Soviet consul in Tabriz, cited in note 18 above.

Chapter 3

1 The population of the Republic, the number of people living in its jurisdiction excluding the three disputed towns of Urmiya, Khoy and Salmas, was estimated by Ghazi Muhammad at 700,000–800,000 (see the Kurdish translation of his interview with *Rahbar*, the Azeri democrat daily, published in *Kurdistan*, no. 69, 28 July 1946). The absence of an official census in Iran before 1955 makes it difficult to verify figures given by Ghazi Muhammad, though figures subsequently given by others for various towns or districts during the same period suggest that he may have overestimated the population of the Republic, and that 500,000 is a more realistic figure. Eagleton, for example, estimates the population of Mahabad under Republican rule at 16,000 (1963, p. 5); see also Seyyid Muhammad Samadi's *Negahi be Tarikhe Mahabad* (A Glance at the History of Mahabad, an unpublished manuscript of 1996), subsequently published under the same title in Mahabad in 1999. In the same interview, in response to a question regarding the jurisdiction and boundaries of the Republic, Ghazi states, 'it is true that our movement spreads from the centre [Mahabad] to

the vicinity of Maku, Shapour (Salmas), Khoy, Rezaiya (Urmiya), Ushno, Sendus (Shahin Dezh), Saqqiz and Serdasht ...' (ibid.). The term 'vicinity' here is carefully chosen to avoid touching on the territorial dispute with the Azeri democratic government over the administration of Urmiya, Khoy and Salmas. For more detail on this issue see note 5 below. Public announcements by various governmental ministries and directorates, especially regarding economic and financial issues published in *Kurdistan*, however, indicate clearly that the jurisdiction of the Republic extended north and north-west to Naqadeh, Ushno and Khana, and south and south-east to Bokan, Baneh and south-west Sardasht. See, for example, a public announcement by Fahimi, the director of Customs and Excise in Mahabad, in late March 1946, on the appointment of officials to head local offices in Naqadaeh and Khana, in no. 28 (27 March 1946). For similar directives and public announcements, especially financial and military, see Izzat 1987 and Emin, 1993.

2　Eagleton, referring to this issue, states that Ghazi Muhammad did in fact authorize Abdulrahman Zabihi and Ali Raihani to contact the British Consul and notify them of the decision of the KDPI to establish an autonomous republic in Kurdistan (1963, p. 61). There may well have been such a contact, but Eagleton's point regarding Zabihi's role is factually unfounded. Evidence suggests that Zabihi had been detained in June 1945 in Tehran and spent nearly eight months in prison in Tehran. He was not released until late February, some time after the inauguration of the Republic. See the news of his release in *Kurdistan*, no. 14, 13 February 1946.

3　FO 371/52702.

4　FO 371/52702.

5　As was seen in the previous chapter, jurisdiction over these three towns remained a major bone of contention between the two republics, significantly affecting their mutual relationship as well as their respective negotiations with the Iranian government regarding their proposed plans for regional autonomy. The actual place of this territorial dispute in the development and demise of the Kurdish Republic is a subject of disagreement among the scholars concerned. For Mobley, for example, the dispute and the persistent refusal of the Azeri leadership to recognize the jurisdiction of the Kurdish administration over these three towns played a pivotal role in the latter's downfall, as it seriously undermined its bargaining powers both in the course of autonomy negotiations with the Iranian government and in the precarious relationship with those sections of the tribal leadership who traditionally had a vested interest in their administration (Mobley, 1979). Eagleton's study supports Mobley's arguments regarding the Azeri leadership's opposition to the Kurdish demands (1963, pp. 61–5). Others assign less significance to this issue, though in varying degrees; see Emin (1993); Yassin (1995); Izzat (1987); Atabaki (2000); Hassanpour (1994). However, the position of the Kurdish leadership at the time, variously reflected in the discourse of *Kurdistan*, seems to be in line with Mobley's view. See, for example, Ghazi Muhammad's speeches in *Kurdistan* nos 45 (8 May 1946) and 62 (27 June 1946), and on return from Tehran negotiations with premier Qawam, no. 72 (30 July 1946). The main cause of the crucial dispute between the Azeri Democrats and the Kurdish leadership, which is omitted by these authors, Mobley included, is that the Azeri leadership was firmly committed to the 'political-administrative' map of Iran, produced by the Pahlavi state in 1940. That is the territorial division (*taqsimat-e keshvari*) of Iran into 10 political-administrative units (*ostans*, 'provinces') to serve a centralized political order tightly run from Tehran. According to this territorial division the bulk of the Kurdish territory, including Mahabad, was part of the province of Western Azerbaijan (Ostan-e Azerbaijan-e Gharbi), the capital of which was Rezaiyeh (Urmiya), and as such it lacked political-administrative autonomy. The central government made this territorial division the framework for autonomy negotiations with the Azeri and Kurdish governments seeking regional autonomy. The Azeri government not surprisingly accepted this arrangement in the autonomy negotiations with the central government. The bulk of the territory over which the Kurdish government claimed jurisdiction was located in the provinces of eastern and western Azerbaijan. This in effect meant that the Kurdish leadership had no autonomous position in negotiations with Tehran; it had been subordinated to the Azeri government in Tabriz and had been deprived of political and tactical initiative *vis-à-vis* the central government.

6   The official documents which have survived the Republic put the number of the regular army at 3,000 in total – 2,000 cavalry and 1,000 infantry. This force seems to have been paid regular salaries by the Republican administration. The command structure and rank and file were both recruited from the urban population, mainly from the petty-bourgeoisie, traditional and modern. See Izzat (1995, vol. 2), esp. documents no. 240, p. 387 and no. 241, pp. 88, 89. The Republican regular forces were mainly equipped with light arms obtained from the Soviet forces stationed in the area, while training was largely provided by the Kurdish officers who had defected from the Iraqi army in the early 1940s and since had been serving the cause of the Kurdish nationalism in eastern Kurdistan. It is widely believed that the term *Peshmerga*, an emotive term denoting readiness to face death and self-sacrifice which subsequently became the common name for Kurdish fighters in different parts of Kurdistan, especially southern and eastern territories, was first coined in Mahabad to refer to the core of the regular forces in the Republic. The small size of the regular force in comparison with that of the tribal contingents, estimated at about 15,000 (Eagleton, 1963), clearly testifies to their relative weight and significance in the structure of political authority in the Kurdish Republic. Emin puts the number of tribal forces, including Barzanis, at 12,750 (1993, pp. 171–5).

7   See the statement by Ahmad Ilmie, the Director of Public Finance – 'it is clear that taxation is the soul of the nation, and if the fiscal conditions are not secured, nothing can be achieved in the administration, no orders can be carried out, nothing will be done' – in *Kurdistan*, no. 6 (21 January 1946). Ilmie presided over the process of collection and procedures were carried out by the former officials of the Iranian Ministry of Finance in Kurdistan under his direction. According to Eagleton, 'all such funds went into the party-government treasury which was in the safe keeping of Ilmie and the Shirkat i Taraqi, an official trading company which controlled the external transactions of the Republic and included on its board the Russian contact, Muhammad Amin Moini, the Minister of Interior' (1963, p. 87). Taxation, though the main source of revenue for the government, could only pay for its daily expenses, mostly wages and salaries. Governmental projects had to

be financed by sources other than taxes and dues. On one occasion the government had to borrow 20,000 Tomans (approximately $4,400) from the Azeri government, which was repaid in sugar produced at the Miandoab refinery (ibid., p. 101). The sale of the annual tobacco crop (1,875,000 kg) to the Soviet army, valued at $800,000 but paid for in Iranian currency, is another prominent example (ibid., p. 88). Financial transactions of this kind were conducted by the Shirkat i Taraqi as instructed by the Central Committee of the KDPI.

8   For a detailed account of taxation regarding agrarian production and land revenue under Reza Shah see Lambton, 1953. For issues related to agrarian property and land rents and government taxes prior to the 1962–3 land reform see also the following: N. Keddie, 'The Iranian Village before and after the Land Reform', *Journal of Contemporary History*, vol. 3, no. 3 (1963); M. Soudagar, *Nezam-e Arbab-Raiyati dar Iran* (Tehran, 1979); A. Vali, 1993, chap. 7.

9   The fiscal structure and administration of the government had been created and put in place by the central committee of the KDPI before the inauguration of the Republic; see the party's directives in *Kurdistan*, nos 5 (6 January 1946) and 20 (21 January 1946).

10   See *Kurdistan*, issues cited in notes 4 and 6.

11   The public announcement by Ahmad Elahie, the Minister of Finance, regarding the creation of the two Tax Commissions further indicates that the Commission for rural areas had been very successful in its efforts, managing to collect taxes in the locality of Shar Veran and among the Mangur and Piran tribes in a period of one week, see *Kurdistan*, no. 15 (16 February 1946). Whatever the actual status of this claim, it does not seem to tally with the subsequent announcements and warnings by the Director of Public Finance regarding the failure/refusal of the landlords and tribal leaders to pay taxes; see *Kurdistan*, nos 13 (11 February 1946), 27 (25 March 1946) and 44 (6 May 1946).

12   See, for example, the KDPI announcement about salaries and overtime pay: 'According to the order given by the central committee [of the KDPI] the Finance Office cannot under any circumstances pay overtime to any governmental office without the approval of the party. This order has been communicated to all government

offices.' *Kurdistan*, no. 68 (18 July 1946). On a different financial issue, see the public announcement of the Central Committee tender leasing out of the revenue of Gebagh Kandi marketplace. Here too the Ministry of Finance is acting as the executive arm of the Central Committee: 'Further to the order no. 24–12–25–2633 of the Central Committee of the KDPI, the ministry of finance in the town of Mahabad is leasing out the revenue of Gebagh Kendi marketplace as of the beginning of the new year [starting1325/21 March 1946]. For this reason we are informing the public ...' *Kurdistan*, no. 28 (27 March 1946). See also the public announcement issued by the Central Committee regarding the cancellation of the order no. 2230 permitting free importation of Iranian goods, mainly textiles, from Iran in *Kurdistan*, no. 46 (11 May 1946).

13 On the existence of conditions pertaining to the emergence of the public sphere in the Republic see also Emin, 1993, pp. 143–69. Emin uses the phrase 'Intellectual Flourish' to define these conditions.

14 The social-occupational structure of the Republican government was as follows:

Ghazi Muhammad, President: Cleric-Landowner

Haji Baba Shaikh, Prime Minister: Landowner

Muhammad Hussein Saif Ghazi, Minister of War: Landowner

Abdul Rahman Ilkhanizadeh (Mohtadi), Minister of Foreign Affairs: Landowner

Ismail Ilkhanizadeh, Minister of Roads: Landowner

Muhammad Amin Mo'eini, Minister of Interior: Small business (Petty-bourgeois)

Ahmad Elahie, Minister of Finance: Small business (Petty-bourgeois)

Karim Ahmadain, Minister of Post, Telegraph and Telephone: Small business (Petty-bourgeois)

Manaf Karimi, Minister of Education: Small landowner and small business

Khalil Khosrawi, Minister of Labour: Small business (Petty-bourgeois)

Haj Mustafa Dawudi, Minister of Trade: Business-Landlord Real Estate (Bourgeois)

Sayyid Muhammad Ayuobian, Minister of Health: Small Business (Petty-bourgeois)

Mulla Hussein Majdi, Minister of Justice: Clergy

Mahmoud Valizadeh, Minister of Agriculture: Business (Bourgeois)

Of the members of the cabinet, Ghazi Muhammad, Haj Rahman Ilkhanizadeh and Haji Baba Shaikh were well educated in the traditional system of *madrasa* and religious seminary, well versed in Islamic theology, logic and philosophy, classical Persian and Arabic literature and language. Haj Mustafa Dawudi is also said to have had a solid traditional education, though he lacked the previous three men's intellectual depth and acumen. The rest were mostly products of the modern education and school system instituted under the Pahlavi rule, though some also had traditional schooling. Mahmoud Valizadeh was to my knowledge the only member of the cabinet with a modern university education. He completed his undergraduate studies at the Daneshsara-yeh Keshavarzi-ye Karaj, Agricultural Training College in Karaj, before joining the cabinet. He is the only member of the Republican government who is still alive at the time of writing this chapter. For the social and occupational structures of the Republican government see, among others, Eagleton, 1963, pp. 61–3; Izzat, 1987, and Emin, 1993, esp. chap. 3, pp. 101–43.

15 The term 'urban notables' was first used by Albert Hourani to define specific sectors of the population in Arab society, which broadly speaking emerged out of intermarriages between groups such as members of civil officialdom, mercantile communities, landowners, and the *ulama*. See 'Ottoman Reform and the Politics of Notables', in A. Hourani, *The Emergence of the Modern Middle East* (Berkeley/Los Angeles, 1981).

16 Shateri in particular was believed to be 'a British spy', recruited earlier in the 1930s when he spent some time in London for medical treatment. The popular perceptions of the two men were often 'corroborated' by the appearance of 'foreign visitors' in Mahabad who were hosted by them, especially Shateri, who was more prominent in this respect. Whether or not popular rumours about their collaboration with foreign powers had any truth to them, their opposition to the leadership of the Republic and their

active co-operation with the central government in Tehran and the Iranian military command in the area were hard to deny. Shateri continued his collaboration with the central government after the fall of the Republic, and especially during the nationalization of oil crisis in the 1950s, when he actively supported the monarchy against the government of Dr Muhammad Mussadeq. Shateri was believed to have been rewarded for his loyalty to the monarchy when he was awarded the concession to establish the first commercial petrol station in Mahabad. The popular perception of Shateri as a collaborator persisted till his death in 1979, soon after the downfall of the Pahlavi monarchy. Only a few mourned his death; among them was Abdulrahman Zabihi, the chairman of Komalay JK, who had returned to Mahabad after 33 years in exile. Zabihi was paying a timely homage to a father figure who had adopted him and raised him in his household when he was orphaned in early childhood. The status of the Shafe'ie clan, their patriarch and his opposition to the Republic is noted among others by Eagleton, 1963, p. 30.

17 Announcement signed by Ilmie, the Director of Public Finance in *Kurdistan*, no. 27 (25 March 1946).

18 *Kurdistan*, no. 44 (5 May 1946).

19 See Bullard's memo to the Foreign Office dated 18 December 1941: 'Kurdish chiefs who were imprisoned by the late Reza Shah were released in accordance with the reforming policy of the new regime and not under any pressure from us nor I believe from the Soviet Embassy' (FO 248/1405). But this expression of good will by the new administration in Tehran does not seem to have affected the tribal leaders' negative perception of and opposition to the Pahlavi rule. A letter signed by 17 tribal chiefs on 1 December 1941 addressed to the British Government asks for 'refuge under British protection'. It reads: 'We the chiefs of Kurdish tribes beg to submit this petition. We have for a long time been suffering from the cruel behaviour of Pahlavi and his officials who have up to now crushed us by their ill treatment ... Now that, thanks to God, the British government has kindly rescued us ... we beg to seek refuge under the British government and request its help in the recovery of our rights so that we may live peacefully and in security ... it is quite impossible, however, for us to accept once more the unjust protection of the wicked and cruel Iranian government. We ask to

be under the kind protection of Great Britain in the same way as many nations enjoying British protection.' (FO 248/1405)

20 A contemporary British diplomatic account of the political allegiance of the Kurdish tribes dated 11 April 1946 states that 'Jellali, Shikkak, Mangur, Mamash, Herki, Suisani and Dehbokri' favoured the Republic, while 'Tilkoo and most tribes of southern Kurdistan are favouring Persian government. Baneh Bagzadeh's are divided. Pizhdar are wavering'. The report further indicates that the political position of 'individual chiefs [was] often at variance with tribal majority'. This point, as was seen in the previous chapters, is of prime importance given the political organization of the tribes, and the structure of command and loyalty in the Kurdish context. Tribal leaders rather than tribesmen and women defined the political orientation of the tribes *vis-à-vis* the Republic and the central government in Tehran (From the Middle East to the War Office, 11 April 1946, WO 106/5961).

21 A number of prominent tribal chiefs, some occupying senior positions in the political and military organizations of the government and even the party, were known to have maintained a cordial relationship with the central government in Tehran, frequently renewing contact to provide information or obtain assurances; among them were Amar Khan Sharifi and Ghassem Agha Debokri. The latter, who was a member of the Kurdish delegation visiting Baku in 1942 and 1945, had become particularly active upon his return from Baku, travelling to Tabriz and frequently sharing views with official sources, especially the British diplomats, warning them of Ghazi's collaboration with the Soviets and their imminent conspiracy to partition Iran and establish a communist government in Kurdistan. The British diplomat reporting the visit to Tehran describes Ghassem Agha as paranoid, his views hysterical and exaggerated. See FO 371/40178 (20 November 1945). The Kurdish leadership in Mahabad and the Soviet officials in Tabriz and Miandoab were aware of Ghassem Agha's activities and identified him as the source of leaks about the Baku visit. Eagleton further states that 'other Chiefs of Dehbokri of Bukan later established contacts with general Homayuni who commanded Iranian army units containing the Republic in the south' (1963, p. 58).

22 *Kurdistan*, no. 11 (6 February 1946).

23 *Kurdistan*, no. 44 (6 May 1946).

24 See *Kurdistan*, no. 54 (6 June 1946).

25 *Kurdistan*, no. 8 (28 January 1946).

26 Saif Ghazi's speech names the hostile elements as Ali Agha Aliyar (tribal landlord), Rahim Vasta Aziz (townsman), Ghafour Mahmoudian (townsman), Hamza Ali Ghawachi (townsman), Mulla Rahman i Surounjdaghi (cleric), Muhammad Abbasi (tribal landlord), Ali Nouzari (tribal landlord), Abdulla Bayiz Agha (tribal landlord), Bayiz Agha Gewirk (tribal landlord), Kak Alla Agha Gewirk (tribal landlord), Qarani Agha Mamash (tribal landlord), Muhammad Faroughi (tribal landlord) (*Kurdistan*, no. 11 [6 February 1946]).

27 In the early days the Republic felt confident enough to take punitive action against the hostile landlords and tribal chiefs. On 10 March 1946, Bayiz i Aziz Agha and Kak Alla Agha, two chiefs from the Gewirk tribe, and Hama Gurga, the former's personal retainer, were detained on a charge of treason against the Kurds and Kurdistan (*Kurdistan*, no. 25 [17 March 1946]).

28 On the Kurdish army officers from Iraq serving in the military institutions of the Republic and the nature of their contribution to the formation and development the regular army see Emin, 1993, pp. 169–201; Izzat, 1995. For Republican documents related to these officers as well as their correspondence with Republican authorities see M.M. Izzat, *The Democratic Republic of Kurdistan: Letters and Documents*, 2 vols (Stockholm, 1992 and 1995). Eagleton also refers to this issue (1963).

29 For figures regarding the organization and approximate number of the regular forces of the Republic see note 3 above. According to Eagleton the regular army was non-tribal, recruited from among the townsmen in Mahabad and its vicinity. At full strength it was led by some 70 officers on active duty, assisted by 40 non-commissioned officers and 1,200 troops. The officer corps, for the most part, was assigned to non-military administrative duties in the government. The regular army was trained by Iraqi Kurdish officers who had defected to the Republic, the experienced Barzani fighters, as well as by a Soviet army officer, Captain Salahaddin Kazimov, known as Kakagha (see Eagleton, 1963, pp. 88–90). The

actual extent of Soviet military aid to the Republic has already been discussed in the previous chapter.

30 The four were Muhammad Hussein Sheif Ghazi, Mulla Mustafa Barzani, Omar Agha Sharifi and Muhammad Rashid Khan Khanzadeh (Hama Rashid Khani Baneh); see Emin, 1993, p. 172. In his discussion of this issue Martin van Bruinessen contends that the Republican military command included three generals; see 'Kurdish Tribes and the Iranian State: the Case of Semko's Revolt', in R. Tapper (ed.), *The Conflict of Tribe and State in Iran and Afghanistan* (London, 1983). See Hassan Ghazi's corrective in his Farsi translation of van Bruinessen's article in *Studia Kurdica*, no. 2 (1986), p. 29.

31 Barzani's arrival is reported in *Kurdistan*, no. 21 (2 March 1946). According to this report Barzani and his armed men entered Mahabad on 1324.12.9 (November 1945) and, after a meeting with Ghazi Muhammad lasting for two hours, declared allegiance to him. For this see also FO 371/37291 (26 April 1946). According to Eagleton, 10,000 Barzanis entered Iranian Kurdistan, including women and children. Of these some 3,000 could bear arms, and of these 1,200 were individually accountable to Mulla Mustafa himself (1963, p. 54; Roosevelt, 1980, p. 141; McDowall, 1994, pp. 241–4). For an emotional eyewitness account see Ghani Blorian's memories, *Alekok* (Stockholm, 1997). For a less sympathetic view of the role of the Barzani force and actual aims and intentions of its leadership, in particular Mulla Mustafa himself, see Emin, 1993, pp. 175–80.

32 See sources cited in note 30 above.

33 For the Soviet suspicion of Barzani see Telegram, Kermanshah to Tehran (4 February 1946), FO 371/52702. What this and other FO documents regarding the Soviet perception of Barzani do not reveal is that the Soviets suspected Barzani not only of having secret contacts with the Iranian regime, but also of having collaborated with the British authorities in Iraq ever since the start of his political career. On the rise of Mulla Mustafa and his political career also see Jwaideh, 1965 and McDowall, 1994.

34 A British Foreign Office document, 'The Summary Report, Persian Kurdistan, General Background', dated 3 April 1946, refers to the existing rift in the cabinet between Ghazi and Amar Khan, to

whom it refers as the minister of war. It further indicates that General Homayuni, the commander of the Iranian Army in the region, is aware of this 'division in the military command of the Republic'. According to the report, General Homayuni further asks the British Consul in Kermanshah to advise the Iraqi government to co-operate with him by posting 'strong garrisons in Qaleh Dizeh opposite Sardasht and Shilar opposite Baneh whose commanders should be instructed to maintain the closest possible liaison with the Persian military authorities in Sardasht and Baneh'. He also considered that it would be a very good move for the Iraqi government to invite Hama Rashid to Dares Khan with the promise of security, and also if possible to make overtures to Mulla Mustafa Barzani who would probably consider returning if the death sentence now standing against him were revoked. 'Both these leaders, though outwardly supporting Ghazi Mohammad of Mahabad, have not yet irretrievably committed themselves to any definite hostility against the Persian government' (FO 371/ 3049). No more than two weeks after this communication the British Consul in Kermanshah reported to Tehran on Hama Rashid Khan's response: 'Hama Rashid has offered to come over to the Persians if they will give him Buneh and a monthly subsidy of 171,000, but these terms are unacceptable since the occupation of Buneh by Hama Rashid at the present juncture would be a grave danger if his loyalty was not sure.' (FO 371/3444); on this last issue see FO 371/36251.

35 Kermanshah to Tehran, 4 February 1946, FO 371 /52702.

36 See notes 33 and 34 above.

Chapter 4

1 Of the surviving issues of *Kurdistan* that I traced while researching this chapter, 15 are in the Library of Congress in Washington, DC (nos 15–29 inclusive), and 6 in the library of the School of Oriental and African Studies, University of London (nos 20–5 inclusive). The remainder are held in private collections mostly in the Kurdish diaspora; these include nos 1, 9, 10 and 43, nos 66–79, and no. 85. I am grateful to Hassan Ghazi for providing me

with photocopies of the existing 67 issues held in various libraries and private collections. Recently, however, a new classified and annotated collection containing 82 issues (nos 1–63, 65–73, 75–9, 85, 87, 88, 92) was published jointly by Zhin and Aras publishing houses in Sulaimaniya and Erbil in 2007. See R. Saleh and S. Saleh (eds), *Rojnamay Kurdistan: Mahabad, 1324–25 Hatawi (1946)* (Binkay Zhin, 2007). Rafiq Saleh and Sadiq Saleh, editors of this collection, state in the introduction to the volume that of the 82 issues included, 79 were kept in the private collection of the late Rashid Bajalan in Baghdad, donated to the Zhin publishing house by his daughter Behar Bajalan. The surviving 67 issues that were consulted in this study have all been reproduced in the new collection, except for issue 74. Although the 2007 edition reached me when this chapter had already been completed, I nonetheless consulted the additional issues of *Kurdistan* included in the collection, referring to them where appropriate. The editors of the new collection put the total number of issues published in the lifetime of the Republic at 112, while information available to me suggests that there were 113 issues in all. See, for example, J. Khaznedar, *Rabari Rojnamagari Kurdi* (1973), p. 52. Unfortunately, given the fact that the last surviving issue is dated 3 October 1946, nearly three months before the fall of the Republic, there is at present no way of verifying the accuracy of these claims or accounting for the apparent discrepancy. This can only be decided in the light of fresh evidence in the future. I am grateful to Djene Bajalan for giving me a copy of the new collection.

2   These articles are often authored by local Kurds, mostly with modern schooling, in the 1920s and 1930s; see, for example, leader articles by Hassan Ghizilji: 'Fedakari ya Serchaway Peshkawtin', in *Kurdistan*, no. 4, 17 January 1946, and 'Ema Dalain Chi?', in *Kurdistan*, no. 6, 21 January 1946. This incipient nationalism and emotional response to national oppression is variously expressed in the following articles in *Kurdistan*: Muhammad Majdi, 'Sekalayek Legal Kewa Berzekani Kurdistan' (no. 3, 15 January 1946); Mulla Muhammad Ayyubi, 'Hayrani Dayki Nishtiman' (no. 5, 20 January 1946); Abdul Rahman Imami, 'Ewa Adalet Bu' (no. 13, 11 February 1946); Seyyid Muhammad Hamidi, 'Hawarek la Dimokrasi' (no. 23, 6 March 1946); Aziz Mowlavi, 'Kar' (no.

28,27 March 1946); Kubra Azimi, 'Xoshbaxti' (no. 11, 6 February 1946). The absence or marginal use of conceptual language and clear-cut ideological orientation is not confined to early nationalist discourse, but such language is more often found in writing dealing with social-economic issues. For example, Mowlavi in his article perceives Kar/Labour not as an economic category but as a natural property/quality with which man is endowed. This trend also prevails in the field of international politics: Muhammad Majdi's article 'Molotov, Burns and Bevin', written in mid-February 1946, after the breakdown of the anti-fascist alliance, is surprisingly free of 'Cold War ideology', referring to the foreign ministers of the three powers in the same vein, regarding them equally as the 'gardeners in the garden of liberty ... who want to found the future world on justice, liberty and equality' (*Kurdistan*, no. 11, 6 February 1946). Muhammad Mahmoud's article 'Kurd u Paymani Atlantik' follows the same line of argument. Written at the end of March 1946 when the Soviet Union was already under pressure to end its military presence in Kurdistan, the author welcomes the Atlantic Treaty as 'heralding freedom for small and colonized nations' (*Kurdistan*, no. 28, 27 March 1946). Ahmad Elahie's article celebrating May Day in Kurdistan shows the persistence of this largely non-ideological perception of politics in the higher echelons of the party government. There is in Elahie's article a curious amalgam of this incipient nationalism with pro-Soviet political statements along with references to Islam and the prophet Muhammad. Elahie concludes a lengthy praise of the Soviet Union, Stalin, the Red Army, and an appreciation of freedom and the Kurdish commitment to the national cause, with the following words: '... for, according to the prophet's Shari'a as well as the laws of the modern world, he who does not have a sense of nationalism and patriotism in him is better dead than alive' (*Kurdistan*, no. 46, 11 May 1946).

3   See, for example, the article from *Rahber* translated from Azeri into Kurdish: 'Nehzati Azerbaijan u Kurdistan, Seratay Nejat u Istiqlali Miletani Rojhelati Nawarast', in *Kurdistan*, no. 66, 9 July 1946, in which social class categories dominate the Soviet-inspired analysis of the two movements in the regional and international contexts. Also the article by Showan, an Iraqi

Kurd, entitled 'Skalay Kurd', in the same issue, which, using the categories of class and relations of production, focuses on an analysis of the conditions of Kurdish peasantry. Also in the same vein is Abdul Ghadir Ahmad's 'Dostiman Keya u Dujmniman Keya?', in *Kurdistan*, no. 67, 14 July 1946. This article shows the direct influence of Cold War ideology and the Soviet/Tudeh perspective on international relations, and hence the division of the world into two antagonistic camps: colonial-imperialist and anti-colonial-liberation, which informs the analysis. The influence of Marxism-Leninism, especially Soviet Marxism, on the discourse of the Republic will be considered in more detail in the following sections of this chapter.

4   See, for example, the appearance of class categories in the article by Hashem Khalilzadeh on the occasion of May Day. The author addresses class exploitation and antagonistic class relations and argues for the alliance of the peasants and workers in the struggle against imperialism led by the USSR, but at the same time resorts to religion, invoking religious vocabulary in order to substantiate his argument; see *Kurdistan*, no. 43, 4 May 1946. See also contributions by Abdullah Dabaghi and Dilshad Rasuli in the same issue, which similarly attempt a class analysis of politics. Rasuli's argument in his later article 'Kurd u Shorish' is more representative in this respect. He writes: 'I believe in so far as the bourgeoisie is holding power and government in its hands, humanity will not be able to realize its heartfelt wishes and aims.' This article also contains the first systematic ideological statement of the Soviet view on the advent of the Cold War: 'Today everywhere in the world, a great war has begun between colonialism and freedom, there is now a powerful confrontation between oppression and justice.' (*Kurdistan*, no. 45, 8 May 1946). In this connection, it is also interesting to note the emergence in the writings of the local Kurdish intelligentsia of the rudiments of an idea of 'Internal Colonialism', referring to Kurdistan as an internal colony ruled by Turks, Arabs and Persians, thus anticipating the concept of 'Kurdistan: An Interstate Colonialism', which was subsequently developed by Ismail Besikci in the 1980s. See, for example, articles by Hemin 'Siyasati Shoum' in *Kurdistan*, no. 16, 18 February 1946, and Hassan Ghizilji, no. 6, 21 January 1946.

5   See, for example, Ghazi Muhammad's exposition of the conditions of the formation of the Republic in his inaugural speech. The brief genealogy of this event involves no reference to the Komalay JK. The KDPI is thus depicted as the force which initiated the nationalist political process leading the Kurdish nation to independence and freedom (*Kurdistan*, no. 11, 6 February 1946).

6   On the formation of the KDPI see Chapter 2, in particular note 1.

7   Mobley in his study (1979) indicates that the bazaar in Mahabad depended on a rural population of three million, who used it as the main centre for the purchase and sale of goods. This view is also variously confirmed by Eagleton (1963) and Jwaideh (1965).

8   See, for example, the definition of the Kurdish nation in Ghazi Muhammad's speech in the 'independence celebration' in *Kurdistan*, no. 10, 4 February 1946. This 'objective' definition of the Kurdish nation as a historical construct is politically compatible with the nationalist discourse of liberation and independence, but does not square with the autonomist discourse of the KDPI or the Republic.

9   See, for example, the leader comment 'Kurd Laber Chi Ghiyami Kird?', *Kurdistan*, no. 3, 15 January 1946.

10 See, for example, Ghazi's remarks in 'conversation' with the editors of the press in Tehran shortly before the declaration of the Republic. Asked whether it was true, as was being said in Tehran, that 'the Kurds under your leadership want separation and independence [from Iran]', Ghazi responds, 'No, it is not true, this is because we want the Iranian government to implement the constitutional law, we want to live autonomously under the Iranian flag.' Further, when asked to explain the position of the KDPI, he states, 'The Kurdish nation in Iran should be free to administer its own affairs and live within the Iranian borders.' (*Kurdistan*, no. 1, 11 January 1946).

11 In *Kurdistan*, nos. 1, 11 January 1946 and 2, 13 January 1946.

12 *Kurdistan*, no. 50, 27 May 1946.

13 *Kurdistan*, no. 50, 27 May 1946. It is interesting to note that the Kurdish leadership had a rather positive attitude towards Prime Minister Qawam, as a person who was better disposed towards the Kurds and was, in contrast to the hostile position of some members of his government, more inclined to negotiate with them to consider their demands for regional autonomy. They openly

speak about division and rift in the government, going so far as to warn Qawam about the conspiracy of the hostile elements to overthrow his government. In this respect the Kurdish leadership seems to be echoing the Soviet-Tudeh and Azeri positions regarding the division of opinion and authority in the government. The existence of disagreements, rifts and factionalism in the central government notwithstanding, it may also have been played on and exaggerated in the course of the autonomy negotiations to influence the Kurdish positions. See also the article by Delshad Rasuli, 'Tahrikati Ew Xainaney Ke Dayanawe Eran Mahwbetawe', in the same issue.

14 See the same article, *Kurdistan*, no. 60, 20 June 1946.

15 See Ghazi's speech expounding the content and significance of the 'Tehran-Tabriz' agreement in *Kurdistan*, no. 62, 27 June 1946. For the text of the agreement see Kurdistan no. 6.

16 *Kurdistan*, no. 72, 30 July 1946. However, writings expounding the idea that the Republic constituted an independent Kurdish state were by no means an unfamiliar feature of the discourse of *Kurdistan*, at times appearing alongside articles which explicitly argued for regional autonomy. This popular but unfounded idea was often assigned an evolutionary form, preceded by regional autonomy since the collapse of Reza Shah's rule in September 1941. An article entitled 'Unity Led Us to [the realization of] Our Wish' thus reads: 'Under the leadership of the president of Kurdistan, his Excellency Ghazi Muhammad, after four and half years of regional autonomy in free Kurdistan, the foundation of independence has now been laid and its sacred banner has been hoisted and the Kurd has realized his wish ... The Kurdish nation has demonstrated its ability to the whole world, and safeguarding the previous autonomy and the establishment of the present independence is an example of its ability ... Kurdistan has shown the world that it can administer its own affairs according to the Atlantic Charter [which says that] any nation which shows the ability to administer its own affairs has the right to be free and should not be subjected to foreign rule ...' (no. 11, 6 February 1946).

17 See relevant articles in *Kurdistan* nos. 52, 2 June; 65, 2 July; 66, 9 July; 67, 14 July; 69, 21 July; 72, 30 July; 73, 4 August; 79, 22 August 1946.

18 See articles by Ibrahim Naderi, Muhammad Hamidi and Muhammad Hussein Saif Ghazi in *Kurdistan*, nos 74, 6 August and 75, 11 August 1946.

19 In the issues available to me the first clear reference to Marx and Engels as the founders of communism is found in J. Bestoun's article 'Millati gawray Rous' (The Great Russian Nation), in Kurdistan no. 30, 1 April 1946. The reference makes a second appearance in an article entitled 'Ishtiraki chi'a?' (What is Communism?), no. 74, 6 August 1946. In both articles Marxism is perceived not as a specific modern ideology with specific conceptual structure and theoretical formation, but as the official ideology of the Soviet state. The appearance of articles with Marxist orientation or simply deploying class categories steadily increases after June 1946, but Marxist theoretical categories do not touch on crucial socio-economic and political issues such as tribes and tribalism, social reform, land reform etc. Nor are they used to define the political programme or ideological stance of the party. The emergence of the anti-imperialist discourse does not change the KDPI's orientation, although there are sometimes isolated attempts to give a new framework to the ideological representation of the movement and define its aims and objectives with reference to the struggle against imperialism, though almost always rhetorically. See sources cited in nos 3 and 4 above, also articles in *Kurdistan*, nos 72, 73, 74, dated 30 July, 4 August and 6 August 1946.

20 Theoretically, conceptualization of the relationship between nation and class has remained the Achilles heel of Marxist discourse on nationalism and national self-determination. Numerous Marxist theorists since the founding fathers have tried unsuccessfully to account for the class character of the nation and nationalism without falling into the trap of economism and reductionism. In Marxist discourse the modernity of the nation and its political character are both derived from its assumed class basis, the modern industrial bourgeoisie. The nation, it is thus believed, signifies the political form of modernity, and the nation state is as such a transitory phenomenon. Class essentialism and the discursive primacy of the category of labour have undermined attempts by Marxists to conceptualize nation, national rights and nationalist struggles as autonomous juridical-political categories with their

own efficacy. Lenin was the first to attempt to break the mould, borrowing the doctrine of national rights to self-determination from democratic theory to account for the pivotal status of the nation in the context of anti-imperialist national liberation movements, which he thus baptized. Lenin's contribution was facilitated by his theory of imperialism, which he deployed as the intersection of horizontal national and vertical class relations in the social formation. Lenin's theorization, if carried to its logical conclusion, may potentially lead the way out of a chronic crisis in Marxist theory, but it is seriously undermined by his ideological orthodoxy and commitment to the discursive primacy of the category of class and class relations. He thus refuses to sanction the autonomy of the national question, subordinating the discussion of national culture to the exigencies of class relations and subverting the theoretical premises of his own analysis. Of the Marxist theorists writing on the issues of nation and nationalism, Otto Bauer and Karl Renner are distinguished by their innovative approach, coming nearest to politically admitting the autonomy of the national question. See E. Nimni, *Marxism and Nationalism: The Theoretical Origins of a Political Crisis* (London, 1994), and P. James, *Nation Formation: Towards a Theory of Abstract Community* (London, 1996).

21 In the issues of *Kurdistan* available to me general references to the Soviet Union as the friend and supporter of the oppressed and hence of the Kurds are plentiful. It is interesting to note that in these general references the political stance of the Soviet Union and its anti-colonialist policies are almost never attributed to or derived from its Marxist-Leninist ideology. This connection is only made in more doctrinaire contributions permeated with Marxist class categories. The first three relatively systematic expositions of the Soviet anti-colonialist stance in *Kurdistan*, written by H. Khalilzadeh, M. Maaroufzad and A. Khosrawi respectively, represent this so-to-speak 'non-ideological' position; see no. 9, 2 February 1946.

22 *Kurdistan*, no. 72, 30 July 1946. Speech delivered on the occasion of his trip to Urmiya. Ghazi begins his address by reciting from the Quran.

23 See, for example, articles cited in note 4 above.

24 For example, articles by the Azeri democrat, and Abdul Ghadir Ahmad, the Iraqi Kurdish communist cited in note 3 above,

represent this position. Ahmad's article is particularly representative. It argues for a bi-polar view of the world, a world divided into two antagonistic blocs: colonial-imperialist versus anti-colonial-liberationist, led by the Soviet Union, and the necessity of siding with the latter against the former. The article by the Azeri democrat, on the other hand, defines the Azeri and the Kurdish movements as national-liberation and hence anti-colonial and anti-imperialist movements. In both articles Marxist class categories are deployed to identify political actors and their interests, and inter-class relations and conflicts are linked with the global conflict between the two colonial and anti-colonial camps. Abdul Ghadir Ahmad follows the same line of argument in his article 'Yek u Yek Deka Du' (One and One Make Two) as does Anwar Dilsoz's contribution 'Chman La Taran Dawe' (What Do We Want from Tehran), in *Kurdistan*, nos 56 and 57, 11 and 13 June 1946. For the growing influence of this view on the members of the KDPI see Seyyid Muhammad Hamidi's article 'Kurdistan Xo Radashkene u Besar Hamu Berhalistekda Zal Dabit', Hemin's speech and Ibrahim Naderi's contribution in *Kurdistan*, nos 41, 56 and 57, dated 29 April, 11 June and 13 June 1946.

25 See, for example, contributions cited in note 4 above. Similarly an article on the notion of democracy in no. 73, 4 August 1946, attempts a genealogy of the notion and explains its evolution in social class terms. But social class analysis and explanation of economic and political relations, as was pointed out earlier in this section, does not signify the position of the leadership in the Republic. It is almost invariably used by the younger generation of the Kurdish nationalists, and by no means in a uniform manner. The ideological orientation of the younger generation varies widely. For example, no. 85, 5 September 1946, contains another article by Seyyid Muhammad Hamidi on the subject of democracy and democratic rule, which is written strictly in liberal-democratic language. Hamidi's contribution aspires to a liberal-democratic government and there is no trace of Marxist class categories in his exposition.

26 The evidence of the strength of religion in the intellectual formation and outlook of the nationalist intelligentsia is too massive to ignore. The articles deploying class categories and analyses are mostly

permeated with popular Islamic discourse. There is, however, a clear difference in the invocation and use of religion and religious precepts and notions in the nationalist discourse between the old and new generations of the nationalist intelligentsia in the ranks of the government and the organizational structure of the party. Education and ideological orientation, rather than social and cultural factors, seem to be the main reason for this difference. In the writing of the older generation with traditional schooling, such as Mulla Hussein Majdie, Haji Baba Shaikh, Ahmad Elahie and Ghazi Muhammad himself, references to Islam and Islamic precepts and notions are an integral component of a political discourse steeped in nationalism and a limited perception of democracy and quest for civic rights and liberties. See, for example, the leader comment 'Destachilay Kurdi Pak' in *Kurdistan*, no. 7, 26 January 1946. Attempting to construct a historical national origin for the Kurds with reference to the Quran, it argues: 'It appears from the verses of the Quran that prophet Ibrahim was a Kurd.' Ghazi Muhammad's speech, on the occasion of his departure to Urmiya for negotiation with Azeri authorities on jurisdiction over three disputed towns, is another example. Here Ghazi starts his argument about the legitimacy of the Kurdish national rights and quest for freedom and progress by citing verses from the Quran; see *Kurdistan*, no. 72, 30 July 1946. See also Ahmad Elahie's article 'Saadati Beshar Bechiya?'; he repeatedly invokes the authority of the Quran to support his moral critique of personal gain and profiteering in public duties and community work (*Kurdistan*, no. 78, 18 August 1946). For the new generation of the nationalist intelligentsia with modern schooling who were also more widely exposed to modern secular ideologies, in particular versions of Soviet Marxism, the use of religion serves a tactical purpose often defined by their own brand of left-wing populism. In this respect see the writings of Seyyid Muhammad Hamidi, Dilshad Rasuli, Abdullah Dabaghi, Hashem Khalilzadeh, Muhammed Majdie and Hemin in issues of *Kurdistan* already cited variously in notes above. This point is discussed further below.

27 *Kurdistan*, no. 10, 4 February 1946. See also Ghazi Muhammad's orders, relayed by Muhammad Lahijani, the director of Owqaf (Religious/Islamic Charitable Foundations), regarding public

prayers at the end of the month of Ramazan and Eid celebrations (Gejni Ramazan) in *Kurdistan*, no. 78, 18 August 1946.

28 See: Ratification of Penal Code, in *Kurdistan*, no. 41, 29 April 1946.

29 I have discussed this issue in detail elsewhere in my works, see, for example, 'The Kurds and Their Others: Fragmented Identity and Fragmented Politics', *Comparative Studies of the Middle East, Africa and South East Asia*, vol. 18, no. 2 (1998) and 'Genealogies of the Kurds: Constructions of the Nation and National Identity in the Kurdish Nationalist Discourse', in Abbas Vali (ed.), *Essays on the Origins of Kurdish Nationalism* (Costa Mesa, 2003).

30 The tribal landlords, we have seen, did not form a homogeneous political bloc, and their positions regarding the Republic and the KDPI varied considerably. Some, like the Harki and Shikak and some Debokri Aghas, continued their collaboration with the central government throughout the brief existences of the Republic. Others, such as some prominent figures among the Mangur and Mamash Aghas, began shifting their allegiances as they started sensing the decline of the Republican power after the departure of the Red Army and in the course of the unsuccessful negotiation with Tehran. This latter group were also among the welcoming party who met General Homayouni in Miandoab on 14 December, a day before Ghazi Muhammad's surrender to the government forces. But there was a small group of tribal leaders with known nationalist credentials who remained loyal to the Republic, its leadership and its ideals. Fayzollabagi and some Gewirk Aghas were prominent among the loyalist Aghas who subsequently paid for their loyalty to the Republic by their lives. See McDowall, 1996 and Eagleton, 1963. On the pro-republican nationalism of the Fayzollabagi leadership, see 'Nalay Daroun u Hawari Brayani Fayzollabagi u Saqqizi – Rola Azadixozakani Kurdistan', in *Kurdistan*, no. 79, 22 August 1946.

31 See Atabaki, 2000, pp. 168–78 and Abrahamian, 1982.

Selected Bibliography

Unpublished Sources

Official Great Britain Unpublished: Public Record Office, London
Series FO 248, FO 371 (Diplomatic Reports and Correspondence)
1921–40, 1941–7

FO 248 nos: 1224, 1225, 1226, 1246, 1278, 1331, 1400, 1405, 1410,

FO 371 nos: 3858, 4147, 4192, 4930, 5067, 6347, 6348, 6434, 6442, 7781, 7802, 7803, 7805, 7806, 7807, 7808, 7824, 7826, 7827, 7835, 7844, 9009, 9010, 9018, 10097, 10098, 10128, 10158, 10833, 10481, 10842, 11484, 11491, 12264, 12265, 12288, 12291, 13027, 13760, 13781, 16063, 16076, 17912, 17915, 18987, 20037, 23261

FO 371 nos: 42582, 27080, 27155, 27244, 27245, 31351, 31388, 31390, 31391, 31394, 31402, 31414, 34940, 35057, 35071, 35072, 35092, 35093, 40219, 40038, 40041, 40173, 40177, 40178, 45340, 45346, 45440, 45447, 45448, 45450, 45459, 45462, 45488, 45503, 52369, 52667, 52698, 52702, 61678, 61986

Kurdish Sources

1. Newspapers and Journals

Nishtiman, issues 1–9 printed July 1943–December 1944; issues 1–6 repr. in J. Nebez, *Gowari Nishtman: Zimani Hali Komalai J.K.* (Stockholm, 1985); issues 7–9 in private collections.

Kurdistan: 82 surviving issues printed during December 1945–December 1946 in Mahabad, repr. in R. Saleh and S. Saleh (eds), *Rojnamay Kurdistan: Mahabad, 1324–1325* (Sulaimani, 2007).

Gzing, nos. 13, 14, 15 (Stockholm, 1996, 1997).

2. Books and Articles

Ahmad, Kemal Mazher, 'Komari Mahabad u Kitebakay Eagleton', *Beyan*, no. 5 (February 1971).

——, *Chand Laparek la Mejuy Gali Kurd*, vol. 1 (Baghdad, 1985).

——, *Kurd u Meju* (Baghdad, 1983).

——, *Tegayishtni Rasti: Sheweni la Rozhnamanusi Kurdida* (Baghdad, 1978).

Ali, K., *Soviet u Bzutnawey Nishtimani Kurd* (Salzburg, 1986).

Awlia, Chalabi, *Kurd la Mejuy Drawsekanida, Sayahat Namay Awlia Chalabi* (Baghdad, 1979).

Ayubzadeh, A., *Chep le Rojhelati Kurdistan: Komala u Dozi Nasionali Kurd* (n.p., 2002).

Blorian, G., *Alekok, Be Sar Hatekani Siyasi Jiyanim* (Stockholm, 1997).

Emin, N.M., *Hokumati Kurdistan (Rebandani 1324/1946-Sermawazi 1325/1946): Kurd La Gamaey Soviet Da* (Utrecht, 1993).

Gaftan, S., *Mejuy Nataway Kurd* (Baghdad, 1969).

Ghassemlou, A.R., *Chil Sal Khabat la Penawi Azadi; Kurtayek la Mejuy Hizbi Demokrati Kurdistani Iran*, vol. 1 (n.p., 1985).

Gohary, H., *Komalay Jiyanawai Kurdistan* (Stockholm, 1999).

Jabari, A.M., *Mejuy Rozhnamagari Kurdi* (Sulaimani, 1970).

Jalil, J., *Hinde Simay Jiyani Komalayati we Kulturi Kurd La Kotayi Saday Nozda u Saretay Saday Bistemda* (Stockholm, 1993).

Hawar, M.R., *Shaikh Mahmoudi Garaman u Dawlatekay Khwaraway Kurdistan* (London, 1990).

——, *Ismail Aghay Shokak u Bezutnaway Kurd* (London, 1997).

Hemin (M.A. Shaikh Al-Islami), *Tarik u Roun* (Baghdad, 1974).

Hussami, K., *Kómár-í Demokrát-í Kurdistán yá Khud-Mukhtárí?* (Stockholm, 1986).

——, *Le Bireweriyekanim*, 11 vols (Stockholm, 1990–2001).

——, *Peda Chuneve: Bezutnevey Nishtimani Kurd la Kurdistani Eran 1947–1978*, vol. 2 (Stockholm, 1997).

Izzat, M. Mulla, *Komari Milli Mahabad* (Stockholm, 1986).

Karimi, A., *Jiyan u Beserhati Abdulrahman Zabihi 'Mamosta Ulema'* (Goteborg, 1999).

Kurdo, Q., *Tarixa Edebiyata Kurdi* (Stockholm, 1983).

——, *Hendek Biru Bawari Hala la Baray Zeman u Mejuy Kurdi* (Baghdad, 1974).

Lazariyev, M.S., *Keshay Kurd (1896–1917)*, 2 vols (Baghdad, 1989).

Mala Sahib, M.B., *Peshawa Ghazi Muhammad u Komari Mahabad* (Sulaimani, 1971).

Mukriani, H.H., *Kurdistani Mukrian ya Atropatiyan* (Rawanduz, 1938).

——, *Dawleti Jumhoori Kurdistan*, 2 vols (Stockholm, 1992, 1995).

Nebaz, J., *Biry Natawayi Kurdi* (Stockholm, 1984).

——, *Kurdistan we Shoreshakany* (Stockholm, 1985).

——, *Gowari Nishtiman* (Stockholm, 1985).

Sabir, R., *Kultur u Nasionalism* (Stockholm, 2003).

Sajjadie, A., *Mejuy Adabi Kurdi* (Baghdad, 1971).

——, *Shoreshakani Hurd u Kurdo Komari Iraq* (Baghdad, 1959).

——, 'Roushanbiri Kewn u Neu la Kurdistanda u Pelay aw Roushanbiray la Derawe', *Gowari Kori Zanyari Kurd*, no. 4 (1976).

Samadi, S.M. (ed.), *Komalay J. K. Chí bu, Chí Dawíst, u Chí lé Ba-Sarhát?* (Mahabad, 1981).

Shamzini, A., *Julaneway Rizgari Nishtimani Kurdistan* (Sulaimani, 1998).

Vasiliyeva, I.E., *Kurdistani Xareway Rojhelat La Saday Hevda ta Saretay Saday Nozda* (Hawler, 1997).

Zaki, M.A., *Tarikhi Kurd Kurdistan* (Baghdad, 1936).

Persian Sources

Adamiyyat, F., *Fekr-e Demokrasi-ye Ejtemai dar Nahzat-e Mashrutiyyat-e Iran* (Tehran, 1354/1975).

——, *Andisheh-ye Taraghi va Hokumat-e Ghanun* (Tehran, 1351/1973).

——, *Majlis-e Awwal va Bohran-e Azadi* (Tehran, 1370/1992).

——, *Ideology-ye Nahzat-e Mashrutiyyat-e Iran* (Tehran, 1354/1975).

Adl, Mustafa (Mansur al-.Saltaneh), *Huquq-e Asasi ya Osul-e Mashrutiyyat* (Tehran, 1327/1948).

Ahmadi, H., *Gowmiyyat ve Gowmgerai dar Iran, Az Afsaneh ta Wageiyyat* (Tehran, 1378/2000).

Ardalan, M., *Lob al-Tawarikh* (Tehran, 1356/1978).

Asnad-i Tarikhi-ye Junbesh-ye Kargari, Susyal-Dimukrasi va Kumunisiti-ye Iran, 5 vols (Florence, 1353/1974).

Badal, S., *Tarikhche-ye Junbeshha-ye Melli-ye Kurd* (KDPI Publications, 1363/1985).

Bahar, Muhammad Taqi (Malek ush-Shu'ara), 'Hezb-e Demokrat-e Azerbaijan', *Iran-e Ma* (16 September 1945/1324).

——, *Tarikh-e Mukhtasar-e Ahzab-e Siyasi-ye Iran* (Tehran, 1st edn, 1322/1944; repr. 1356/1978).

Bedlisi, Amir Sharaf Khan, *Sharafnama: Tarikh-e Mofasal-e Kurdistan* (Tehran, 1344/1965).

Behnam, J., *Iraniyan va Andisheh-ye Tajadod* (Tehran, 1375/1997).

Behrami, A., *Tarikh-e Siyasi va Ejtemai-ye Iran Az Zaman-e Naseraddin Shah ta Akhar-e Selseleh-ye Qajariyyeh* (Tehran, 1344/1966).

Berard, V., *Enghelabat-e Iran* (Tehran, 1356/ 1977).

Etehadiyyeh, M., *Peydayesh va Tahawol-e Ahzab-e Siyasi-ye Mashrutiyyat: Dowreh-ye Awwal va Dowom-e Majlis-e Shora-ye Melli* (Tehran, 1361/1983).

Iransky, S., et al., *Enghelab-e Mashrutiyyat-e Iran va Rishehayeh Ejtemai va Eghtesadi-ye An* (Tehran, 1330/1951).

Iskandar, Beg-e Monshi, *Tarikh-e Alam Aray-eyh Abbasi*, 2 vols (Tehran, 1334/1955, 1335/1956).

Jalaiepoor, H.R., *Kurdistan, Ellal-e Tadawom-e Bohran pas az Ingilab-e Islami* (Tehran, 1372/1994).

Kambakhsh, Abd us-Samad, *Nazari be Junbesh-e Kargari va Kumunisti dar Iran*, 2 vols (Stockholm, 1351–3/1972–4).

Kasravi, A., *Tarikh-e Hizhdah Sale-yeh Azerbaijan* (Tehran, 1346/1967).

——, *Tarikh-e Mashruteh-ye Iran* (Tehran, 1340/1961).

Kuhi-yi Kirmani, H., *As Shahrivar-e 1320 ta Faji'eh-ye Azerbaijan va Zanjan*, 2 vols (Tehran, n.d.).

Majd ul-Eslam Kermani, *Tarikh-e Enhetat-e Majlis* (Esfahan, 1356/1978).

Mahdawyi, A., *Táríkh-e Rawábit-e Kháridjí-e Irán: Az Ibtidá-e Dawrán-e Safavieh tá Páyán-e Jang-e Duham-e Jihání* (Tehran, 1368/1990).

Malekzadeh, M., *Tarikh-e Engelab-e Mashrutiyyat-e Iran*, 3 vols (Tehran, 1363/1985).

Mardukh, A., *Ghiyam-e Shaikh Ubaidallah-e Shamzini dar Kordestan* (Tehran, 1355/1977).

Mastoreh Kurdistani (Mah Shraf Khanim Gaderi), *Tarikh-e Ardalan* (Tehran, 1343/1965).

Melikov, A.S., *Esteghrar-e Diktatori-ye Reza Khan dar Iran* (Tehran, 1358/1981).

Mirza, Shokrallah Sanandaji, *Tohfeh-ye Naseri* (Tehran, 1366/1988).

Mohit-e Tabatabai, M., *Tarikh-e Tahlili-ye Matbua'at-e Iran* (Tehran, 1366/1988).

Molla Muhammad, Sharif Ghazi, *Zobdaaltawarikh: Sanandaj dar Tarikh-e Kurdistan* (Tehran, 1379/2001).

Pesyan, N.G., *Marg Bud Bazgasht Ham Bud* (Tehran, 1326/1947).

——, *Az Karaneha-yeh Aras ta Mahabad-e Khoonin*, (Tehran, 1327/1948).

Samadi, S.M., *Neghi Digar be Komala-e J. K.* (Mahabad, 1984).

——, *Tarikhche-yeh Mahabad* (Mahabad, 1984).

Sepehr, A.A. (Muvarrekh al-Dauleh), 'Qiyam-e Pishehvari', *Salnamih-ye Dunya*, vol. 14 (1337/1958).

Shaji'i, Zahra, *Namayandigan-e Majlis-e Shaura-ye Milli dar bist-u-yik Daurih-ye Ghanunguzari* (Tehran, 1344/1965).

——, *Vizarat va Vaziran dar Iran*, vol. 1 (Tehran, 1976).

Sharifi, A., *Ashayer-e Shikak ve Sharhe Zendeghi-ye Anha be Rehbari Ismail Agha Semko* (Tehran, 1348).

Soudaghar, M., *Nezam-e Arbab va Rayyati dar Iran* (Tehran, 1357/1979).

Tabari, E., *Jameh-ye Iran dar Douran-e Reza Shah* (Tudeh Publications, 1356/1978).

Yasami, R., *Kurd ve Rishe-yeh Najadi Uo* (Tehran, 1334/1956).

Yazdani, S., *Sour-e Esrafil: Nameh-ye Azadi* (Tehran, 1386/1908).

English Sources (Books and Articles)

Abrahamian, E., 'The Crowd in Iranian Politics 1905–1953', *Past and Present*, vol. 41 (December 1968).

——, 'Communism and Communalism in Iran: The Tudeh and the Firqah-i Demukrat', *International Journal of Middle Eastern Studies*, vol. 1, no. 4 (October 1970).

——, 'Factionalism in Iran: Political Groups in the 14th Parliament (1944–6)', *Middle Eastern Studies*, vol. 14, no. 1 (January 1978).

——, 'The Strength and Weaknesses of the Labour Movement in Iran in 1941–53', in Michael Bonine and Nikkie Keddie (eds), *Continuity and Change in Modern Iran* (Albany, 1981).

——, *Iran Between Two Revolutions* (Princeton, 1982).

Acheson, D., *Present at the Creation: My Years in the State Department* (New York, 1969).

Afary, J., *The Constitutional Revolution in Iran, 1906-1909* (New York, 1996).

Agamben, G. *Homo Sacer: Sovereign Power and the Bare Life* (Chicago, 1998).

——, *State of Exception* (Chicago, 2005).

Aghajanian, A., 'Ethnic Inequality in Iran: An Overview', *International Journal of Middle East Studies*, no. 15 (1983).

Alaolmalki, N., 'The New Iranian Left', *Middle East Journal*, vol. 41, no. 2 (1987).

Algar, H., *Mirza Malkum Khan: A Study in the History of Iranian Modernism* (Berkeley and Los Angeles, 1973).

——, *Religion and State in Iran, 1785–1906* (Berkeley and Los Angeles, 1969).

Allouche, A., *The Origins and the Development of the Ottoman-Safavid Conflict (906–1061/1500-1555)* (Berlin, 1983).

Amirarjomand, S., 'The Constitutional Law', in E. Yarshater, *Encyclopaedia Iranica*, vol. 6 (Costa Mesa, 1993).

Anderson, Benedict, *Imagined Communities: Reflections on the Origins and Spread of Nationalism* (London, 1984).

Arfa, Hassan, *The Kurds: A Historical and Political Study* (London, 1966).

Ashraf, A., 'Bazaar-Mosque Alliance: "The Social Bases of Revolts and Revolutions"', *International Journal of Politics, Culture, and Society*, vol. 1, no. 4 (1988).

——, 'Theocracy and Charisma: New Men of Power in Iran', *International Journal of Politics, Culture and Society*, vol. 4, no. 1 (1990).

Atteridge, A., et al. (eds), *Post-Structuralism and the Question of History* (Cambridge, 1988).

Avery, P., *Modern Iran* (London, 1965).

Avery, P.W., and Simmons, J.B., 'Persia on a Cross of Silver 1880–1890', *Middle Eastern Studies*, vol. 10, no. 3 (1974).

Azimi, F., *Iran: The Crisis of Democracy in Iran* (New York, 1989).

Banani, A., *The Modernization of Iran, 1921–1941* (Stanford, 1961).

——, 'Modernization and Reform from Above: the Case of Iran', *Journal of Politics*, vol. 32 (1970).

Baram, P., *The Department of State in the Middle East, 1919–1945* (Philadelphia, 1978).

Barnett, M., 'Identity and Alliances in the Middle East', in Peter J. Katzenstein (ed.), *The Culture of National Security. Norms and Identity in World Politics* (New York, 1996).

Barth, Fredrik, *Principles of Social Organization of Southern Kurdistan* (Oslo, 1953).

——, *Nomads of South Persia: the Basseri Tribe of the Khamseh Confederacy* (Oslo, 1961).

Bayat, M., *Iran's First Constitutional Revolution: Shi'ism and the Constitutional Revolution of 1905–1909* (London, 1991).

Beetham, D., *Max Weber and the Theory of Modern Politics* (Cambridge, 1987).

Beiner, R. (ed.), *Theorizing Nationalism* (Albany, NY, 1999).

Benhabib, S., *Democracy and Difference* (New York, 2001).

Benjamin, W., 'Critique of Violence', in W. Benjamin, *Reflections* (New York, 1968).

Bhabha, H., *Nations and Nationalism* (London, 1990).

Bharier, J., *Economic Development in Iran, 1900–1970* (London, 1971).

Bill, J.A., *The Eagle and the Lion: The Tragedy of American-Iranian Relations* (New Haven, CT, 1988).

Bill, J., 'The Study of Middle East Politics 1946–1996: A Stocktaking', *Middle East Journal*, vol. 50, no. 4 (1996).

—— and Roger Louis, W. (eds), *Mussadiq, Nationalism and Oil* (Austin, 1986).

Binder, L., *Iran: Political Development in a Changing Society* (Berkeley, CA, 1962).

Bishop, I.L.B. *Journeys in Persia and Kurdistan*, 2 vols (London, 1891).

Bois, T., 'Kurds and Kurdistan: History from 1920 to the Present', in C.E. Bosworth et al. (eds), *Encyclopaedia of Islam* (Leiden, 1986).

Bonine, Michael, and Keddie, Nikki R. (eds), *Modern Iran: The Dialectics of Continuity and Change* (Albany, NY, 1981).

Bosworth, C.E. (ed), *Iran and Islam* (Edinburgh, 1971).

Breiner, P., *Max Weber and Democratic Politics* (Ithaca, NY, 1996).

Brown, L.C., *International Politics and the Middle East: Old Rules, Dangerous Game* (Princeton, 1984).

Browne, E.G., *The Persian Revolution of 1905–1909* (Cambridge, 1910.

Brubaker, R., *Nationalism Reframed: Nationhood and the National Question in the New Europe* (London, 1996).

Bruinessen, Martin van, 'The Kurds between Iran and Iraq', *Middle East Report*, no. 41 (1980).

——, 'Popular Islam, Kurdish Nationalism and Rural Revolt: The Rebellion of Sheikh Said in Turkey', in J.M. Bak and G. Beneche (eds), *Religion and Rural Revolt* (Manchester, 1984).

——, 'The Ethnic Identity of the Kurds', in P.A. Andrews (ed.), *Ethnic Groups in the Republic of Turkey* (Wiesbaden, 1989).

——, *Agha, Shaikh and State: On the Social and Political Structures of Kurdistan* (London, 1992).

Bryson, T.A., *American Diplomatic Relations with the Middle East, 1784-1975: A Survey* (New Jersey, 1977).

Brzezinski, Z.K., *The Grand Chessboard: American Primacy and Its Geostrategic Imperatives* (New York, 1998).

Buci-Glucksmann, Christine, *Gramsci and the State* (London, 1980).

Bullard, Sir Reader, *Britain and the Middle East: From the Earliest Times to 1950* (London, 1951).

——, *The Camels Must Go: An Autobiography* (London, 1961).

——, 'Persia in the Two World Wars', *Journal of the Royal Central Asian Society*, vol. 50 (1963).

Bullock, J., and Morris, H., *No Friends but the Mountains: The Tragic History of the Kurds* (London, 1992).

Burton, H., 'The Kurds', *The Journal of the Central Asian Society*, vol. 31, pt 1 (January 1944).

Calhoun, C. (ed.), *Habermas and the Public Sphere* (Cambridge, MA, 1992).

Chaliand, G. (ed.), *People without a Country: The Kurds and Kurdistan* (London, 1980).

Chaqueiri, C., *The Soviet Socialist Republic of Iran, 1920–1921: Birth of the Trauma* (Pittsburgh, 1995).

Chatterjee, Partha, *Nationalist Thought and the Colonial World: A Derivative Discourse?* (London, 1988).

Coan, F.G., *Yesterdays in Persia and Kurdistan* (Claremont, CA, 1939).

Connor, W., *The National Question in Marxist-Leninist Theory and Strategy* (Princeton, 1984).

Cottam, Richard, *Nationalism in Iran* (Pittsburgh, 1964).

——, 'The United States, Iran and the Cold War', *Iranian Studies*, vol. 3, no. 1 (Winter 1970): pp. 2–22.

——, *Nationalism in Iran: Updated through 1978* (2nd edn, Pittsburgh, 1979).

——, *Iran and the United States: A Cold War Case Study* (London, 1988).

Cruickshank, A., 'International Aspects of the Kurdish Question', *International Relations*, vol. 3, no. 6 (1969).

Curzon, G.N., *Persia and the Persian Question*, 2 vols (London, 1969).

Dean, M., *Governmentality: Power and Rule in Modern Society* (London, 1999).

——, *Critical and Effective Histories: Foucault's Methods and Historical Sociology* (London, 1994).

Derrida, J., 'Force of Law: The Mythical Foundations of Authority', in P. Cornell et al. (eds), *Deconstruction and the Possibility of Justice* (London, 1992).

Douglas, W.O., *Strange Lands and Friendly People* (New York, 1951).

Driver, G.R., 'The Name Kurd and Its Philological Foundations', *Journal of the Royal Asiatic Society*, vol. 8 (1921).

Eagleton, W. Jr., *The Kurdish Republic of 1946* (London, 1963).

Edmonds, C.J., *Kurds, Turks and Arabs: Politics, Travel and Research in North-Eastern Iraq 1919–1925* (London, 1957).

——, 'Kurdish Nationalism', *Journal of Contemporary History*, vol. 6, no. 1 (1971).

Elphinston, W., 'The Kurdish Question', *International Affairs*, vol. 22, no. 1 (January 1946).

Elwell-Sutton, L.P., 'Political Parties in Iran: 1941–1948', *Middle East Journal*, vol. 3, no. 1 (1949).

——, 'The Iranian Press, 1941–1947', *Iran*, vol. 6 (1968).

Emerson, R., *From Empire to Nation: The Rise to Self-Determination of Asian and African People* (Cambridge, MA, 1960).

Entesar, N., 'The Kurdish Mosaic of Discord', *Third World Quarterly*, vol. 11, no. 4 (October 1989).

——, *Kurdish Ethnonationalism* (Boulder, CO, 1992).

Entner, M.L., *Russo-Persian Commercial Relations, 1828–1914* (Gainesville, TX, 1965).

Esman, M.J., and Rabinovich, I. (eds), *Ethnicity, Pluralism and the State in the Middle East* (Ithaca, NY, 1988).

Eskandar Beg Monshi, *History of Shah Abbas the Great* (Boulder, CO, 1978).

Fateh, M., *The Economic Conditions of Persia* (London, 1926).

Fatemi, F., *The U.S.S.R. in Iran: The Background History of Russian and Anglo-American Conflict in Iran, Its Effects on Iranian Nationalism, and the Fall of the Shah* (London, 1980).

Fatemi, N., *Diplomatic History of Persia, 1917–1923* (New York, 1952).

——, *Oil Diplomacy: Powder Keg in Iran* (New York, 1954).

Fawcett, L., 'The Struggle for Persia: The Azerbaijan Crisis of 1946', unpublished Ph.D. dissertation (University of Oxford, 1988).

——, 'Invitation to the Cold War: British Policy in Iran, 1941–1947', in Ann Deighton (ed.), *Britain and the First Cold War* (London, 1990).

——, *Iran and the Cold War: the Azerbaijan Crisis of 1946* (Cambridge, 1992).

Fishman, J.A., et al., *Language Problems of Developing Nations* (New York, 1968).

Forbes-Leith, F.A.C., *Checkmate: Fighting Tradition in Central Persia* (London, 1927).

Foucault, M., *The Order of Things* (London, 1974).

——, *Discipline and Punish: The Birth of the Prison* (London, 1977).

———, *The History of Sexuality*, vol. 1 (London, 1979).

———, *Society Must Be Defended* (London, 2003).

Fox, R.G. (ed.), *Nationalist Ideologies and the Production of National Culture* (Washington, DC, 1990).

Gause, F.G., III, 'Sovereignty, Statecraft and Stability in the Middle East', *Journal of International Affairs*, vol. 45, no. 2 (1992): pp. 441–67.

Gavan, S.S., *Kurdistan: Divided Nation of the Middle East* (London, 1958).

Gellner, E., *Nations and Nationalism* (Oxford, 1986).

Ghassemlou, A., *Kurdistan and the Kurds* (London, 1965).

Ghods, M.R., *Iran in the Twentieth Century: A Political History* (London, 1989).

———, 'The Iranian Communist Movement Under Reza Shah', *Middle East Studies*, vol. 26, no. 4 (October 1990).

Gokalp, Z., *Turkish Nationalism and Western Civilisation* (London, 1959).

Goode, J.F., *The United States and Iran 1946–51* (London, 1989).

Goode, L., *Jurgen Habermas: Democracy and the Public Sphere* (London, 2005).

Gramsci, A., *Selections from the Prison Notebooks* (London, 1971).

Gupta, R.N., *Iran: An Economic Study* (New Delhi, 1947).

Habermas, J., *The Structural Transformation of the Public Sphere: An Inquiry into a Category of Bourgeois Society* (Cambridge, MA, 1989).

Hackforth, J.C., 'The Kurds and Their Future', *World Affairs*, vol. 12 (1964).

Haddad, W., and Ochsenwald, W. (eds), *Nationalism in a Non-National State: The Dissolution of the Ottoman Empire* (Columbus, OH, 1977).

Halliday, F., 'The Middle East, the Great Powers and the Cold War' in A. Sayigh and Shlaim (ed.), *The Cold War and the Middle East* (Oxford, 1997).

Hamilton, A.M., *Road through Kurdistan* (London, 1937).

Hamzavi, A.H., 'Iran and the Tehran Conference', *International Affairs*, vol. 20, no. 2 (April 1944).

Harris, G., 'Ethnic Conflict and the Kurds', *Annals of the American Academy of Political and Social Sciences*, no. 433 (1977).

Hassanpour, A., *Nationalism and Language in Kurdistan, 1918–1985* (San Francisco, 1992).

——, 'Kurdish Studies: Orientalist, Positivist and Critical Approaches', *Middle East Journal*, vol. 47, no.1 (1993).

——, 'National Movements in Azerbaijan and Kurdistan', in John Foran (ed.), *Iran: A Century of Revolution* (Minneapolis, 1994).

Hay, W.R., *Two Years in Kurdistan: Experiences of a Political Officer* (London, 1921).

Hayman, A., *Elusive Kurdistan: The Struggle for Recognition* (London, 1988).

Hazen, W., 'Minorities in Revolt: The Kurds of Iran, Iraq, Syria, and Turke', in R.D. McLaurin (ed.), *The Political Role of Minority Groups in the Middle East* (New York, 1979).

Hesse, G.R., 'The Iranian Crisis of 1945–6 and the Cold War', *Political Science Quarterly*, vol. 89, no. 1 (1974).

Helfgott, L.M., 'The Structural Foundations of the National Minority Problems in Revolutionary Iran', *Iranian Studies*, vol. 8 (1980): pp. 1–4.

Heyd, U., *Foundations of Turkish Nationalism: The Life of Ziya Gokalp* (London, 1950).

Higgins, P.J., 'Minority-State Relations in Contemporary Iran', *Iranian Studies*, vol. 17, no. 1 (1984).

Hinnebusch, R., *The International Politics of the Middle East* (Manchester, 2003).

Hobsbawm, Eric, *Nations and Nationalism since 1780* (Cambridge, 1990).

Hourani, Albert, *Minorities in the Arab World* (Oxford, 1947).

——, *A Vision of History: Near Eastern and Other Essays* (London, 1961).

——, *The Emergence of the Modern Middle East* (London, 1981).

Howell, W., 'Soviet Policy and the Kurds: A Study of National Minority Problems in Soviet Policy', unpublished Ph.D. Dissertation (University of Virginia, 1965).

Hurewitz, J., *Middle East Dilemmas: The Background of United States Policy* (New York, 1953), vols 1 and 2.

Irani, R., *American Diplomacy: An Option Analysis of the Azerbaijan Crisis, 1945–1946* (Strategic Studies Institute, US Army War College, 1978).

Issawi, C. (ed.), *The Economic History of Iran: 1800–1914* (Chicago, 1971).

Jabar, F.A., and Dawod, H. (eds), *The Kurds: Nationalism and Politics* (London, 2006).

James, P., *Nation Formations: Towards a Theory of Abstract Communities* (London, 1996).

Jwaideh, W., *The Kurdish National Movement: Its Origins and Development* (Syracuse, NY, 2006).

Karpat, K.H., *An Inquiry into the Social Foundations of Nationalism in the Ottoman Empire* (New Jersey, 1973).

Katouzian, H., *Mussadeq and the Struggle for Power in Iran* (London, 2002).

Keddie, Nikki R., *Religion and Rebellion in Iran: The Tobacco Protest of 1891–1892* (London, 1966).

———, *An Islamic Response to Imperialism: Political and Religious Writings of Sayyid Jamal ad-Din 'al-Afghani'* (Berkeley, CA, 1968).

———, *Historical Obstacles to Agrarian Change in Iran* (Claremont, CA, 1960).

———, 'The Iranian Village Before and After the Land Reform', *Journal of Contemporary History*, vol. 3, no. 3 (1963).

———, *Roots of Revolution* (New Haven, 1981).

Kedourie, E. (ed.), *Nationalism in Asia and Africa* (New York, 1970).

Kellas, J., *The Politics of Nationalism* (London, 1991).

Kinnane, D., *The Kurds and Kurdistan* (London, 1964).

Kohn, H., *The Idea of Nationalism* (New York, 1967).

Kolko, G., and Kolko, J., *The Limits of Power: The World and United States Foreign Policy, 1945–1954* (New York, 1972).

Koohi-Kamali Dehkordi, F., 'The Republic of Kurdistan: Its Rise and Fall', unpublished MA dissertation (University of Oxford, 1986).

———, *The Political Development of the Kurds in Iran: Pastoral Nomadism* (Basingstoke, 2003).

Kreyenbroek, P.G., and Sperl, S. (eds), *The Kurds: A Contemporary Overview* (London, 1992).

Kritzman, L. (ed.), *Michel Foucault: Politics, Philosophy and Culture* (London, 1988).

Kuniholm, B., *The Origins of the Cold War in the Near East: Great Power Conflict and Diplomacy in Iran, Turkey and Greece* (Princeton, 1980).

Kushner, D., *The Rise of Turkish Nationalism, 1876–1908* (London, 1977).

La Feber, W., *America, Russia and the Cold War in Iran 1945-1984* (New York, 1985).

Ladjevardi, H., 'The Origins of U.S. Support for an Autocratic Iran', *International Journal of Middle East Studies*, no. 15 (1983).

Lambton, A.K.S., 'Iran in the Middle East: A Political and Economic Survey', *Royal Institute of International Affairs* (London, 1950).

——, *Landlord and Peasant in Iran* (Oxford, 1953).

Lassman, P., and Speir, R. (eds), *Weber: Political Writings* (Cambridge, 1994).

Lenczowski, G., *Russia and the West in Iran 1918–1948: A Study in Big Power Rivalry* (Ithaca, NY, 1949).

Llobera, J.R., *The God of Modernity: The Development of Nationalism in Western Europe* (Oxford, 1994).

Lockhart, L., 'The Constitutional Laws of Persia: An Outline of Their Origin and Development', *The Middle East Journal*, vol. 8, no. 4 (Autumn 1959).

Louis, W.R., *The British Empire in the Middle East 1945–1951: Arab Nationalism, The United States and Postwar Imperialism* (Oxford, 1984).

Lytle, M.H., *The Origins of the Iranian-American Alliance 1941–1953* (New York, 1987).

McCrone, D., *The Sociology of Nationalism: Tomorrow's Ancestors* (London, 1998).

McDaniel, R.A., *The Shuster Mission and the Persian Constitutional Revolution* (Minneapolis, 1974).

McDowall, D., *A Modern History of the Kurds* (London, 1994).

Machalski, F., 'Political Parties in Iran in the Years 1941–1946', *Folia Orientalia*, vol. 3, nos 1–2 (1961).

Maier, C.S. (ed.), *Changing Boundaries of the Political: Essays on the Evolving Balance between the State and Society, Public and Private in Europe* (Cambridge, 1987).

Malcolm, Sir John, *The History of Persia*, 2 vols (London, 1815).

Marshal, T.H., *Citizenship and Social Class* (Cambridge, 1950).

Martin, J., *Gramsci's Political Analysis: A Critical Introduction* (Basingstoke, 1998).

Marx, K., *Capital*, vol. 1 (Moscow, 1965).

Meinecke, F., *Cosmopolitanism and the National State* (New Jersey, 1970).

Mobley, R.A., 'A Study of the Relations between the Mahabad Republic and Azerbaijan Democrat Republic: Turbulent Alliance and Its Impact upon the Mahabad Republic of 1946', seminar paper submitted in partial fulfilment of the requirement of the course on 'Modernisation in the Islamic World' (Georgetown University, Washington, DC, 1979).

Mouffe, C. (ed.), *The Challenge of Carl Schmitt* (London, 1999).

Nancy, J.-L., *The Inoperative Community* (Minneapolis, 1991).

——, *The Birth to Presence* (Stanford, CA, 1993).

Natali, D., *The Kurds and the State: An Evolving National Identity in Iraq, Turkey, and Iran* (Syracuse, NY, 2005).

Nimni, E., *Marxism and Nationalism: The Theoretical Origins of a Political Crisis* (London, 1994).

O'Brien, C.C., *Godland: Reflections on Religion and Nationalism* (Cambridge, MA, 1988).

Olson, R., *The Emergence of Kurdish Nationalism and the Sheikh Said Rebellion 1880–1925* (Austin, 1989).

——, 'Five Stages of Kurdish Nationalism: 1880-1990', *Journal of the Institute of Muslim Minority Affairs*, vol. 12, no. 2 (July 1991).

——(ed.), *The Kurdish Nationalist Movement in the 1990s* (Lexington, 1996).

——, *The Goat and the Butcher* (New York, 2005).

Periwal, S. (ed.), *Notions of Nationalism* (Budapest, 1995).

Perry, J.R., 'Forced Migration in Iran during the 17th and 18th Centuries', *Iranian Studies*, vol. 8, no. 4 (1975).

Ramazani, R., 'The Autonomous Republic of Azerbaijan and the Kurdish People's Republic: Their Rise and Fall', *Studies on the Soviet Union*, vol. 11, no. 4 (1971).

——, *Iran's Foreign Policy 1941–1973: A Study of Foreign Policy in Modernizing Nations* (Charlottesville, 1975).

——, 'The Republic of Azerbaijan and the Kurdish Peoples' Republic', in T. Hammond (ed.), *The Anatomy of Communist Takeover* (New York, 1975).

Rezun, M., *The Soviet Union and Iran: Soviet Policy in Iran from the Beginning of the Pahlavi Dynasty until the Soviet Invasion in 1941* (Geneva, 1981).

Roosevelt, A. Jr., 'The Kurdish Republic of Mahabad', *The Middle East Journal*, vol. 1, no. 3 (July 1947); repr. in G. Chaliand (ed.), *People Without a Country* (London, 1980).

Rossow, Robert Jr., 'The Battle of Azerbaijan, 1946', *The Middle East Journal*, vol. 10, no. 1 (Winter 1956).

Rothschild, J., *Ethnopolitics: A Conceptual Framework* (New York, 1981).

Rubin, B., *Paved with Good Intentions* (New York, 1980).

——, *The Great Powers in the Middle East, 1941–1947: The Road to the Cold War* (London, 1980).

Safrastian, A., *Kurds and Kurdistan* (London, 1948).

Schmidt, D.A., *Journey Among Brave Men* (Boston, 1964).

Schmitt, Carl, *The Crisis of Parliamentary Democracy* (Cambridge, MA, 1985).

——, *Political Theology: Four Chapters on the Concept of Sovereignty* (Cambridge, MA, 1986).

——, *The Concept of the Political* (Chicago, 1996).

Seton-Watson, H., *Nations and States: An Enquiry into the Origins of Nations and Politics of Nationalism* (Boulder, CO, 1977).

Shuster, William Morgan, *The Strangling of Persia* (New York, 1912).

Sicker, M., *The Bear and the Lion: Soviet Imperialism and Iran* (New York, 1988).

Smith, A., *The Ethnic Origins of Nations* (Oxford, 1988).

Strohmeier, M., *Crucial Images in the Presentation of a Kurdish National Identity* (Leiden, 2003).

Sykes, P., 'Persia and Azarbaijan', *Soundings* (1947).

Tapper, R. (ed.), *The Conflict of Tribe and State in Iran and Afghanistan* (London, 1983).

Taylor, C., *The Sources of the Self: The Making of Modern Identity* (Cambridge, 1989).

Teich, M., and Porter, R. (eds), *The National Question in Europe in Historical Context* (Cambridge, 1993).

Thompson, Rt. Rev. W.J., 'Iran, 1947, Conditions of Daily Life', *Journal of the Royal Central Asian Society*, vols 35–6, nos 3–4 (1948–9).

Tilly, C. (ed.), *The Formation of National States in Western Europe* (Princeton, 1975).

Tivey, L. (ed.), *The Nation State: The Formation of Modern Politics* (Oxford, 1981).

Upton, Joseph M., *The History of Modern Iran: An Interpretation* (Cambridge, MA, 1960).

US Department of State, *Foreign Relations of the United States* (Washington, DC, 1941–53).

Vali, A., *Pre-Capitalist Iran, A Theoretical History* (London, 1993).

——, 'Genèse et structure du nationalisme kurde en Iran', *Peuples Mediterranéens*, nos 68–9 (1994).

——, 'The Making of Kurdish Identity in Iran', *Journal for Critical Studies of the Middle East (Critique)*, no. 7 (1995).

——, 'Nationalism and Kurdish Historical Writing', *New Perspectives on Turkey*, no. 14 (1996).

——, 'Kurdish Nationalism in Iran: The Formative Period, 1942–1947', *The Journal of Kurdish Studies*, vol. 2 (1997).

——, 'The Kurds and Their Others: Fragmented Identity, Fragmented Politics', *Comparative Studies of South Asia, Africa and the Middle East*, vol. 18, no. 2 (1998).

—— (ed.), *Essays on the Origins of Kurdish Nationalism* (Costa Mesa, 2003).

Wilber, D., *Iran: Past and Present* (Princeton, 8th edn rev., 1978).

Westermann, A., 'Kurdish Independence and Russian Expansion', *Foreign Affairs*, vol. 24, no. 4 (1946).

Yasin, B., *Vision or Reality? The Kurds in the Policy of the Superpowers 1941–1947* (Lund, 1995).

INDEX

Abbasi, Muhammad 74, 168n
Abrahamian, E. 140n, 146n, 180n
Absolutism 15, 117, 119–21, 125 (see also Pahlavi absolutism)
Adl, M. 140n, 165n
Agrarian production 2, 163n; disruption of 12; pre-capitalist structure of 6, 7, 15, 88, 111, 118; in tribal lands 7, 8; in Kurdish Republic 61, 68, 77
Agrarian property 118, 163n
Agricultural produce 15, 118
Ahmad, Abdul Ghadir 173n, 177n, 178n
Ahmad, Kamal Mazhar 139n, 146n
Aliyar, Ali Agha 73, 168n
Allouche, A. 144n
Amir Asa'd, Ali Agha 74
Amirarjomand, S. 140n
ancien regime 6, 12
Anderson, Benedict xv

Anti-colonialism 30, 55, 101–3 passim, 173n, 177n, 178n
Anti-fascist alliance 36, 39; breakdown of 172n
Anti-imperialism 30, 102; in discourse of *Kurdistan* 100 passim, 176n, 177n
Arab states 36, 39
Arabic (language) 103, 165n
Arabs 173
Ardalan (family) 73, 142n, 144n
Ardalan, Saifallah Khan 73
Arfa, H. 147n
Armenians 13, 94
Assyrians 13, 21, 94
Atabaki, Touraj 141n, 161n, 180n
Atba' 3
Atlantic Charter/ Treaty 25, 149n, 172n, 175n
Ayuobian, Sayyid Muhammad 164n
Ayyubi, Mulla Muhammad 171n
Azerbaijan 6, 14, 33, 36, 39, 55, 60–1, 68, 72, 74, 94, 96–7, 110, 141n, 154–6n

Azerbaijan (Democrat) Republic
36, 42–3, 50–60 passim, 67,
111, 158n, 179n
Azerbaijan Democratic Party 54,
101
Azerbaijan National Assembly 52
Azerbaijan-Tehran agreement 94
Azeri (language) 60, 156n
Azeris 7, 13; democrats 54, 56,
58–9, 96, 161n, 177–8n;
government 58–9, 74, 93,
97, 160n, 161–2n; leadership
160–1n; Shi'i community
125; 'Azeri model' 40
Azeri-Kurdish agreement 57, 59
Aziz, Rahim Vasta 168n

Badir Khan 66
Bagherov, M. J. 50–2
Bagzadeh (tribe) 167n
Bakhtiari (tribe) 15
Baku 38–9, 43, 49–52, 67, 156n,
158n, 167n
Balance of power 40; national
security and 134; political
and military 9
Bana 79, 157n, 158n
Baneh 42, 44, 49, 160n, 167n,
170n
Barclay, G. 143n
Barth, F. 143–4n
Barzani force 78, 80, 162n,
169n
Barzani, Mulla Mustafa 78–80,
169–70n
Baskale 141n
Bauer, Otto 177n
Bayat, M. 140n

Bayiz Agha Gewirk 157n, 168n
Bayiz Agha Mangur 78
Besikci, Ismail 173n
Bestoun, J. 176n
Blorian, Ghani 150n, 169n
Bokan 44, 49, 154n, 160n
Bourgeoisie 29–31, 67, 132,
145n, 153, 173n; democratic
29, 30; mercantile 2, 12,
14, 20, 27, 34, 40, 44, 46,
63–6, 67, 88; petty 20, 30,
40, 44, 55, 63–5, 70, 75,
88, 162n; in Republican
government 164–5n
British: foreign policy in Iran
54, 157–8n; towards USSR
32–3, 101, 157–8n; Foreign
Office papers 35, 37–8,
154–6n, 159n, 166n, 169n;
Confidential Report 157n;
diplomats 73, 167n; Consul
in Kermanshah 56, 79–80,
170n; Consul in Tabriz 54,
56, 143n, 153n; Embassy/
Minister in Tehran 153n;
political officers stationed
in Kurdistan and Azerbaijan
72; British-Soviet occupation
153–4n, 155n
Browne, E.G. 140n
Buci-Glucksmann, C. 146n
Bukan 167n
Bullard, Sir R.W. 36, 153n, 166n

Capitalism 30; in Iran 2, 15, 17;
and nationalism 29–30, 33;
backwardness of in Kurdistan
75, 111

Centralization, political and administrative 9, 15, 17, 70, 71, 75, 114, 118, 119, 120, 124, 161n

Chaldiran, battle of 144n

Chieftains (Kurdish) 6, 7, 10, 34, 37, 51, 70–4, 76, 80, 89, 134, 142n, 143n, 150n, 166–8n

Christian inhabitants of Kurdistan 20

Churchill, Winston 149n

Citizenship 3, 4, 11, 95, 107, 128–9, 131; conditions of 3, 4, 95–6; Iranian 95–6; rights of 95, 130; subject-citizenship in the Iranian Constitution 3, 132

Civil and democratic rights 4, 84, 106, 119, 127, 130, 137, 179n

Civil society 19, 20, 63–5, 90, 118, 120, 126

Class 102, 108, 132, 172n, 178n; categories 21, 31, 103–4, 172–3n, 176–8n; domination 145n; essentialism 176n; essentialist 29, 32; exploitation 102, 173n; identity 30; ideology 29; interests 31; and nation 102, 176n; relations 30–1, 33, 103, 177n; antagonistic 173n

Clayton, Vice-Consul 141n

Cold War 35, 50, 134, 151n, 173n; ideology 172–3n

Colonialism: internal 173n

Comintern 67, 102 (see also Third Communist International)

Commodity relations 6, 15, 20, 75

Communism 21, 67–8, 103, 176n; Soviet 101

Communist 34, 177–8n; agenda 148n; alliance 17; parties 101; regime 40

Communist Party of Iran, see Tudeh Party

Communist Party of Iraq 101

Communist Party of the Soviet Union (CPSU) 36, 50

Constitution, Iranian (of 1906) 3, 4, 5, 10, 58, 90–6, 98–9, 115–16, 120–1, 128–32, 135, 140–1n; abrogation of 122; discourse of 3; and language 4

Constitutional: era xi, 5, 6, 10–12, 113, 116, 142–3n; government 10–11, 116, 132; monarchy 2; politics 121, 131; state 4, 116–17, 140n, 142n; sovereignty 116–17

Constitutional forces 12, 116

Constitutional Law (of 1906) 3, 25, 91–6, 115, 140n, 174n

Constitutional Revolution (of 1905) 2, 10, 11, 12, 99, 114, 116, 120, 136, 145n

Constitutionalist movement 3, 5–6, 12, 14, 118, 140n, 142n

Coup d'état 116

Curzon, G.N. 141n, 143n

Dabaghi, Abdullah 173n
Dares Khan 170n
Dawudi, Haj Mustafa 164–5n
Debokri (tribe) 73, 142n, 167n,
    180n
Debokri, Ghassem Agha 167n
Decentralization of power 90,
    94–5; device for 91
Decentralized political
    administration 91, 140n;
    political structure 9; state
    structure 134
Decentralizing forces 5
Democracy 97, 131–3, 135–7,
    178–9n; principles of 94;
    struggle for 92; in the
    Kurdish Republic 63; and
    the 1906 Constitution 94–5,
    131–3, 135
Democratic Party of Iranian
    Azerbaijan 101
Democratic Party of Kurdistan,
    see Kurdistan Democratic
    Party of Iran
Democratic theory 3, 135, 176n;
    and citizenship in Iran 3–4;
    and ethnicity 4, 95–6
Derrida, J. 116
Dictatorship 122; military 71;
    Pahlavi 91; Reza Khan's 94;
    theocratic-military 137
Difference 113–15, 125, 131,
    137; cultural and linguistic
    123–5; democratic
    recognition of 137;
    discursive primacy of 114;
    ethnic 4, 18, 92, 99–100;
    ethnic and cultural 31, 128,
130; ethnic and linguistic
    xiv, 125–6; ethno-nationalist
    92, 99–100; expression of
    65; and identity 126; and
    Iranian subject-citizen 130;
    language of 19; lineage
    of xii; Kurdish xii; and
    Kurdish identity xii, xiii;
    of the Kurds 19; national
    31; public expressions of
    19; religious 132; religious
    and ethnic 90–1; socio-
    economic and political
    23–4, 99–100; suppressed
    136
Dilsoz, Anwar 178n
Directive Concerning Taxes and
    Expenditures 63
Director of Public Finance 62,
    69, 162–3n, 166n
Dizeh, Qaleh 170n

Eagleton, W. 50–3, 56–7, 60, 64,
    66, 76–7, 147n, 149n, 151n,
    154n, 158–63n, 165–9n,
    174n, 180n
Eden, Sir Anthony 36, 38
Education 67, 179n; and
    intelligentsia 19, 107;
    language of 4, 94; madrasa
    107; modern 55, 165,
    107, 131, 165n, 179n;
    national 18; primary 18;
    secular 5, 12, 20, 118,
    124; traditional 106, 165n,
    Western 120
Eid celebration (Gejni Ramazan)
    179–80n

Elahie, Ahmad 163–4n, 172n,
    179n
Elite: governmental 119; local
    33; modernizing 119;
    political 65, 119; ruling 66
Emin, N.M. 147n, 151n,
    160–2n, 164–5n, 168–9n
Empiricist epistemology xv;
    historiography 151
Entner, M.L. 154n
Erbil 149n, 171n
Essentialism xii; class 176; of
    historicist discourse xii; of
    the Soviet analysis of Kurdish
    society 33
Essentialist xv, 1, 32, 113, 115,
    131, 136–7; class 29, 32;
    tradition 152n
Ethnicity: Kurdish xiii–xiv, 4,
    10–11, 16–19, 23–4, 30–1,
    55, 86, 90, 92, 97, 99–100,
    105–6, 114–15, 125–6;
    non-Persian 4, 65, 95, 129;
    as difference 4–5, 18–19,
    30–1, 65, 86, 99, 105, 115,
    124–6, 129–30; and the 1906
    Constitution 5, 10, 58, 90–6,
    115, 128–30, 131, 132; and
    identity 10, 11, 16, 18–19,
    55, 86, 114, 121, 125–6, 134,
    135; and class 30, 31; and
    nationalism 24, 27, 86, 87,
    89–90, 99–100, 105, 114,
    125–8; and sovereign power
    129–130, 131, 132, 135–7

Fahimi (director of Customs and
    Excise in Mahabad) 160n

Faroughi, Muhammad 74, 168n
Fascism 50, 102, 145n
Fateh, M.K. 154n
Fayzollabagi (tribe) 142n, 180n
Feudal: social structures in
    Kurdistan 6, 8, 10, 75; Soviet
    views of 32–3
figh 107
Firouz-Pishevari agreement 59–
    60, 93, 96–8
First World War 12, 50, 116
Foroughi, M.A. 16, 147n
Foucault, Michel 140n;
    Foucauldian theory xiii, 139n
French Revolution 145n

Gellner, Ernst xv
Gender 4
Genealogy 173n, 178n; of
    Kurdish identity xii, xvi
Germany 38, 156n
Gewirk (tribe) 168n, 180n
Gewirk, Kak Alla Agha 168n
Ghaderi, Mah Sharaf Khanom
    (Mastooreh Kurdistani) 144n
Ghassemlou, Abdul Rahman
    139n, 142n, 146n, 150–2n
Ghawachi, Hamza Ali 74, 168n
Ghazi Fattah 142n
Ghazi, Hassan 147n, 155n,
    169–70n
Ghazi Muhammad 47, 50–6, 64,
    66–8, 70, 72–4, 78–80, 90–2,
    97–8, 102, 107, 108, 110,
    142n, 149–50n, 157n, 159–
    61n, 164–5n, 167n, 169–70n,
    173–5n, 177n, 179n, 180n;
    surrender of 111–12, 180n

Ghazi, Muhammad Hussein Saif
74, 92, 164n, 168–9n, 176n
Ghazi, Rahim Saif 156n
Ghizilji, Mulla Ahmad
(Turjanizadeh) 13, 146n
Ghizilji, Hassan 171n, 173n
Gilan 14
Gohary, H. 147n, 150n
Gramsci, Antonio: passive
revolution 12, 145n
Great Britain 54, 148n, 166n
(see also British)
Gurga, Hama 168n
Gzing 149n, 152n

Haji Baba Shaikh 164–5n, 179n
Hamedan 154n
Harki (tribe) 79, 109, 167n,
180n
Hashemite rule 16
Hassanpour, A. 141n, 143n,
146–7n, 150–2n, 154n, 161n
Hawar (journal) 157n
Hawar, M.R. 146n
Hegemony 88, 145n
Hemin 173n, 178–9n
Historical discourse xi, xii, xv;
nationalist 141n, 174n, 179n
Historicism xi, xii, 1, 113, 115
Hobsbawm, Eric xv
Homayuni, General 80, 111,
169–70n; in Miandoab 167n
Hourani, Albert 165n

Ibrahim (prophet) 179n
Ilkhanizadeh, Abdul Rahman
(Haj Rahman Ilkhanizadeh)
164–5n

Ilkhanizadeh, Ghassem Agha 51
Ilkhanizadeh, Ismail 164n
Ilmie, Ahmad 69, 162n, 166n
Imami, Abdul Rahman 171n
Iran xi, 1, 2, 3, 45–7, 50–2,
54–5, 58, 71, 75, 77, 84,
89–95, 97–9, 101, 105, 109,
110–11, 113–14, 117, 120,
127, 132, 134–9, 142–3n,
145n, 148n, 150–4n,
158–9n, 161n, 164n, 167n,
174n; citizenship 3–4,
94–6, 120, 127–32; economy
of 2, 7, 75, 111, 119–20;
government 13, 15, 36, 37,
42–3, 52, 56, 58–60, 62,
68, 72–3, 79–80, 87, 89–92,
96–8, 110, 133, 135, 141n,
143n, 150n, 152–4n, 157n,
160–1n, 165–7n, 174n,
175n, 180n; identity 2, 4,
10, 12, 17–20, 86, 95–6,
100, 113–15, 126, 129–30;
intelligentsia 7, 136; military
forces 34, 42, 49, 74, 77,
79–80, 87, 88, 109–10,
111–12, 157n, 165n, 167n,
169n; nationalism in 2–3,
5, 18–19; political culture
in 57, 62, 83, 91, 92, 94,
101, 117, 131–3, 136; and
sovereign power xii, xiii, 60,
65, 95–6, 100, 115, 121,
122, 130, 135, 137; see also:
Persia, Persian language,
Kurdistan
Iranian Constitution, see
Constitution

Iranian foreign policy 36–9;
Turkey 16–17; Soviet Union
33, 50, 89; GB 36–7, 54;
US 36
Iranian Revolution (of 1979) 27,
131–2
Iranian state xii, xiii, 1, 15, 16,
25, 37, 70, 86, 90, 105, 111,
114, 127, 134–6; Islamic xiii,
137; relations with Kurdish
tribes 8–10, 15, 70, 72–3,
79, 80, 110
Iraq 16, 36, 39, 169; army 76,
162; Communist Party of
101; government 39, 78,
170n; KDP 150n; Iraqi
Kurdistan 79, 143n; Kurds
from 84, 168n, 172n,
177–8n
Isfahan 142n
Islam: and Komalay JK 21,
147–8n; in political discourse
of Republic 106–8, 165n,
172n, 178–9n; Sunni 40;
Twelver Shi'ism 4, 129, 132
Issawi, C. 154n
Izzat, Mahmoud Mulla 57,
150n, 152n, 160–2n, 165n,
168n

Jabbari, Abdul Jabbar Muhammad
141n, 142n, 146n
Jacobins 145n
James, P. 177n
Jellali (tribe) 167n
Jiana Kurd society, see Komalay
JK
jin be jine 108

Juridical power: processes/
practices in Republic 107–8;
and the state 114–25 passim,
134; violence of 121–3; and
concept of minority 58,
124–5, 129–30, 132, 137;
and citizenship 3, 11,
129–30
Jwaideh, Wadie 66, 70, 139n,
141–2n, 146n, 154n, 169n,
174n

Karaj (Agricultural Training
College) 165n
Karimi, Ali 147n, 149–50n,
152n, 157–8n, 164n
Karimi, Manaf 164n
Kasravi, A. 142n, 146n
Katouzian, H. 146n
Kazimov, Captain Salahaddin
(Kakagha) 168n
Keddie, N. 141n, 146n, 163n
Kermanshah 56, 79–80,
169–70n
Khalilzadeh, Hashem 177n, 179n
Khana 160n
Khanzadeh, Muhammad Rashid
Khan (Hama Rashid Khani
Baneh) 169n
Khaznedar, J. 146n, 171n
Khosrawi, A. 177n
Khosrawi, Khalil 164n
Khoy (Khoi) 43, 57, 59, 61,
159–60n
Khoybun 55
Kirmanshah 94, 142n
Knatchbull-Hugessen, Sir
Hugh 38

Komala (see Komalay JK)
Komalay JK 20–4, 25–7,
40–7, 147n, 150n; agrarian
populism 22, 26, 40, 86;
dissolution of 25–7, 51,
84, 149n, 152n; formation
of 20, 29; leadership of 45,
47, 156n; and KDPI 25–7,
51, 84–6, 150n, 151–2n,
173–4n; and nationalism
20, 22–4, 30, 43–4, 46, 86,
125, 127–8; organizational
structure of 43–5, 47, 158n;
politics of 20–4, 37, 40–1,
43–7, 86, 127, 148n, 156–7n;
and Soviet Union 40–3;
social structure of 20, 29,
44–7, 159n
Komalay Shorishgeri
Zahmatkeshani Kurdistani
Iran 27, 150n
Kurdish (language) xiv, 4, 13,
18–20, 83–4, 94, 103, 124–6,
136, 149n, 165n; as language
of otherness 19; Sorani
dialect 13; writing in 20
Kurdish community xiv, 68,
70, 88, 108, 114, 115,
122–3, 127; conditions
of the transformation of
121; ethnic and linguistic
unity of xiii; boundaries
of 126; constitutive of
xiii; construction of xiv;
foundations of 6, 11,
development 114; economic
supremacy in 88; historical
encounters between the
sovereign power and xii,
115; historical transformation
of 114; lack of a uniform
ethnic identity in 134;
political backwardness and
cultural isolation 116;
social structure of the
emergent public sphere
in 65; sovereign power
as constitutive outside
of 114; sovereign power
to secure domination xii,
126; structure of political
authority and administration
in 47; subjugation of xiii,
122–4, 126
Kurdish ethnicity xiv, 16–17,
124–5; denial of 19, 124,
126 politicization of 89, 92,
100, 114, 121, 125–6
Kurdish historical writing 1, 14,
141n
Kurdish identity: formation of
xi, xii, 1, 113–14, 125; in
Firouz-Pishevari agreement
97; genealogy of xii, xvi; and
KDPI; in nationalist discourse
55, 81, 127; and the
Republic 100; suppression
of 19, 136; boundaries of 31;
construction of 30; in the
discourse of Komala JK 127;
in the discourse of *Nishtiman*
85–6; in the discourse of
Kurdistan 84, 87, 99–100; in
Iran 113, 148; redefinition
of 105; and sovereign power
113, 121, 126–7, 131, 136

Kurdish intelligentsia 5, 7, 14,
19–20, 27, 84, 173n; see also
nationalist intelligentsia
Kurdish leadership 51, 55, 75,
91–3, 96–7, 101, 130–3,
148n, 161n, 167n, 174n
Kurdish middle class 4, 30, 34,
118–20, 124, 126; dissenters
119–20
Kurdish (nationalist) movement
33; dynamics of 114–15;
national identity in 29; Soviet
support for 42
Kurdish nation 22–4, 46, 65,
72, 74, 86, 90, 94, 99, 141n,
173–5n; absence of the idea
as sovereign 14; authority
of 89; constructions of the
conceptions of 87; ethnic-
nationalist conception of 89;
essentialist conception of 1;
political sovereignty of 90;
sovereignty of 65
Kurdish national entity 127
Kurdish national rights 127,
179n
Kurdish national state 35
Kurdish nationalism 11, 13,
65, 73; class analysis of
152n; crystallization of 84;
development of xi, 13, 39,
150n; in Eastern Kurdistan
162n; emergence of 19;
idea of 40; genesis of 13;
in Iran 1, 28, 50, 84; in
Iranian Kurdistan 19; and
modern middle class 124;
and Shaikh Ubaidollah

141n; and Soviet policy
35–43 passim; and tribal
landowners 71
Kurdish nationalists 40–1,
55–6; and Azeri democrats
59; and Azeri plan 57;
autonomy project of 40;
from Iraq 76; in Mahabad
58; next generation of
112; and the Soviets 60,
154–5n; in the Republican
administration 103;
quest for an autonomist
government 52–3; younger
generation of 104, 178n
Kurdish peasantry 172n; mass of
60, 68
Kurdish principalities 8, 9, 134,
143–5n; administrative and
fiscal autonomy of 144n;
forced destruction 8, 9,
144n; recognized domains of
declining 133–4
Kurdish Question (in Iran) 16,
17, 50, 93–4, 97, 136–7,
148n, 155n; formation
and persistence of 136;
misrepresentation of 133–5;
Soviet approach to 50
Kurdish rebellions xiv, 12, 19,
111, 133–4
Kurdish Republic (in Mahabad)
xi, xiv, xvi, 1, 2, 23, 25–9, 31,
33, 41–2, 49–50, 52–4,
56–81, 83–5, 87–92, 95,
97–104, 106–11, 113, 128,
130, 133, 136–7, 139,
141–2n, 147n, 149–52n,

155n, 157n, 159–71, 173–5n, 178n, 180n; armed forces 61, 75–7, 161n, 168n; Republican government 57–68 passim, 72, 73, 75, 77–9, 87, 103, 110, 111, 151n, 161n, 162n, 165n; social composition of government 65, 66, 164n; leadership 42, 64, 66, 67, 70, 71, 73, 88–90, 106–7; end of Republic 110; taxation 61–2, 162–3n

Kurdish territory 5, 12, 16, 41, 45, 49, 53, 61, 87, 112, 133; in Iran 5, 90, 148n, 161n; in Iraq, Iran and Turkey 143n; Iranian Kurdistan as most underdeveloped part of 7; and the Soviet army 34–5, 37

Kurdish tribes 7–9, 15–17, 37, 78, 143n, 153n, 156n, 166–7n

Kurdish urban centres 9, 17, 37, 88, 124; culture 10, 20

Kurdish-Azeri agreement 57, 59–60

Kurdish-Azeri front 59

Kurdistan (journal) 26–7, 30, 61, 63, 69, 73, 83–5, 87–95, 98–101, 103–6, 139n, 141n, 143–4n, 147n, 149–51n, 157n, 159–64n, 166–80n

Kurdistan xiii, 5–7, 8, 11,12, 14–17, 20–4, 26, 28, 38, 43, 52, 54–5, 57, 62, 68, 71–4; 77, 80, 84, 92–4, 97–9, 109–10, 122–3, 126–7, 130, 141n, 143–4n, 146–7n,

153–6n, 158n, 160n, 162n, 172–3n; 175n; cultural and linguistic difference in 123; first division of Kurdistan 8; historical specificity of nationalist politics in 35; modern state in 20; nationalist idea of a united and independent 13; non-tribal agriculture in Kurdistan 7; polygamy in 108; popular democratic cause of the nationalist movement in 29; revival of civil society in 20; sovereign order in 122; sovereign power in 124, 126, 136; state-tribal relations in 9; Greater Kurdistan 43, 55, 57, 86, 100, 127, 148n

Kurdistan Democratic Party of Iran (KDPI) 23, 25–9, 41 49–57, 62–3, 65, 69, 74, 79, 83–5, 87, 91, 107–8, 131, 149–52n, 157n, 160n, 163n, 173–4n, 176n, 178n, 180n; authority of 69; autonomist discourse of 174n; autonomist political programme of 72; birth of 47; central committee of 26, 45, 55–6, 62–3, 108, 163–4n, 174n; conditions of the formation of 28–9, 43, 49, 85; conservative traditionalism 28; discourse of 128; formation of 29, 49–50, 84, 88; 148–9n, 152n; leadership 27, 52–5, 57, 62–3, 108; nationalist political process by 30; opposition

to 68; position of 174n; pre-
history of the creation of 85;
programme of 91, 96; radical
nationalists in 55

Lahijani, Muhammad 179n
Lake Urmiya 1
Lambton, A.K.S. 143n, 163n
Land reform 163n, 176n
Land revenue 2, 8, 61, 163n
Landownership: in Iran 2,
8–9, 15, 117–18, 120; in
Kurdistan 2, 6–7, 8–9, 10,
12, 21, 25, 65, 68, 165n;
large landowners 2, 12,
66, 117; middle 66, 71;
privileged position of 68;
small 70–1; tribal 15, 17,
71, 75
Landowning class (Kurdish) 2,
6, 7, 12, 17, 21, 23, 25, 27,
30, 32, 40–1, 46–7, 62, 65,
67–9, 71, 73, 86–9, 102,
104, 109, 111, 143n, 146n,
152n, 159n
Law 107, 117, 121, 172; formal
116; martial 122; and order
15, 67; and power 116–17;
rule of 11; and sovereign
identity 116; and sovereign
power 124–5; and violence
130
League of Nations 16
Lenin 21, 101–2, 147n, 176–7n
Liberal: democratic ideal 11;
intelligentsia 14; political
culture 19
Literacy 4

Lockhart, L. 140n
London 165n

Maaroufzad, M. 177n
Mahabad (town) xi, 20, 23,
42–4, 49, 51–3, 57–9, 62, 64,
67, 78–9, 91–2, 107, 109,
111–12, 114, 142n, 149n,
154n, 157n, 159–61n,
164–70n, 174n
Mahabad Republic, see Kurdish
Republic
mahalli 58
Mahmoud, Muhammad 172n
Mahmoudian, Ghafour 168n
Maisky, J. 38
Majdi, Muhammad 171–2n,
179n
Majdi, Mulla Hussein 107, 164n,
179n
Majlis 14–5, 26, 147n
Maku 57, 159n
Malekzadeh, M. 142n
Mamash (tribe) 167n, 180n
Mamash, Gharani Agha i 74, 78,
109, 157n, 168n, 180n
Mamash, Mam Aziz 78
Mangur, Abdullah Agha 74,
157n
Mangur, Alijani 74
Mangur 109, 163n, 167n, 180n
Mardukh, Shaikh Muhammad,
144n
Marx 120; and Engels 176n
Marxism 101, 103, 176n; of
the Tudeh Party 55, 132; in
discourse of Kurdistan 84,
103–4, 176n, 177–8n; and

nationalism 176–7n (see also Soviet Marxism)

Marxism-Leninism 104, 173n; and ideological formation of Komala 22, 148n; in Azerbaijan 67

Marxist: analyses of Kurdish politics 27–35 passim, 151n;

May Day 173n; in Kurdistan 172n

Mazuji, Hamid 64

McDowall, David 142–3n, 154n, 169n, 180n

Mercantile bourgeoisie, see bourgeoisie, mercantile

Miandoab 49, 56, 79, 111, 167n

Miandoab refinery 163n

Ministry of Finance (Iranian) 162n

Ministry of Finance (Kurdish Republic) 62, 163–4n

Ministry of War (Kurdish Republic) 108

Mobley, R.A. 41, 57, 155n, 158n, 160–1n, 174n

Modernity 45, 81, 109, 151n, 176n; discourse of 19; of the nation xv, 176n; paradox of 110, 112; in Iran 1, 2, 4, 5, 111

Modernization: in Iran, and political centralization 5, 16; and absolutism 14–15, 119; authoritarian 19, 118–19, 123–4, 134, 140n

Mo'eini, Muhammad Amin 162n, 164n

Molotov 36, 38, 172n

Monshi, Eskandar Beg 144n

Moscow 38

Mowlavi, Aziz 171n, 172n

Muhammad (prophet) 172n

Muhammad Ali Shah 3

Mussadeq, Dr Muhammad 166n

Muzaffaradin Shah 3

Nancy, Jean-Luc 130

Naderi, Ibrahim 175n, 178n

Naqadeh 49, 160n

Nasir al-Din Shah 144n

Nation xiv, xv 3, 24, 93, 94, 103, 106, 109, 110, 141n, 162n, 175n, 176n; authority of 90; boundaries of 90, collective will of 11; concept of 90, 99, 141n; definitions of 86; ethnic and cultural diversity of 5; nationalist political process 89; rights of 93; sellers 74

Nation state 135; ethnic foundations of political rationality in 136; juridico-political framework of 134–5; political form of 176n; sovereignty and integrity of 135

National identity xv, 3, 30, 31, 33, 46, 60, 65, 81, 96, 111; of citizens 95; conception of 18, 99, 141n; constituent elements 4, 31; constitutive of 31; construction of 29, 31, 127; contours of 31, 85; discourse of 18; historicist readings of 115; boundaries of 30, 31; in Iranian Kurdistan 24; in Kurdistan 33; in modern Iran xi; modernity of xv; political field 117; of Republic 98; sense of 18

National memory 55, 85

National question 102, 177n; Soviet approach to 101

National rights 14, 25, 106, 126, 127,176n; conceptions of 127; political character of 128; rhetoric of 128

National sovereignty 18; redeployment of 117; concept of 135

Nationalism xiv–xv, 141n, 179n; in Marxist/ Leninist theory 29–33, 102, 176–7n; conception of 141n; ethnic conception of 135; (see also Kurdish nationalism, Iranian nationalism; modernity of) xv, 1, 2, 14, 20, 47, 90, 109, 146n

Nationalist discourse (Kurdish) 30–1, 65, 89, 100, 127, 179n; early 84, 172–3n

Nationalist forces (Kurdish) 37, 40–1, 89; in Kurdish urban centres 37

Nationalist history 14, 24, 141n, 152n; development of 85

Nationalist intelligentsia 34, 100–2, 106–7, 178–9n; immaturity of 83; younger generation of 107

Nationalist movement (Kurdish) 152n; discursive and non-discursive conditions of possibility of formation of 2; in Iranian Kurdistan 1, 29–35 passim, 45, 47, 84, 86, 101, 107, 139n, 152n; on Iraqi Kurdistan 39; among Kurdish tribes 16; see also Kurdish national movement

Natural rights theory 84

Nebez, J. 51, 147–9n

Nikitine, Basil 139, 142n

Nimni, E. 177

Nishtiman 21, 147–8n; discourse of 21–2, 85, 87, 100, 104; Kurdish people and Kurdish nation in the discourse of 22, 86; national identity in the discourse of 30, 85, 99, 100; nationalist politics and nationalist history in the discourse of 46

Noshirwan, Emin 57, 147n, 151n, 160–2n, 164–5n, 168–9n

Nouzari, Ali 168n

October Revolution 147n

Office of Public Finance (of Kurdish Republic) 62–3

Olson, Robert 139n, 141n

Ottoman Empire 1, 5, 7, 9, 16, 154n

Ottoman Kurds 7

Owqaf (Religious/Islamic Charitable Foundations) 179n

Pahlavi: absolutism xi, 1, 11–19 passim, 68, 71, 110, 111–23 passim, 126, 146n; absolutist rule xii, 18, 68, 91, 131–2, 153n, 166n

Passive revolution 12; concept of 145n

Persia, see Iran

Persian (ethnicity) 18–19, 31, 65, 92, 95–6, 105, 126, 129–32, 135; as 'other' to Kurds 31, 99–100, 105

Persian (language) 3–4, 25, 83, 103, 165n; dominance of 18; influence on Kurdish 83–4; as language of sovereign 4; as official language 4

Peshmerga 162n

Pesyan, N. 142n

Petty-bourgeoisie, see bourgeoisie, petty

Pezeshkan, Colonel 73

Piran 163n

Pishevari 52, 54, 56–7, 60 (see also Firouz-Pishevari)

Pizhdar 167n

Population of the Republic 159

Populism 21, 102, 104; agrarian, 22, 24, 127; of Komala 27, 40, 46, 86; and nationalism 71

Pre-capitalism: in Iran 2; in Kurdistan 47, 75, 118

Provincial and District Councils 91–6, 129–30, 133, 140n

Qajar rule 2, 10, 116, 121, 144n

Qashqai (tribe) 15

Qawam, Ahmad (Prime Minister of Iran) 57, 161; government of 60, 98, 174n

Quran 21, 106, 177n, 179n

Rahbar 159n, 172n

Raihani, Ali 160n

Rasuli, Delshad 173n, 175n, 179n

Reasons of the state 113, 123, 133–5

Red Army 34, 39–40, 42, 54, 156, 172n; departure of 74, 180n; presence of 42, 49; see also Soviet military

Regional autonomy 25, 30, 40, 96, 98, 141n, 160–1n, 174n; in the discourse of *Kurdistan* 92; Kurdish demand for 98, 174n; Kurdish quest for 90–1; politics of 92

Renner, Karl 177n

Reza Shah 14–16, 19, 34, 153n, 166n; abdication of 20

Rezaiyeh 57–8, 159n, 161n

Rich, C.J. 143, 145n

Roj i Kurd (journal) 146n; political discourse of 14

Roosevelt, T. (USA president) 149n

Roosevelt, A. 55, 147n, 151n, 158–9n, 169n

Rossow, Robert Jr. 60

Sa'd Abad treaty (Saadabad Pact) 17, 41

Safavid dynasty 9, 144n

Saleh, Rafiq 171n
Saleh, Sadiq 171n
Salmas 43, 59, 61, 159–60n
Samadi, Seyyid Muhammad
    147n, 154n, 150n, 159n
Sanandaji, Mirza Shokrollah 144n
Saqqiz 42, 44, 49, 73, 77, 142n,
    154n, 159n
Sardasht 42, 44, 49, 56, 79,
    158n, 160n, 170n
Saujbulaq 142n
Schmitt, Carl 121
Second World War 28, 35
Self-determination 55, 99, 100,
    176n; democratic doctrine
    of 128
Semko Shikak, see Shikak, Semko
    (Ismail Agha)
Semko's movement 13–14, 16,
    133, 146n
Sendus (Shahin Dezh) 159n
Senna 94, 142n
Seyyid Muhammad Hamidi
    171n, 175n, 178–9n
Shafe'ie (tribe) 67, 166n
Shafe'ie, Haji Rahmat 67
Shahin Dehz 79, 159n
Shahrvand 3
Shaikh Mahmoud 55
Shaikh Said's movement in
    Turkey 16
Shaikh Ubaidollah's movement
    1, 66, 139n; nationalism of
    141n
Shaji'i, Z. 147n
Shamzini, A. 147n
Shar Veran 163n
Shari'a 107–8, 172n

Sharif Pasha, General 148n
Sharifi, Amar Khan 78–9, 167n,
    169n
Sharifi, Omar Agha 169n
Shateri (tribe) 67
Shateri, Haj Salih 67, 165–6n
Shi'ification 9
Shikak (tribe) 79, 109, 167n,
    180n
Shikak confederacy 12–13,
Shikak, Ja'afar Agha i 142n
Shikak, Semko (Ismail Agha),
    12–13, 16, 17, 66, 142n,
    146n (see also Semko's
    movement)
Shilar 170n
Showan 172n
Smart, Walter 143n
Soudagar, M. 163n
Sovereignty 3, 8, 12, 19, 60, 95,
    116, 117, 119–20, 122–3,
    125, 135; absolutist 117–19;
    autocratic 11; difference 113,
    115; domination 122–3, 126;
    ethnicity 95–6; identity of xii,
    xiii, 18–19, 100, 116, 125–6,
    129, 131–2, 136; Iranian xiii,
    57, 60, 90, 99, 130, 132,
    155n; juridical conditions of
    11; jurisdiction 55; of Kurdish
    nation 14, 65; language of 4,
    60; opposition to 125; person
    of the sovereign 119, 122;
    state of Iran 37, 58, 99; and
    use of violence 122
Sovereign power xii, xiii, xiv,
    114–17, 120, 122–6, 129–30,
    134, 136 ; absence of 134;

construct of 133; ethnic
definition of 131, 135,
137; identity of 125, 135–6;
Iranian 115; and Kurdish
community xii, 121–2,
123, 126; in Kurdistan 124;
opposition to 125; and
Persian ethnicity 131; and
its political and cultural
significations 125–6;
structural weakness of 116;
violence 125, 130
155n; policy in Kurdistan 29,
31–41, 57, 157n
Soviet authorities 54, 152–3n; in
Tabriz 54, 56, 57, 156–67n,
159n
Soviet military 34, 42, 57, 76,
88, 162, 163, 168 (see also
Red Army and Soviet forces)
Soviet Marxism 84, 101, 103,
179n
Soviet Union 21, 26, 28–9, 35,
39, 41–3, 50–1, 88–9, 93,
101–2, 111, 148n, 151n,
172n, 177–78n; active
support of 88; Anglo-
American pressure on 89;
political stance of 103;
regional considerations of 27,
28, 33, 36, 39, 50, 103,
Stalin 38, 101, 104, 149n,
152n, 172n; on nation and
nationalism 33; Stalinist
revisionism 29
Suisani 167n
Sulaimaniya 158n, 171n
Sunni Islam 40

Supplementary Constitutional
Law 3, 140n
Suppression of Kurdish ethnic
identity 16, 18
Surounjadaghi, Mulla
Abdulrahman i 74n, 168n

Tabriz 58, 61, 109, 146n,
167n; fall of 110–11;
re-conquest of 111;
University of 153n
Tabriz government 64, 93
Tabriz-Mahabad agreement 98
Tajirbashi family 154n
Tapper, Richard 145–6n, 169n
Tax Commission (Tax Association
of Mahabad Republic) 62,
68, 163n
Tax regime in Iran 5, 12, 15; in
the Republic 61, 62, 68
Tehran 56, 59, 60, 93
Tehran-Tabriz agreement 97–8
Territorial centralism 12, 16–17,
134, 153; in Kurdistan 69;
politics of 16–17, 19, 117,
123
Territorial division (Taqsimat-e
Keshvari) xiii, 161n
Third Communist International
102 (see also Comintern)
Tilkoo (tribe) 167n
Tribal landlordism 17, 110,
123
Tribalism 11, 16, 32, 87, 143n,
176n; in 15; in Kurdistan
80
Tsarist army 142n
Tsarist power 116

Tudeh Party 43, 55, 101, 132, 175n; endorsement of 93
Turkey, Republic of 154n; and Kurds 15–16, 37, 143n, 155–6n; in regional politics 36, 38

Ulama 165n
United Kingdom, see Great Britain
United Nations 149–50n
Urban centres 2, 4, 7, 44–6, 49,
Urban notables 67–8, 159n, 165n
Urmiya 13, 43, 59, 61, 109, 142, 146n, 159–61n, 177n, 179n
Urquhart, R.W. 153
US official reports 41–2, 155
USA 54, 101, 155n; foreign policy 35–6, 72–3
Ushno 49, 159–60n
USSR, see also Soviet Union

Vali, Abbas 145n, 147n, 163n, 180n
Valizadeh, Mahmoud 165n
van Bruinessen, Martin 143–6n, 154n, 169n
Versailles Peace Conference 148n

welayat-e faqih 131
Western Azerbaijan (Ostan-e Azerbaijan-e Gharbi) 50, 57–8, 161n
Woods, J.E. 144n

Yaghma 147n
Yalta Conference 149n
Yassin, Borhanedin 55, 57, 151n, 155n, 158n, 161n

Zabihi, Abdulrahman 26, 44, 51, 147n, 149–50n, 152n, 156–60n, 166n
Zanjan 109
Zero Beg 79